# UNDERSTANDING

# The Internet

*Bruce J. McLaren*
*Indiana State University*

**JOIN US ON THE INTERNET**
WWW: http://www.thomson.com

**South-Western Educational Publishing**

*an International Thomson Publishing company*  I⟨T⟩P®

Cincinnati • Albany, NY • Belmont, CA • Bonn • Boston • Detroit
Johannesburg • London • Madrid • Melbourne • Mexico City
New York • Paris • Singapore • Tokyo • Toronto • Washington

Team Leader: Steve Holland
Managing Editor: Carol Volz
Marketing Manager: Larry Qualls
Editor: Mark Cheatham
Art Coordinator: Mike Broussard
Consulting Editor: Jeanne Busemeyer
Production House: Litten Editing and Production

ISBN: 0-538-72132-4

3 4 5 6 7 8 9 10 D 02 01 00

Printed in the United States of America

International Thomson Publishing

# Preface

*Understanding & Using the Internet* is about accessing information on the Internet with a personal computer. It is based on the Windows graphical user interface and is designed for use on a variety of Internet software packages. Although this book is aimed at those who can directly access the Internet from an office computer or a microcomputer lab, it also explains how to obtain the telecommunications tools to dial in to the Internet. Although the book appears with screens from Windows 95, Windows 3.x users can also take advantage of this textbook.

## Why This Book?

It is my intention to offer a book that not only teaches how to use the Internet, but also examines the larger issues dealing with information found on the Internet. Students are first walked through simple activities. Then, more advanced concepts are presented in realistic scenarios with an emphasis on *why* rather than simply *how*. The writing style is straightforward and friendly.

This book serves an important role in that it unifies the approach to Internet tools under Windows. In many cases, when students use software offered as shareware, they have no available documentation. This book fills that need by providing explanations for essential use of the most popular client tools.

*Understanding & Using the Internet* serves as part of the *Internet Series* published by South-Western Educational Publishing (see pages xiv–xv for information about other products in this series). This text can be used alone, in combination with other books in the series, or to supplement any other book in a course where a knowledge of the Internet is desired.

## What's New in This Edition

This edition adds coverage of the latest available versions of the Internet client software tools. In particular, the book includes Netscape Communicator 4.0 and Microsoft Internet Explorer 4.0. All units use screens from Windows 95 software. There are more guided activities in this edition.

Unit 5, a new unit, covers searching for Web sites and personal information on the Internet using search engines. Unit 8 on building home pages is based both on HTML and on Netscape Composer. Unit 9 is strengthened by its enhanced coverage of electronic commerce and recent Internet news, including the Telecommunications Act of 1996 and Intranets. The unit on Gopher clients was deleted; Gopher servers can be accessed by Web browsers.

# Content Highlights

*Understanding & Using the Internet* consists of nine independent chapters called units.

**Unit 1: Development of the Internet** serves as an introduction to Internet terminology and presents an overview of basic Internet applications such as e-mail, FTP, Telnet, news groups, Gopher, and the World Wide Web. Directions are given to locate the shareware software used in this book.

**Unit 2: Connecting to the Internet** covers technical issues associated with connecting to the Internet and is of primary interest to those who must dial in to an Internet service provider. Dial-up users will find instructions on how to create a dial-up PPP connection under Windows 95. Users who have access through an office or microcomputer lab can skip this unit.

**Unit 3: Electronic Mail—The Basic Internet Tool** explains how to use e-mail with Eudora Light, a widely used Windows-based e-mail client. Basic and advanced e-mail features are presented.

**Unit 4: Hypertext and the World Wide Web** is the second largest unit in the book. It uses Netscape Communicator and Microsoft Internet Explorer to demonstrate how World Wide Web services can be used with hypertext and multimedia data. The unit was moved closer to the front of the book, reflecting its importance to Internet access.

**Unit 5: Searching for Information on the Web** is new to this edition. It covers use of search engines such as Yahoo and Lycos to locate Web sites of interest. This unit also contains a section on finding business and personal information such as phone number, address, and e-mail address.

**Unit 6: Discussion Groups—News Groups and Mailing Lists** provides an overview of news groups and mailing list discussion groups found on the Internet. Examples show how to use these tools to find information about a multitude of topics as well as to respond to areas of interest.

**Unit 7: File Transfer Protocol (FTP) and Telnet** presents the basics of file transfers and remote terminal sessions. This short unit covers enough material to enable students to use FTP and Telnet, but also points users to the advanced tools available in the World Wide Web.

**Unit 8: Creating Web Documents in HTML** serves as an introduction to creating home pages for the Web. It introduces HTML formatting tags for building home pages with Notepad. It also demonstrates how to create a Web document with Netscape Composer.

**Unit 9: Electronic Commerce and the Future of the Internet** highlights emerging areas of personal and business applications on the Internet. It includes many examples of innovative use, including Intranets. The unit features a discussion of security issues for transmitting such sensitive information as credit card data.

# How to Use This Book

See pages xii–xiii for an illustrated guide to the features of the student textbook. This book is designed so that you can read Unit 1 and then go through remaining units in any order. Unit 2 provides technical material for dial-up users. We strongly suggest that the user work through *all* of the Guided Activities while sitting at the computer. You may learn this material best by practicing it actively. Each unit contains the following features:

- **Learning Objectives** at the beginning of each Unit comprise the knowledge you will acquire and skills you will develop as you master the unit content.

- **Net Ethics** features ask you to consider the unique ethical concerns that have arisen as the Internet continues to expand its role in our lives. Topics include use of copyrighted material, privacy issues, and competitive practices within the software industry. Discuss these issues with your peers as you apply your sense of ethics to a new arena.

- **Guided Activities** are step-by-step, hands-on, illustrated activities. They are embedded in key locations within the text material to allow for immediate re-inforcement of chapter concepts. The activities contain *Checkpoints* which ask critical thinking questions to increase your knowledge and understanding while you work. (Answers to Checkpoints are in an Appendix within the student text.)

*End-of-Unit Material:*

- **Command Reviews** at the end of each Unit are the keyboard and mouse commands covered in the unit in the format of a quick-reference table.

- **Vocabulary Exercises** ask you to review key terms and concepts within each unit. Through this feature you will master a new vocabulary for success with the Internet.

- **Review Questions** are designed for reinforcement and to test your knowledge of Unit content. These can serve as a Unit quiz and are excellent preparation for Unit tests.

- **Exercises** are additional assignments to give you practice. Some exercises have specific instructions, while others are less structured. Most exercises will use the computer.

- **Projects** are open-ended minicases. Projects tend to be more challenging than exercises in that they not only draw upon the skills you learned within the Unit but often ask you to be creative by extending beyond what you have learned. The *Team Option* encourages you to work with your peers to solve problems as you may do within a team in a business setting.

*Other Features:*

- The **Glossary Of Internet Terms** is a list of important Internet terms with definitions at the end of the textbook. This is a quick key to your new Internet vocabulary.

- **Answers To Checkpoints** and **Selected Review Questions** are included as an appendix to the student text. Checkpoints within the Guided Activities pose critical thinking questions, and these answers allow for a self-check.

- The **Electronic Instructor** contains general teaching suggestions with sample syllabi; solutions to Review Questions, Exercises, and Projects; and test questions.

- The **Web Home Page** is a comprehensive Web page that has been developed for this textbook. It is frequently cited in exercises and activities. The Web page contains breaking news about the Internet, updates to the textbook, current hot links to the Internet references, and links to the Internet shareware software used in the textbook. Its URL address is *computered.swep.com*. Select the Resources link.

## A Note of Thanks

- To Connie, my wife and colleague, for her steady encouragement, suggestions, and careful reading of this manuscript. Without her support this book would not exist.

- To my children, Anne and Cathy, who have unlimited patience with my writing habit, even on family vacations.

- To Dean Donald Bates and my colleagues in the School of Business at Indiana State University for their support.

- To Mark Cheatham of South-Western Educational Publishing for initiating the concept and keeping the book on track.

- To Jeanne Busemeyer, Malvine Litten, and others involved in the production of this book. Their professionalism and careful attention to details have made this an enjoyable task and a learning experience for me.

- Finally, to my students, who inspire me to write in a way that they can understand.

*B. J. M.*
*Terre Haute, Indiana*

# About the Author

**Bruce J. McLaren** is Professor of Systems and Decision Sciences at Indiana State University. He holds a BS degree in Aeronautical Engineering and a Ph.D. in Operations Management from Purdue University. He has been a consultant to many organizations in the integration of management information systems, and he has served on numerous computing committees at ISU. He formerly was a faculty member at the University of Virginia's Darden School.

Bruce teaches courses in management information systems, database management, telecommunications, network management, advanced microcomputer applications, and operations management. He has been recognized for outstanding teaching at Indiana State University.

He is the author of a column, "Your Business and the Internet," found in the *Terre Haute Journal of Business.* McLaren has authored more than twenty textbooks in the computer and business areas. He would like to hear from users of this book, and can be contacted by e-mail at *B-McLaren@indstate.edu.* His personal home page can be found at *http://www.indstate.edu/mclaren/home.html/.*

# CONTENTS

# Using This Book

**Learning Objectives** at the beginning of each Unit comprise the knowledge you will acquire and skills you will develop as you master the unit content.

**Key Terms** are listed on the unit opener and highlighted in color within the text narrative so you can quickly learn the vocabulary of the Internet.

---

## Connecting to the Internet

This unit describes the ways you can connect a client station to the Internet. Most of the unit deals with technical details about conducting dial-up sessions away from a lab environment. If you have already established an Internet connection, you may skip this unit and proceed to Unit 3.

### Learning Objectives

At the completion of this unit, you should be able to

1. explain the role of TCP/IP and Winsock software,

2. describe the various methods of connecting to the Internet,

3. list the advantages of using the dial-up method,

4. install Windows 95 Dial-Up Networking,

5. configure the Windows 95 TCP/IP settings,

6. create a Windows 95 PPP connection,

7. establish a PPP connection to the Internet.

### TCP/IP Software

As mentioned in Unit 1, the TCP/IP protocol provides a method for delivering data packets through the Internet from your computer to the server and vice versa. You must have a software package for your computer that understands how to communicate with the Internet. Any computer that is connected to the Internet must have a TCP/IP program.

#### TCP Protocol

TCP stands for Transmission Control Protocol and represents the part of the system that transmits your message from computer to computer across the Internet. It breaks down your message into

**14**

### Key Terms

The following terms are introduced in this unit. Be sure you know what each of them means.

Asymmetric Digital Subscriber Line (ADSL)
Authentication
Chameleon Sampler
Dial-up connection
Direct connection
Domain name server (DNS)
Internet Protocol (IP)
Internet service provider (ISP)
IP address
ISDN
Ping
Point to Point Protocol (PPP)
Routing
Serial Line Internet Protocol (SLIP)
Shell account
TCP/IP stack
Transmission Control Protocol (TCP)
Trumpet
V.9.0 (56 Kbps)
V.32bis (14.4 Kbps)
V.34 (28.8 or 33.6 Kbps)
Web TV
Winsock

---

### Net Ethics    *Sharing Your Internet Account*

Some individuals have opened an account with an Internet service provider, agreeing that they will abide by the rules and regulations associated with the account. Yet they make the user name and password available to others for a fee, effectively "sharing" the account in violation of the agreement. Is it ethical for several individuals to use one account when ordinarily they would have to purchase their own account? How is this different from "stealing" cable TV signals by wiring two apartments together on one account?

#### Installing Dial-Up Networking

The next step is to install the Dial-Up Networking utility in Windows 95 if it is not already installed on your computer. You will use the Add/Remove Programs program in the Control Panel to add this utility to your Windows configuration. The following Guided Activity will lead you through each of the steps.

### GUIDED ACTIVITY

#### 2.1    Installing Dial-Up Networking in Windows 95

In this activity you will check for dial-up networking and install it if necessary.

1. Make sure that you are running Windows 95 on your computer and that your modem has been installed in Windows 95.

**CHECKPOINT 2A**  How can you tell if a modem has been installed in your computer?

2. At the Windows 95 desktop, open the *My Computer* window by double-clicking its icon. Check for the Dial-Up Networking icon as shown in Figure 2.1. If it is already present, skip directly to Guided Activity 2.2.

**FIGURE 2.1**
*My Computer window*

Check for this icon

3. Next you will install Dial-Up Networking. You will need the original Windows 95 CD-ROM or floppy installation disks. Double-click the Control Panel icon in the My Computer window to open the Windows 95 Control Panel.

---

**Net Ethics** features ask you to consider the unique ethical concerns that have arisen as the Internet and new technologies continue to expand their role in our lives. Topics include use of copyrighted material, privacy issues, and competitive practices within the software industry. Discuss these issues with your peers as you apply your sense of ethics to a new arena.

**Guided Activities** are step-by-step, hands-on, illustrated activities embedded in key locations within the text material. They immediately reinforce chapter concepts. The activities contain *Checkpoints* which ask critical thinking questions to increase your knowledge and understanding while you work.

## End-of-Unit Material

**Summaries** provide a quick overview of each Unit.

**Command Reviews** at the end of each Unit are the keyboard and mouse commands covered in the unit in the format of a quick-reference table.

**Vocabulary Exercises** ask you to review key terms and concepts within each unit.

## SUMMARY

This unit contains a detailed discussion of the TCP/IP protocol, including IP addresses. The domain name server converts a name address into the 16-bit IP address. It is necessary to have a TCP/IP stack on your computer in order to connect to the Internet. In Windows, the Winsock software represents the TCP/IP stack.

There are three main ways to connect to the Internet. Direct connections are the fastest, using a dedicated connection to your school, campus, or office. Dial-up connections are the most common way to connect to the Internet, using a modem to connect to an Internet service provider. Shell accounts use a terminal connection to a text-based host.

The unit contains a step-by-step discussion of creating a dial-up connection in Windows 95 to an ISP. First add Dial-Up Networking, and then add the TCP/IP protocol. Next create a PPP connection to a specific ISP, and then use that connection to make the link. The unit includes a short demonstration of the Ping TCP/IP utility to test the connection and concludes with directions for disconnecting.

### Command Review

| | |
|---|---|
| Ping (MS-DOS) | Test the TCP/IP connection, returns IP address |
| Start→Programs | Launch a Windows program from the taskbar |
| Start→Settings→Control Panel | Open Windows Control Panel for making configuration changes |

### Vocabulary Exercise

*Write a short definition for each term in the following list.*

| | | |
|---|---|---|
| Asymmetric Digital Subscriber Line (ADSL) | Chameleon Sampler | Domain name server (DNS) |
| Authentication | Dial-up connection | Internet Protocol (IP) |
| | Direct connection | Internet service provider |

---

### Review Questions

1. What is the World Wide Web?
2. Explain the concept of hypertext.
3. What types of multimedia information can be viewed from Web documents?
4. What are Internet Explorer and Netscape Communicator?
5. Explain the following World Wide Web terms.
   a. home page
   b. URL
   c. HTTP
   d. link
   e. .GIF file
6. Explain how bookmarks or favorites can be used in your browser. Explain how to customize your bookmarks or favorites list.
7. What Web protocols or services are available through your browser? Briefly define the use of each protocol.
8. Explain how to play a multimedia file through your browser.

### Exercises

*You should use your own Web browser for these exercises. Keep in mind that the World Wide Web is constantly changing, and that information may appear in different formats and in different places over time. For the latest updates, see the textbook home page at http://computered.swep.com and select the Resources link.*

1. Use your Web browser to access your school or organization home page. Make a list of the important things that appear on the opening page.
2. Use your Web browser to access the home pages for the following sites. Print a copy of the home page for each site. Make a note of the important items on each opening page.

**Review Questions** are designed for reinforcement and to test your knowledge of Unit content. These can serve as a Unit quiz and are excellent preparation for Unit tests.

**Exercises** are additional assignments for reinforcement. Some exercises have specific instructions, while others are less structured. Most exercises require use of the computer.

**Projects** are open-ended minicases that summarize the activities of the unit. Projects tend to be more challenging than exercises. The *Team Option* encourages you to work with your peers to solve problems as you will do within a team in a business setting.

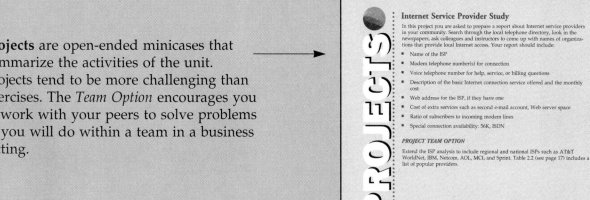

## PROJECTS

### Internet Service Provider Study

In this project you are asked to prepare a report about Internet service providers in your community. Search through the local telephone directory, look in the newspapers, ask colleagues and instructors to come up with names of organizations that provide local Internet access. Your report should include:

- Name of the ISP
- Modem telephone number(s) for connection
- Voice telephone number for help, service, or billing questions
- Description of the basic Internet connection service offered and the monthly cost
- Web address for the ISP, if they have one
- Cost of extra services such as second e-mail account, Web server space
- Ratio of subscribers to incoming modem lines
- Special connection availability: 56K, ISDN

### PROJECT TEAM OPTION

Extend the ISP analysis to include regional and national ISPs such as AT&T WorldNet, IBM, Netcom, AOL, MCI, and Sprint. Table 2.2 (see page 17) includes a list of popular providers.

# See These Other Texts About the Internet!

## *Internet Explorer 4.0* by Dennis O. Gehris
This product is an introductory text to the Microsoft Web browser Internet Explorer 4.0.

| Product | ISBN |
| --- | --- |
| Student Text | 0-538-68597-2 |
| Electronic Instructor Package | 0-538-68598-0 |

**Table of Contents**

## *FrontPage 98* by Mark Ciampa
This text introduces Microsoft® FrontPage 98 and allows users to create Web pages with ease.

| Product | ISBN |
| --- | --- |
| Student Text | 0-538-68601-4 |
| Electronic Instructor Package | 0-538-68602-2 |

**Table of Contents**

## *Internet Concepts and Activities* by Barksdale, Rutter, Rand
This popular text delivers the Internet in a fun and colorful format. It is an Internet quick-start that focuses on the practical side of the 'Net to answer the question, "What does it mean to me?"

| Product | ISBN |
| --- | --- |
| Student Text (perfect bound) | 0-538-72166-9 |
| Student Text (spiral bound) | 0-538-72088-3 |
| Electronic Instructor Package | 0-538-72131-6 |

**Table of Contents**

## *Internet Custom Modules*

Need to include Internet topics in your curriculum? Our Internet modules offer an up-to-date, concise overview of Internet technology topics with introductory concepts. Illustrated with screen captures and figures, each short (30-to-60-page) module also includes glossary terms and exercises. The modules you choose will be combined into a custom textbook available within days of your order. Or, bundle one or two modules with another South-Western title for even more versatility. Call 1-800-245-6724 for more information.

Instructor support materials available on Web site (for instructors only; password protected) include approximately 4 pages per module of teaching tips, lecture notes, background information, and answers to the student exercises.

Internet Custom Modules:

South-Western
Educational Publishing

**Join Us on the Internet**
**WWW: http://www.swep.com**

# Development of the Internet

This unit serves as an introduction to the "information superhighway" called the Internet. It presents the basics of networks and describes the development of the Internet. It concludes with an overview both of information found on the Internet and of the tools you can use to access this information.

## Learning Objectives

At the completion of this unit, you should be able to

1. describe the basics of networks,

2. explain how the Internet evolved,

3. describe how data packets are transferred across the network,

4. list the kinds of information found on the Internet,

5. discuss the tools used to access information found on the Internet.

## Network Basics

Networks are composed of computers and various computing devices such as printers and disk drives. Networks are connected with some **communications channel** in such a way that all users can have access to the resources found in that network. The channel is typically a copper telephone wire or fiber optic cable but can also include high-speed wireless microwave and satellite connections.

The individual user's computer is called a **workstation** or **client**. The workstation or client

## Key Terms

*The following terms are introduced in this unit. Be sure you know what each of them means.*

10Base-T
Anonymous FTP
Bandwidth
Browser
Client
Communications channel
Discussion group
Download
Driver
Electronic mail (e-mail)
FTP
Gateway
Home page
Host
Hypertext
Information superhighway
Internet
Local area network (LAN)
Mid-level network
Network
Packet
Server
Shared resource
Stand-alone computer
Store and forward
Surfing the Internet
Telnet
Viewer
Wide area network (WAN)
Workstation
World Wide Web (WWW)

typically has its own CPU, hard disk and other local storage, video, and keyboard. The client computer is usually an IBM-compatible PC or a Macintosh computer that can also stand alone (a **stand-alone computer**) and work independently of the network. The client computer could be a UNIX workstation that could also function as a server.

Computers that contain information that others can access are called **hosts** or **servers**. A server typically contains a large hard drive so that it can provide information, software, and data to be shared with client stations. It may also have other **shared resources** such as CD-ROMs, tape drives, image scanners, high-speed or specialty printers, and communication links. A server can also function as a client in certain network configurations.

## Local Area Networks

Most networks use a system of dedicated wires called a **local area network (LAN)**. The LAN may be limited to a single room, building, or several buildings. Some LANs even work across a metropolitan area. When a large number of users are connected to a network, it is often subdivided into several smaller interconnected LANs for efficiency purposes. That way, fewer users on a single LAN segment compete for available transmission time.

Figure 1.1 shows a schematic diagram of a local area network. The server computer typically has a significant amount of hard disk storage space and acts as a **gateway** for communications with other networks outside the LAN. The LAN may feature other shared resources such as laser and specialty printers, fax capability, tape drives for backups, and image scanners.

**FIGURE 1.1**
*Local area network diagram*

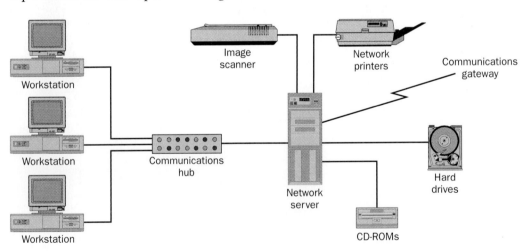

The most popular kind of network connection uses inexpensive telephone wiring. The standard is called **10Base-T**, referring to the *10* Mbps (megabits per second) data transmission rate using *baseband* transmission and connecting with *twisted pair* telephone wire. In many cases the organization can use existing (but unused) telephone wiring that has already been laid to each office. Typically, the most expensive part of a local area network is the cost of installing and troubleshooting the network cable itself. 100Base-T represents baseband transmissions at 100 Mbps.

Most networks break a message into **packets** of information traveling between a source and a destination. Each packet contains data and additional identifying information that allows it to be routed error-free to the ultimate destination. Unit 2 will describe in more detail the TCP/IP packets used over the Internet.

## Wide Area Networks

A wide area network (WAN) includes networks and computers that span a wide geographic area, typically across a city or state or even between countries. In most cases the WAN uses a communications channel that is rented from a telephone company or data communications carrier. Some large firms employ their own dedicated communications channels for wide area voice and data communications. The Internet is an example of a WAN. We'll talk more about the Internet later in this unit.

## Workstation Requirements

To connect your workstation to a local area network, you must have a network connection and a network interface device. Most desktop computers will use a network interface card (NIC) that plugs into an expansion slot in a manner similar to a modem. The NIC will have a connection at the back that allows you to attach a cable, connecting it with the network outlet. To connect using the 10Base-T standard, plug in the RJ-45 cable, which resembles an RJ-11 standard telephone cord with a modular connector at each end. Some networks use a *coaxial* (coax) cable that resembles a cable TV connector.

Home workstations will not be connected to a LAN but instead must use a modem to connect to a network. Rather than a network interface card, the computer will use the modem to dial through the telephone and make the connection. Even with today's high-speed modems, this method is much slower than having a direct network connection. The modem option is discussed in more detail in Unit 2.

After the hardware connection is established, each workstation must also have network access software, called a driver. The network driver informs the computer of the specific network hardware and also allows it to communicate with the network using additional commands. The drivers must be prepared for the specific model of network card, and must match the network operating system in use. Windows 95 drivers are discussed in Unit 2.

## *The Internet*

The Internet is a network of networks. There are more than one hundred thousand networks—and more being added every day—connected to the Internet. Think of it

---

**Net Ethics**          *Using the Words of Others*

The Internet provides easy access to the ideas of others. It provides you with the ability to cut and paste text or pictures into a document of your own in an instant. However, just because this information is easy to use, do not assume that you can present it to others as being your own. If you use the ideas of others in your own writing, you should include a note about where that information came from, just as if you had found it in a book. Why do you think it is unethical to present the ideas of others as being your own? What harm could result from doing this?

as a high-speed highway system that connects regions. Each region has its own networks with many connected organizations. In effect, each organization has its own local area networks with individual users' workstations. Some users connect via the local area network; others connect with a modem via telephone lines.

To send a message over the Internet, you must connect to a local network. It, in turn, will be connected to a regional network, which connects to the main "backbone" lines connecting the regional networks. If the destination for your message is within the local network, the message will not be routed to the regional network. However, if the message is destined for a distant location, it will be routed on appropriate links until it is delivered. Some people like to think of the Internet as the information superhighway, a term that has entered the language and culture of today.

# Early History

Although we would like to think that there is a grand plan for the design, implementation, and expansion of the Internet, it actually has happened over time almost by accident. The early network experience was primarily with local area networks. Wide area networks that connect other networks were much less successful.

## ARPANET

The original Internet began in the 1960s as a U.S. Department of Defense network called ARPANET. This was designed to support military research about how to build networks that could withstand partial cable outages from military attacks. As a result, the network was implemented using a store and forward procedure. This means that each piece of information was split up into packets and transmitted from one network node to another, ultimately ending up at the destination. A complete and direct path from sender to destination was not needed. If part of the network became damaged, the network was able to resend the packets over an alternate path to assure their delivery.

Soon research and academic users were connecting to ARPANET and using it for more than just military research. Much of the early Internet work was conducted at colleges and universities. One important fact soon emerged—the network must allow for a wide variety of client and server computers.

## CSNET

As the UNIX operating system became popular among computer science departments at universities, another WAN was established to allow researchers to communicate with one another. Called CSNET, this network was instrumental at bringing institutions of all sizes together electronically. Enthusiastic professors and students using CSNET were an important factor in bringing about the implementation of the full Internet at many campuses.

## NSFNET

Another development in the 1980s provided more reasons for connectivity. The National Science Foundation (NSF) funded five supercomputer centers at major universities, making these important resources available to scholars who could establish a need. The NSFNET network was built to provide this connectivity between universities. This network operated at 56,000 bits per second and quickly became very popular. The NSF grants were given to schools that promised to encourage development of widespread use of the network. In time, the NSFNET became saturated as more users saw its advantages.

## The Internet Today

In 1987 the NSF central network was upgraded significantly with faster telephone lines and bigger computers. In 1995 NSF gave up control of the central network. Today this central backbone is maintained by commercial telecommunications companies. It comprises 15 sites and provides for high-speed communications across the country. These 15 sites are called mid-level networks. Figure 1.2 shows the interconnection of these 15 sites and other points in North America.

**FIGURE 1.2**
*Visualization study of mid-level backbone network*

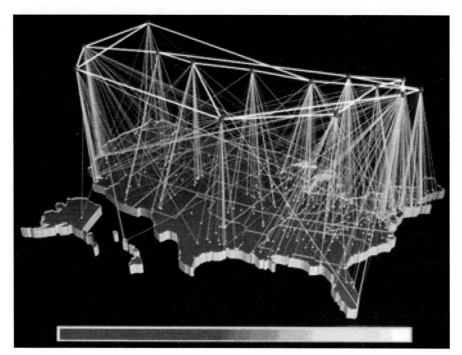

In 1983 the Internet connected fewer than 600 computers. By 1997 it had exploded to connect more than 50 million users and some 19 million host computers around the world. Every six months the number of users doubles! There are more than 4.5 million commercial addresses on the Internet with more joining each day.[1] Companies like General Electric, Hewlett-Packard, Volvo, Bank of America, the Home Shopping Network, and more are setting up Internet pages for customers and potential customers.

## National Technology Grid

In 1997 the National Science Foundation established funding for a new high-speed grid to link more than 50 educational, research, and defense institutions. Led by the University of Illinois' National Center for Supercomputing Applications

---

[1] For more information on Internet size, see the Internet Domain Survey produced by Network Wizards. The data is available on the Internet at *http://www.nw.com/*.

(NCSA), the grid will function as a new backbone, running at 600 Mbps. This high-speed connection will benefit the scientific and engineering communities that need higher bandwidth links. For more information, see the NCSA Web site at *http://alliance.ncsa.uiuc.edu/news/press_prototype.html.*

## The Global Internet

Today the Internet extends to more than 200 countries on every continent. Many other countries can connect to other networks, and thus connect indirectly to the Internet. Although you can sit at home and access Internet sites all over the world, it may take longer to communicate with overseas sites. The bandwidth, or channel capacity, is limited in many areas of the world. Even with limited bandwith, however, when servers in North America are busy in the daytime, similar information stored in Europe or Asia may be retrieved faster because it is nighttime at those sites.

English seems to be the universal language used on the Internet. You can access FTP sites in Germany or France and see the same program names and the same menu prompts as in the United States.

## *Overview of Information on the Internet*

There is *so* much information available through the Internet that few people can make use of it easily. A new term, surfing the Internet, has come into use to describe the way many people work with the Internet. They come across a particularly interesting address, open the information found there, and then follow a link to another interesting piece of information and so forth. Many times they end up in a completely different place from where they began—happily lost, or just browsing, in the jungle of computerized information.

## The Information Superhighway

The phrase *information superhighway* has been used, perhaps incorrectly, as a synonym for the Internet. It became popular in 1993 when the Clinton administration presented a position paper describing the development of the National Information Infrastructure (NII) in this country. It proposes that any citizen would have affordable access to information resources, regardless of where he or she lives or works. The proposal estimates that accelerated deployment of the NII will increase the U.S. gross domestic product (GDP) by $194 billion by the year 2007 and increase productivity by 20 to 40 percent.

## Electronic Mail

Perhaps the most common use of the Internet is to transport electronic mail (e-mail) between users. E-mail is a method of sending messages electronically from sender to receiver. The sender is able to create a letter at one computer, edit it electronically, and then send it to one or more users at other locations with the push of a button. The message is sent on its way without further intervention by the sender. The receiver is able to read the message and then print the message on paper or prepare a reply to it. Users can place attachments to the original message such as word processing documents, spreadsheets, and graphic images. Unit 3 contains an in-depth discussion of e-mail.

## Discussion Groups

The Internet provides thousands of discussion group forums where users can pose questions or read responses from other Internet users who have common interests. These discussion groups are sometimes called Listserv groups or news groups and are covered in more detail in Unit 6. Discussion groups exist for nearly any possible topic. Many Internet software packages have special news reader software programs to help users wade their way through the groups.

## Transferring Data—FTP

An enormous amount of data of all kinds is readily available on computers attached to the Internet. You can download (retrieve) data stored there by using FTP, or File Transfer Protocol. With FTP you can connect to a server somewhere on the Internet, identify the file to transfer to your own disk drive, and then initiate the transfer. Many sites allow anonymous FTP transfers, meaning that you can log in as an anonymous user or visitor, without previous approval. Other sites require that you have a valid account on that machine before gaining permission to transfer files. FTP is covered in more detail in Unit 7.

## Remote Log Ins—Telnet

It is also possible to use the Internet to connect to a server or host computer somewhere else on the Internet and conduct a regular session as if you were physically present at its location. The Telnet program allows you to initiate the contact and act as a terminal over the network. For example, you might begin a Telnet session with the Library of Congress information system called Marvel and search through its computerized library catalog. Telnet is covered in more detail in Unit 5.

## World Wide Web

The most popular way to access information on the Internet is through the World Wide Web (WWW). The Web is the part of the Internet used for multimedia documents containing text, pictures, animation, video, and sounds. It is based on hypertext, a method of presenting and linking related information. To use the Web, you must have a Web viewer or browser. The two most popular viewers are Netscape Navigator and Microsoft Internet Explorer. They display information on a Web home page, or opening screen. The home page shows various text and graphical items. Some of the items appear in a different color or are underlined, signifying they represent links to more information about that item. The Web is the fastest-growing part of the Internet and represents the single most popular way of accessing and viewing information on the Internet. We present more about the Web in Units 6–9.

## Unlimited Information on the Internet

You will find the content of a great many newspapers, magazines, books, and pictures on the Internet, presented in a readable and searchable format. You can peruse electronic want ads and look for a job on the Internet. You can check stock market quotes and read company reports. Government documents from the IRS and Social Security may be accessed from the Internet. You can tour a college campus by visiting its World Wide Web home page, as shown in Figure 1.3.

**FIGURE 1.3**

*Indiana State University World Wide Web home page*

You can shop on-line from individual businesses and from multiple stores at electronic shopping malls. You can search flight schedules and make airline reservations on-line. You will find a generous supply of (mostly) humorous one-liners on the Internet. Most of the information sources are free, but some products are available on a subscription-only basis. Most of these products have a free trial period during which you can evaluate them.

## More About the Internet

So much information is available today that you might be overwhelmed by the possibilities and not know just where to start. You have made the right decision so far by starting with this book. We will guide you through getting started with the Internet and take you far enough so that you will be able to help yourself.

Perhaps the most obvious place to look for information about the Internet is on the Internet itself. Units 4–9 contain references to many information sources. You can view text, graphics, and videos, and even listen to explanations about the Internet through your PC or Mac. With innovative features like Chat, CU-SeeMe, and Internet Phones, you can communicate live with others. Unit 9 presents a

NET TIP
**Web Addresses**

Current links to most Web sites in this book can be found on the *Understanding & Using the Internet* Home Page. Choose **Resources** at **computered.swep.com**. Remember that a Web address may change at any time. An address given in this book as an example may no longer be valid. If this is so, either access the Home Page for the current link or do a search to find a similar site (see Unit 5 for a discussion of search methods).

view of the future of the Internet, including a discussion about business and commercial uses.

# Obtaining the Software Used in This Book

This book illustrates the Internet using Windows 95 and Windows NT software. Although your specific operating software might be different from what we are using, the principles are essentially the same. Windows 3.1 and Macintosh users can find nearly identical versions of most of the packages listed below.

Some of the software is available on the Internet itself, while other portions may be purchased at low cost at a bookstore. Your institution may have already made the investment in Internet software. If you plan to connect to the Internet from a dial-up connection, this section shows where to find some of the components. We recommend that you cover Unit 7 on FTP *before* attempting to obtain any of this software by FTP. The textbook's home page can be found by visiting Resources at *computered.swep.com.* This home page contains current links to the latest versions of these programs, along with short descriptions of the new versions.

## Commercial Internet Service Providers

If you want to use a commercial information service provider such as Prodigy or America Online, obtain the software from those sources. AOL in particular gives away the software with a ten-hour free trial. Prodigy has a similar program but doesn't generally send out free disks. Look for a guest membership packaged with your modem. CompuServe also has a free trial membership and often comes packaged with your modem.

## Trumpet Winsock TCP/IP

The Trumpet Winsock TCP/IP package is a useful tool for dialing in to an Internet Service Provider under Windows 3.1. If you are using Windows 95, install its built-in TCP/IP protocol instead, as explained in Unit 2. You can obtain Trumpet via FTP at *ftp://ftp.trumpet.com.au/ftp/pub/winsock/.* This is an Australian address, and it might take some time to connect. An alternate FTP location is *ftp://papa. indstate.edu/winsockl/winsock/.* The file is called twsk30d.exe. This is not a free program; you can use it for educational purposes for a trial period but must pay a small fee to the developer if you continue to use it.

## Eudora Light

Unit 3 uses Eudora Light to demonstrate e-mail concepts. If you want to obtain your own copy, download it from *http://www.eudora.com/eudoralight/.* The Eudora Web page contains much information about the shareware version of Eudora used in this book as well as the commercial version called Eudora Pro. Additional documentation for Eudora is also available in Acrobat PDF format at the same Web site.

## News Xpress 2.0 Newsreader

The News Xpress newsreader client provides support for news groups. You can download an evaluation copy from *http://www.malch.com/nxfaq.html.* Versions for

Windows 3.1 and Windows 95/Windows NT are available. Usenet news groups are covered in Unit 6 of this text.

# WS_FTP32 FTP Client

The WS_FTP32 program is a 32-bit FTP client designed for Windows 95 and Windows NT. A 16-bit version is available for Windows 3.1. You can download an evaluation copy from *http://www.ipswitch.com/*. Although similar to the predecessor version, the new version uses two display windows instead of four windows. The LE (Limited Edition) version may be used for free by academic users; the Pro version, with more capabilities, is available for a fee. The text file that comes with WS_FTP32LE explains license restrictions.

# Netscape Navigator 4.x

Netscape Navigator is the browser we use most often in this book to explore the information found on the World Wide Web. Netscape Navigator is free and can be downloaded via FTP from *ftp.netscape.com/pub/*. From there, navigate to the desired folder. Version 4.03 is about 8 MB in size. Of course, if you have a functional Web browser, you can use the Netscape Web site at *http://home.netscape.com/download/*.

# Netscape Communicator

This is a software suite that includes Netscape Navigator as well as much additional functionality. Communicator adds modules for HTML document development (Composer), e-mail (Messenger), groupware (Collabra), real-time conferencing (Conference), and push broadcasting tool (Netcaster). Download it from *http://home.netscape.com/download/*.

CAUTION **Communicator is a very large product and may take a long time to download via modem.**

# Microsoft Internet Explorer

Microsoft's browser tool is called Internet Explorer (IE). IE is installed with Windows 95 and later versions of Microsoft Office. It is comparable to Netscape Communicator and comes with several optional modules. You can download a copy of Internet Explorer 4.0 at no cost from *http://www.microsoft.com/ie/*.

CAUTION **Internet Explorer 4.0 is a very large product and may take a long time to download via modem.**

# Windows 95 Internet Software

Windows 95 comes with built-in TCP/IP and networking support, including PPP connections to dial-up services. Windows 95 also comes with the following character-based Internet programs to get you started. We will use GUI programs for the rest of this book. Use of the Windows 95 TCP/IP tools is covered in Unit 2.

- Ping (to check the status of your Internet connection)
- FTP (to download and upload files)

- Telnet (to establish a remote terminal session)

- Tracert (to display the names of intermediate routers between your PC and an Internet host)

- WinIPcfg (GUI tool to display the TCP/IP configuration status while connected)

# SUMMARY

This unit describes basic network concepts and provides an overview of the development of the Internet, from ARPANET to NSFNET. The Internet is an example of a wide area network. It is available in more than 200 countries and on most of the continents. The most common Internet application is electronic mail. Discussion groups allow users to discuss topics of common interest. Discussion groups are similar to e-mail. FTP, or file transfer protocol, is used to move files from one place to another on the Internet. Telnet is a method for doing a remote terminal login to a host computer or server. The World Wide Web is a multimedia section of the Internet that uses hypertext to organize information. A Web browser is necessary to view information found on the Web. The chapter concludes with directions on obtaining copies of the software described in this book.

## Vocabulary Exercise

*Write a short definition for each term in the following list.*

| | | |
|---|---|---|
| 10Base-T | Home page | Shared resource |
| Anonymous FTP | Host | Stand-alone computer |
| Bandwidth | Hypertext | Store and forward |
| Browser | Information superhigh- | Surfing the Internet |
| Client | way | Telnet |
| Communications channel | Internet | Viewer |
| Discussion group | Local area network | Wide area network |
| Download | (LAN) | (WAN) |
| Driver | Mid-level network | Workstation |
| Electronic mail (e-mail) | Network | World Wide Web |
| FTP | Packet | (WWW) |
| Gateway | Server | |

## Review Questions

1. Explain the function of the following network components.

    a. server

    b. workstation or client

    c.  cabling

    d.  packets

2. What are the differences between a LAN and a WAN? Which type of network is the Internet?

3. What are the requirements to connect a personal computer to the Internet?

4. Discuss the role of each of the following networks in the development of the Internet.

    a.  ARPANET

    b.  CSNET

    c.  NSFNET

5. Explain in detail how each of the following Internet services can be useful to a student at school or an employee at work.

    a.  e-mail

    b.  discussion group

    c.  FTP (file transfer protocol)

    d.  Telnet (remote login)

    e.  World Wide Web

6. How can you obtain the Internet software used in this book?

7. What are the most popular Web browsers available today?

8. Explain the type of application associated with each of these software products.

    a.  Eudora Light

    b.  Netscape Communicator

    c.  WS_FTP32

    d.  Internet Explorer

**PROJECTS**

## University Admissions Web Site

Many colleges and universities have developed a comprehensive Web site for admissions and financial aid. Prepare a short report about the admissions and financial aid features of the Web site at a selected institution. Explain the options available to users at the opening screen. Describe the options available from the Admissions menu. What sort of information can a prospective student obtain from this Web site? Does this school have an on-line application? If approved by your instructor, contact the admissions office at this school and find out what features are intended for the site in the future. What additional features or information would *you* recommend?

### PROJECT TEAM OPTION

Visit the Web sites of at least five well known universities and describe the admissions and financial aid information that appears there. Organize a table for main items and indicate which of the six schools (including the school you investigated above) provide that feature at the admissions Web site.

# UNIT 2

# Connecting to the Internet

This unit describes the ways you can connect a client station to the Internet. Most of the unit deals with technical details about conducting dial-up sessions away from a lab environment. If you have already established an Internet connection, you may skip this unit and proceed to Unit 3.

## Learning Objectives

At the completion of this unit, you should be able to

1. explain the role of TCP/IP and Winsock software,

2. describe the various methods of connecting to the Internet,

3. list the advantages of using the dial-up method,

4. install Windows 95 Dial-Up Networking,

5. configure the Windows 95 TCP/IP settings,

6. create a Windows 95 PPP connection,

7. establish a PPP connection to the Internet.

## TCP/IP Software

As mentioned in Unit 1, the TCP/IP protocol provides a method for delivering data packets through the Internet from your computer to the server and vice versa. You must have a software package for your computer that understands how to communicate with the Internet. Any computer that is connected to the Internet must have a TCP/IP program.

### TCP Protocol

TCP stands for Transmission Control Protocol and represents the part of the system that transmits your message from computer to computer across the Internet. It breaks down your message into

## Key Terms

*The following terms are introduced in this unit. Be sure you know what each of them means.*

Asymmettric Digital Subscriber Line (ADSL)
Authentication
Chameleon Sampler
Dial-up connection
Direct connection
Domain name server (DNS)
Internet Protocol (IP)
Internet service provider (ISP)
IP address
ISDN
Ping
Point to Point Protocol (PPP)
Routing
Serial Line Internet Protocol (SLIP)
Shell account
TCP/IP stack
Transmission Control Protocol (TCP)
Trumpet
V9.0 (56 Kbps)
V.32bis (14.4 Kbps)
V.34 (28.8 or 33.6 Kbps)
Web TV
Winsock

pieces called *packets.* Each packet contains header information about where it is from, where it is going, the type of information carried within it, and the information itself. Packets range in size from a few bytes to 1,500 bytes. A byte contains 8 bits and is roughly equivalent to one character.

The packets are numbered, and TCP makes sure the packets are delivered error-free at the destination in the correct sequence. TCP handles the routing of your message. As parts of the network become busy or unreliable, TCP will reroute the packets by finding another path to the ultimate destination. If a packet is not received by a certain time, TCP will request that it be resent. Or, if the packet is received with an error, TCP also will ask that it be resent.

# IP Protocol

IP stands for Internet Protocol and represents the methods for sending and receiving data packets. Each computer attached to the Internet must have a unique IP address, which is formed by four groups of numbers separated by periods. For instance, the main Web server's IP address at Indiana State University is 139.102.15.15. Each group of numbers represents four bits, or decimal values from 0 to 255. With 256 possible values for each group of numbers, there are $256^4$ or more than four billion IP addresses possible. The first number in the group represents the network, in this case 139. Most of the machines at a site will share the same first number in the IP address. Later numbers represent subnets and, eventually, the specific computer on that subnet. No two computers on the Internet will have the same IP address.

For convenience, we usually refer to addresses on the Internet by a name rather than a number. The domain name server (DNS) will automatically convert that name to the actual IP address when you send a message or refer to an Internet resource. You can use the Ping program to find out the equivalent IP address for an Internet site. Table 2.1 shows some Internet addresses and their numeric equivalents. The numeric IP address can change over time.

It is necessary to have a TCP/IP connection to use the Internet. Commonly called a TCP/IP stack (or PPP for modem connections), this software communicates with the Internet and your computer. If your computer does not have its own Internet connection (called a shell account, described later), the host computer that is connected to the Internet will have a TCP/IP connection.

The TCP/IP connection is established as part of the network configuration whether you have a direct connection or are dialing in to an Internet provider. Although you may use Novell NetWare as the network software, a separate TCP/IP driver will be added to allow IP packets to pass through the local server to the Internet.

## TIP

The Ping program is built into Windows 95. If you have a TCP/IP connection established, you can look up an IP address for a domain name address. Open the MS-DOS prompt and type `Ping web. indstate.edu` to see the IP address for the ISU Web server.

---

**NET TIP**
**Web Addresses**

Current links to most Web sites in this book can be found on the *Understanding & Using the Internet* Home Page. Choose **Resources** at **computered.swep.com.** Remember that a Web address may change at any time. An address given in this book as an example may no longer be valid. If this is so, either access the Home Page for the current link or do a search to find a similar site (see Unit 5 for a discussion of search methods).

| INTERNET ADDRESS | NUMERIC IP ADDRESS |
|---|---|
| ftp.netscape.com | 205.216.163.99 |
| web.indstate.edu | 139.102.15.15 |
| www.microsoft.com | 207.68.143.92 |
| cnn.com | 207.25.71.28 |
| www.whitehouse.gov | 198.137.240.91 |
| jazz.trumpet.com.au | 203.5.119.51 |

## Winsock Software

Winsock refers to Windows Socket, a necessary part of the TCP/IP software for Windows users. Winsock is a well-known Windows programming standard and is generally built in to the TCP/IP software. All of the Windows Internet applications covered in this book use the Winsock 1.1 protocol. You will frequently find that Windows Internet software available as shareware is collected under the Winsock label. A new, higher-speed standard called Winsock 2.0 is under development.

Microsoft frequently makes free upgrades to its Windows components available on its Web site for downloading. See *www.microsoft.com/windows95/* for more information about upgrades for the Winsock or dial-up networking components.

# *Methods of Connection*

There are three main methods of connecting to the Internet. The first method uses a direct network connection, and typically is found on a school campus or in a company. The second method involves using a modem to dial in to an Internet service provider. Although much slower, the dial-up method enables you to connect from virtually anywhere through the telephone system. The last method is through a text-only shell account to a UNIX host and limits what you can do on the Internet.

Although not yet widely available, a new kind of Internet connection may be offered by your cable television company. The *Telecommunications Act of 1996* made it possible for the cable TV company to provide two-way interactive services. Likewise, the telephone company will be permitted to provide programming content. Using the high-speed connection already coming to your house or apartment, the cable TV connection will provide significantly higher connection speeds for Internet users.

## Direct Network Connection

Many schools and companies have already connected classrooms, computing labs, dorm rooms, and office computers to the campus network. Once this takes place, it is easy to connect to the Internet. Many local area networks are capable of speeds of 10 megabits per second (Mbps). This direct connection is preferable, particularly when large files or graphic images and sounds are transmitted over the network. Configuration settings can be determined centrally and implemented across the network, making it easier for users. The connection generally is available around the clock. Many Internet users find that nighttime workloads are lower, which speeds up the access times. The direct connection typically is funded at the campus or organization level, with no hourly charges to users for connect time.

# Dialing in to an Internet Service Provider

This method replaces the high-speed network cable with a lower-speed dial-up connection using a modem and the public telephone system. The user runs a special dial-up program to provide for the TCP/IP protocol. This program controls the modem and makes the Internet connection. The Internet service provider (ISP) at the other end of the telephone call maintains a port that resembles the one you might have at your organization. You will probably have the same services available as you have with a direct connection, but the transmission rate will be much slower. Most Internet service providers do not charge for the actual connection time, using a flat monthly fee. Your school or company may have a dial-up Internet port available at little or no cost. We'll demonstrate how to do this in a Guided Activity later in this unit.

There are two kinds of commercial information services. The first kind represents dedicated dial-up Internet connections. If you use one of these companies, you have a full Internet connection but few additional information services. The other commercial providers offer extensive on-line information to their subscribers in addition to possibly limited Internet access. The recent trend is to provide full Internet access to subscribers. All of these companies charge for the Internet connection, some with an initial membership and monthly fees. Some have an hourly charge plan for those who don't use the Internet very much. If it is available to you, use the low-cost dial-up connection to your school or organization.

Table 2.2 shows some of the better-known commercial Internet service providers and lists contact information. Unless otherwise noted, the phone number is a voice line. You can use the Web address shown to obtain more information if you have a working Web browser.

## QUESTIONS FOR YOUR ISP

The competition for the Internet user's ISP business is increasing. Although many ISPs offer the $19.95 unlimited usage package, there are some additional questions

**TABLE 2.2**
*Commercial Internet providers*

| PROVIDER | PHONE NUMBER | WEB ADDRESS |
|---|---|---|
| America Online | (800) 827-6364 | www.aol.com |
| AT&T WorldNet | (800) WORLDNET | www.att.com/worldnet |
| CompuServe | (800) 848-8990 | www.compuserve.com |
| GTE Intelligent Network | (800) 927-3000 | www.gte.net |
| IBM | (800) 821-4612 | www.ibm.net |
| MCI Internet | (800) 550-0927 | www.mci.com |
| Microsoft Network | (800) 373-3676 | www.msn.com |
| Netcom | (800) 353-6600 | www.netcom.com |
| Prodigy | (800) 776-3449 | www.prodigy.com |
| Sprint | (800) 747-9428 | www.sprint.com |

you should ask an ISP before signing on. For more information, see the article "Choosing Your ISP" in PC Magazine Online, *http://www.zdnet.com/pcmag/features/ispchoose/_open.htm.*

- Are there local (non-toll) phone numbers in your area?

- Do you offer an e-mail account with the Internet service? What is the cost of extra e-mail accounts for other family members?

- What is the ratio of subscribers to incoming modem ports? (A ratio above 10 may mean you'll get lots of busy signals.)

- Do you offer Web page space for users who want to create their own home pages? How much space is available?

- Do you offer free software (browser, e-mail) with the subscription? Can I use my own e-mail and browser software?

- Do you offer 56K service? What is the cost of this service? (See the following section on modems.)

- Do you offer ISDN service? What is the cost of this service?

## *MODEM STANDARDS*

Older modem connections generally run at 14,400 bps or 14.4 Kbps, using the V.32bis standard. Newer modems capable of running at 28.8 or 33.6 Kbps use the V.34 standard. Although this may seem fast, even the 28.8 Kbps connection is more than 300 times slower than a direct Internet connection running at 10 Mbps. You will mostly notice the problem with slower speeds when retrieving large files with FTP or when retrieving graphical images from the World Wide Web.

The newest modem technique provides for faster modem speeds when downloading files from a compatible service provider. Two groups are competing for the final standard. 3Com's U.S. Robotics modems use the x2 protocol to achieve up to 56 Kbps download speeds, while Rockwell's K56flex protocol does the same thing with a slightly different technique. In February 1998 the V.90 standard for 56k modems was approved as a compromise between the two groups. Both groups advertise that their modems can be upgraded to the final standard. Of course, your ISP must provide a compatible modem at the other end of your call to make the 56 Kbps speed connection. For a detailed technical discussion of the x2 and K56flex protocols, see *http://x2.usr.com/technology/whitepapers.html* and *http://www.nb.rockwell.com/K56flex/.*

## Net Ethics    *Sharing Your Internet Account*

Some individuals have opened an account with an Internet service provider, agreeing that they will abide by the rules and regulations associated with the account. Yet they make the user name and password available to others for a fee, effectively "sharing" the account in violation of the agreement. Is it ethical for several individuals to use one account when ordinarily they would have to purchase their own account? How is this different from "stealing" cable TV signals by wiring two apartments together on one account?

ADSL (Asymmettric Digital Subscriber Line) is expected to be available in late 1998. This digital telephone connection will allow you to use your home telephone line for 1.5 Mbps transmission speeds *and* use the phone at the same time on the same line.

**To determine whether your phone line supports the x2 and K56 technologies, you can dial a toll-free number with your V.34 modem and follow the directions. Use a terminal program such as the Windows 95 Hyperterminal. The number is 1-888-877-9248. The login name is *Line Test*. About 60 percent of phone lines today support the new modem technology. For more information, see *http://x2.usr.com/connectnow/linetest.html*.**

### ISDN CONNECTIONS

A faster telephone connection is finally becoming available to speed up Internet and other dial-up connections. ISDN stands for Integrated Services Digital Network and represents a significantly faster way to connect, up to 128 Kbps. ISDN is a digital connection directly to the phone company, eliminating the need for an analog modem. ISDN rates are based on a fixed monthly fee plus a charge for connection time or volume of data transmitted and can be expensive. Check with your local telephone company for availability and rates.

ISDN lines require a special modem-like adapter, and the computer at the other end must also have an ISDN connection. ISDN offers the advantage of simultaneous voice and data (limited to 64 Kbps when voice is active) on the same phone line. Some ISDN subscribers use it as a second voice phone line and a high-speed data connection, making the high cost somewhat easier to accept. We will not illustrate how to set up an ISDN connection here.

### DIRECT SATELLITE CONNECTION

You may be able to install a small satellite dish and receive a direct Internet feed at sustained speeds up to 400 Mbps. The DirecPC satellite service provides for a normal telephone link for requests sent *to* the Internet, while downloads *from* the Internet travel over the DirecTV satellite. Transmissions are actually made at 12 Mbps to your dish, but because other people are using the service, your portion operates from 200–400 Mbps. Large Web documents with graphics and file downloads see the biggest benefit from satellite transmission; e-mail shows the least.

The DirecPC package requires a monthly ISP fee as well as an initial startup fee, plus the cost of the dish and the installation. There is even a package that combines satellite TV with the Internet service. For more information, see *http://www.DirecPC.com*.

### TYPE OF MODEM CONNECTION (SLIP AND PPP)

There are two types of dial-up modem connections—SLIP and PPP. SLIP stands for Serial Line Internet Protocol and is the older method of connection. Serial Line refers to a serial port connection, the typical interface for a modem. PPP (pronounced *p-p-p*) is an abbreviation for Point to Point Protocol, which offers more flexibility and reliability than SLIP. Although SLIP is simpler and easier to implement, PPP has become more popular due to its flexibility and technical features. PPP is preferred for noisy lines because of its superior error-correction features.

The dial-up software you use implements the TCP/IP protocol via PPP and then commands the modem to dial the Internet provider. After you are authenticated as a legitimate user, you are given an Internet connection and can proceed as if you were attached to a local port. Because the Internet itself can be slow at times, using a modem at 28,800 or 33,600 bits per second (bps) may not appear to be much slower than the 10 Mbps connection discussed in the previous section. However, when you transfer multimedia graphics, video, and sound, there can be significant delays at slower speeds.

**NOTE** **Some users erroneously use the term** *baud* **to refer to the modem's data transmission rate. Baud actually refers to the modulated telephone signal carrying the data; at higher speeds the baud rate is less than bits per second.**

### WHERE TO FIND WINDOWS TCP/IP DIALING SOFTWARE

Windows 95 comes with its own built-in TCP/IP and Winsock software. We will demonstrate how to install, configure, and use the Windows 95 TCP/IP software later in this unit. For other operating systems, ask your instructor whether your computing center has this software available. My organization put together a package of DOS, Windows 3.1, and Macintosh programs and documentation to make it easier for students to set up their home connection. Several popular packages are available through bookstores and through the Internet via FTP. **Chameleon Sampler** includes the PPP dialer and TCP/IP software and functioning versions of the major Windows applications. **Trumpet** is a TCP/IP stack with Winsock and PPP support. Your local computer center may have versions of these and other packages available for you to download free to your own computer.

### CREATING YOUR TCP/IP SETTINGS

Before you can initiate a PPP or SLIP connection, you must configure the TCP/IP settings according to your Internet service provider. Although each TCP/IP package is different, Table 2.3 shows some of the common settings. Your instructor or ISP can give you values for most of these.

**TABLE 2.3**
*Common dial-up TCP/IP configuration settings*

- Port and speed for your modem (typically already set within Windows)

- Your own IP address (sometimes set automatically) and subnet mask (not always needed)

- Your host name

- Your domain name

- Domain Name Server (DNS) IP address

- Dial-up telephone number(s) for your Internet service provider

## Shell Account

A **shell account** involves connecting your computer as a terminal to a UNIX host computer and running UNIX commands and Internet programs. These programs execute on the host computer. You will see only the results of the commands on your screen. For instance, if you do an FTP file transfer, incoming files will be saved in your account on the host computer's hard drive, not on your local computer. Few of the examples in this book use the shell account method, because it is quite limited. To take full advantage of the Internet features, we assume that you will connect to the Internet with one of the full connection methods previously described.

## Web TV

Some manufacturers are promoting use of a set-top Internet connection device that displays information through your television set. Called Web TV, this approach uses a separate telephone modem connection and eliminates the need for a separate personal computer and modem. Sony and Philips now sell the Web TV box, with additional vendors lining up to join this group. The monthly service charge is $19.95, or $9.95 if you use your own ISP. An advanced version called Web TV Plus with more features is also available. The Web TV home page is found at *http://www.webtv.net.*

# *Making the Dial-Up Connection*

Windows 95 comes with a complete TCP/IP implementation, including a PPP dialer for dial-up users. Setting up Windows 95 for Internet access requires these steps:

1. Install the network adapter or modem.

2. Install dial-up networking if using a modem.

3. Install the TCP/IP protocol and configure its parameters for your ISP.

4. Create a dial-up PPP configuration if you are dialing an Internet service provider.

## Setting Up a Windows 95 PPP Connection

In this section we will demonstrate how to create a dial-up PPP connection under Windows 95 using the TCP/IP protocol. The process is divided into three Guided Activities so that readers can choose which components to install. These activities are *not* necessary if you are running from a computer lab or have a direct connection in an office. Microsoft has released an Internet Wizard that will make setting up a PPP connection easier. Check your version of Windows 95 before attempting these three activities.

## Installing the Modem

In most cases, your modem will already be installed on your computer and in Windows 95. To check for an installed modem, click the *Start* button on the taskbar, choose *Settings*, and select *Control Panel.* From the Control Panel, open the Modems window. In the General tab you should see the make and model of your modem. To close all of those windows at once, hold down the *Shift* key and click the *Close* box.

    To install an internal modem, first shut down your computer. Remove the cover, and then physically install the modem in a free expansion slot. If it is not a Plug N Play device, you will have to manually configure the modem's switches before completing the installation. Replace the cover, and then turn the power on and let the computer boot. If it is a Plug N Play modem, Windows will discover the modem and configure it automatically. In either event, Windows should discover the new modem and add it to the device list.

Installing an external modem is simpler. Shut down the computer. Attach the modem's cable to an available serial port, and then restart your computer. The computer should discover a new modem and add it to your device list.

## Installing Dial-Up Networking

The next step is to install the Dial-Up Networking utility in Windows 95 if it is not already installed on your computer. You will use the Add/Remove Programs program in the Control Panel to add this utility to your Windows configuration. The following Guided Activity will lead you through each of the steps.

### GUIDED ACTIVITY

### 2.1    Installing Dial-Up Networking in Windows 95

In this activity you will check for dial-up networking and install it if necessary.

1. Make sure that you are running Windows 95 on your computer and that your modem has been installed in Windows 95.

**CHECKPOINT 2A**    How can you tell if a modem has been installed in your computer?

2. At the Windows 95 desktop, open the *My Computer* window by double-clicking its icon. Check for the Dial-Up Networking icon as shown in Figure 2.1. If it is already present, skip directly to Guided Activity 2.2.

**FIGURE 2.1**
*My Computer window*

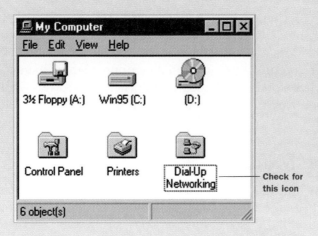

3. Next you will install Dial-Up Networking. You will need the original Windows 95 CD-ROM or floppy installation disks. Double-click the Control Panel icon in the My Computer window to open the Windows 95 Control Panel.

**FIGURE 2.2**
*Control Panel window*

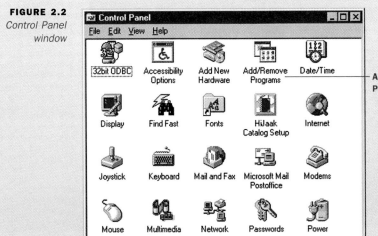

**HINT**  *You can also open the Control Panel by clicking Start → Settings → Control Panel.*

4.  In the Control Panel window shown in Figure 2.2, open the *Add/Remove Programs* application. Click on the *Windows Setup* tab to view the Windows components as shown in Figure 2.3.

**FIGURE 2.3**
*Add/Remove Programs Properties dialog box*

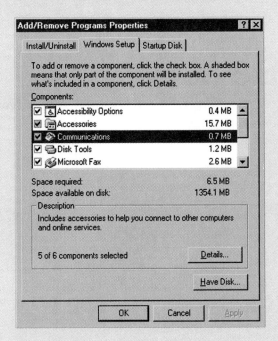

5.  Select *Communications* and click the *Details* button in the lower-right corner. When the *Communications* dialog box opens (as shown in Figure 2.4), place a check next to *Dial-Up Networking*, then click *OK* two times. Windows will prompt you to insert the Windows 95 installation disk and will load the necessary components.

CAUTION **If there already is a check in front of Dial-Up Networking, it is already installed. Removing the check will instruct Windows to remove this component.**

FIGURE 2.4
*Communications
dialog box*

Add check here
to install
component

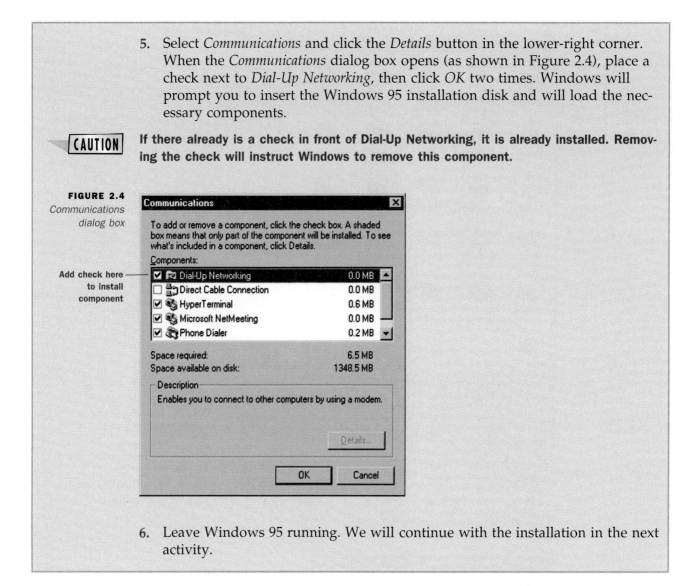

6.  Leave Windows 95 running. We will continue with the installation in the next activity.

## Adding the TCP/IP Protocol

Next you must install the TCP/IP protocol in the Windows 95 Network dialog box. Without TCP/IP installed, client programs on your computer will not be able to communicate with the Internet. The following Guided Activity will explain how to add TCP/IP.

GUIDED ACTIVITY

## 2.2  Adding the TCP/IP Protocol to Windows 95

In this activity you will add the TCP/IP protocol to Windows 95, then configure it with the appropriate settings. Before you begin, obtain the necessary TCP/IP parameters from your ISP or from your instructor.

1. Make sure you are running Windows 95. Open the *Control Panel* window as explained in the previous Guided Activity.

2. Now you need to install the TCP/IP Protocol. In the Control Panel window, open the *Network* application. Make sure that the *Configuration* tab is clicked, as shown in Figure 2.5.

**FIGURE 2.5**
*Network dialog box*

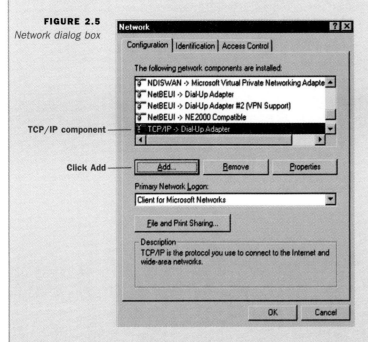

TCP/IP component ———

Click Add ———

3. Look for TCP/IP in the list in the center of the *Network Configuration* window. If it is already present (as shown here), skip directly to the next Guided Activity. If it is not present, click the *Add* button.

**CHECKPOINT 2B**  What is the difference between an *adapter* like Dial-Up Networking and a *protocol* like TCP/IP?

4. Select *Protocol*, and then click the *Add* button. When the next dialog box appears, select *Microsoft* in the left *Manufacturer* pane, and then select *TCP/IP* in the right pane and click *OK*. See Figure 2.6.

**FIGURE 2.6**
*Select Network Protocol dialog box*

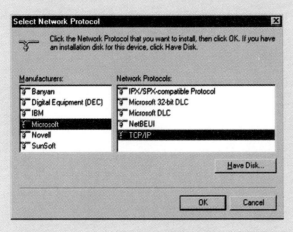

5. Windows will display the Network properties window. Click *TCP/IP* in the middle pane, and then click the *Properties* button to set the properties for your TCP/IP connection.

6. Next you need to fill in the appropriate TCP/IP parameters for your ISP. Click the *IP Address* tab, and either select *Obtain an IP* address automatically, or enter your particular IP address. Most schools will implement the automatic IP address process, as shown in Figure 2.7.

**FIGURE 2.7**
*TCP/IP Properties—IP Address tab*

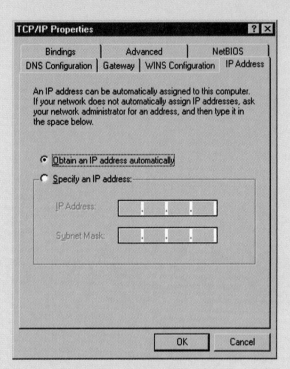

7. Next click the *DNS Configuration* tab, and click the *Enable DNS* option button. Enter your own user name in the *Host:* box, and enter the domain name of your ISP in the *Domain:* box. For ISU, this is indstate.edu, as shown in Figure 2.8.

**FIGURE 2.8**
*TCP/IP Properties—DNS Configuration sheet*

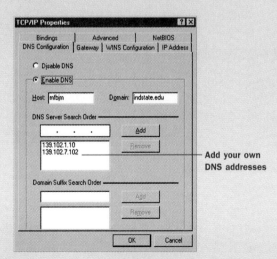

Add your own DNS addresses

8. Now enter the appropriate *DNS IP* address and click the *Add* button. For ISU, there are two Domain Name Servers: 139.102.1.10 and 139.102.7.102. When finished, click *OK* to complete the configuration. Windows 95 will probably read some information from the installation disk and then inform you that you need to restart the computer. Click *Yes.*

**NOTE**   **There is an alternate way to establish TCP/IP settings if you intend to connect to different Internet service providers. In that case, skip steps 6–8 in this Guided Activity. You can enter TCP/IP Settings in the PPP dialog box when you configure a particular connection.**

## Creating a PPP Connection

Once you have installed Dial-Up Networking and the TCP/IP protocol, it is time to create a PPP connection to a particular ISP. This process is very easy—just go through the Add a New Connection Wizard in the Dial-Up Networking application and specify the proper telephone number. The following Guided Activity will show you how to do this.

**GUIDED ACTIVITY**

# 2.3   Creating a Dial-Up PPP Connection in Windows 95

In this activity you will create a dial-up PPP connection for your ISP or school. Make sure you have the necessary parameters from your ISP or your instructor before beginning this activity.

1. Make sure you are running Windows 95.

2. Dial-Up Networking is found in the My Computer window on your desktop. Open the *My Computer* window, and then double-click *Dial-Up Networking.*

**CHECKPOINT 2C**   Is there any other way to start Dial-Up Networking? (*Hint:* It is a Windows accessory.)

3. When the Dial-Up Networking window appears, open the *Make New Connection* icon. The wizard will lead you through the remaining steps.

4. Pick a name for your connection that describes where you are connecting. For example, the default is My Connection. Although your modem should already be installed in the lower box, you will need to change the configuration. Click the *Configure* button, as shown in Figure 2.9.

5. Click the *Options* tab, and then select *Bring up* terminal window after dialing, as shown in Figure 2.10. This will give you a chance to enter your user name and password to gain access to the ISP PPP connection. Also make sure that Display modem status is also checked. Click *OK* to return to the Wizard, and click *Next* to go to the next step.

**FIGURE 2.9**
*Make New Connection wizard*

Name your connection

Configure button

**FIGURE 2.10**
*Modem Properties— configure terminal window for PPP authentication*

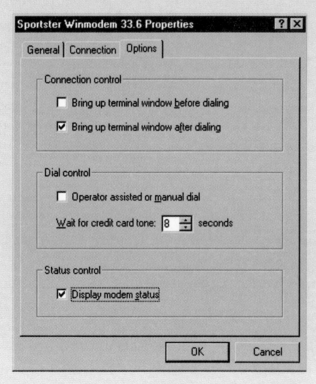

6. In the next box, type the phone number for the ISP connection and click *Next*. If you are satisfied with the name, click *Finish* in the next box to complete the PPP connection. Windows will create a PPP connection in Dial-Up Networking that you can use to connect to your Internet service provider.

# Starting the Dial-Up PPP Software

Once you have installed and configured the appropriate communications software, it is time to make the connection and gain access to the Internet. Because the direct connection is already established for machines in the computer lab, we will illustrate a typical dial-up connection to the ISU Internet service provider.

Several things happen when the phone is answered at the other end. The two modems send a series of signals that test the phone line and indicate what speed and protocols are available. They will connect at the highest speed possible for the phone conditions.

When the line connection is made, an authentication process begins that identifies you as a valid user of that service. In most cases this means a user name and a password must be transferred. Some client dialers already have this information and do it automatically; you will do it manually in the following activity. Finally, when your user identity is validated, you are connected to the Internet and can begin using Internet software packages.

## GUIDED ACTIVITY

## 2.4    Using the PPP Connection to Connect to the Internet

In this activity you will start the PPP connection and then make a PPP connection using dial-up networking. You will go through the authentication process with your ISP and then disconnect from the Internet. Make sure you have your user name and password before starting this activity.

1.  To test the connection, click *Start* → *Programs* → *Accessories* → *Dial-Up Networking*. Then double-click your connection. When the *Connect To* box shown in Figure 2.11 appears, click *Connect* to begin the connection. Your modem will dial the indicated phone number and attempt to make the connection.

**Make sure you use the phone number for your own ISP connection.**

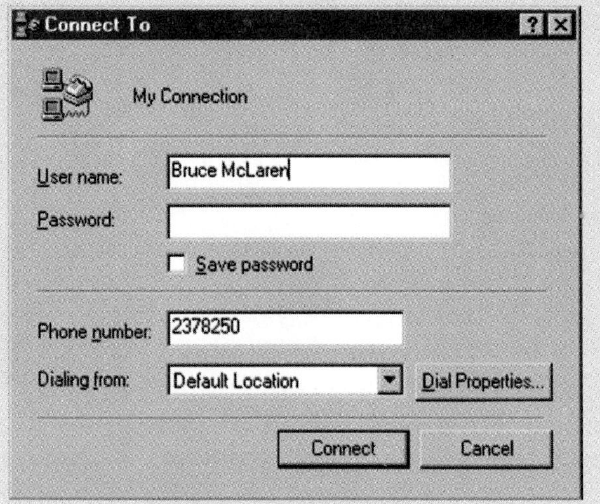

**FIGURE 2.11**
*Connect To dialog box*

Connect To

My Connection

User name:    Bruce McLaren

Password:

☐ Save password

Phone number:    2378250

Dialing from:    Default Location    ▼    Dial Properties...

Connect    Cancel

2. When the modem connection is established, Windows will display a Post-Dial Terminal Screen window where you will identify yourself. Follow the instructions provided by your ISP. At ISU we must press Enter two times, then we will get a Username> prompt. After typing the user name, we get a Password> prompt. See Figure 2.12 for a sample authentication screen. Your screen will not be the same as this.

**FIGURE 2.12**
*Post-Dial Terminal Screen for ISU dial-up connection*

3. After typing the password, we select the PPP connection from a menu and press F7 to continue with the PPP session. Follow the directions for your own organization. The post-dial terminal window will close.

**NOTE** **Your instructor or lab assistant may be able to show you how to create a PPP script that automates the entry of your user name and password. You would no longer need to go through the terminal window.**

4. After a few moments you will see the Connected To dialog box that indicates a PPP connection has been established with your ISP. At this point you can run an Internet client such as an e-mail package, Netscape Navigator browser, FTP client, or other programs. Figure 2.13 shows the Connect to ISU PPP box with a connection speed of 26.4 Kbps.

**CHECKPOINT 2D**     Why is the connection speed shown in Figure 2.13 slower than 28.8 Kbps?

**FIGURE 2.13**
*Connected To dialog box*

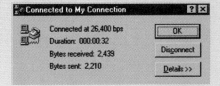

**NOTE**

**If you are using the newer OEM version of Windows 95, the Connected To dialog box does not ordinarily appear on your desktop. A small PPP connection icon appears in the tray on the taskbar, near the clock. Right-click this icon and choose *Display Status* to see the *Connected To* dialog box. Figure 2.13 shows the newer version of the Connected To dialog box.**

5. To test your Internet connection, click the *Start* button, select *Programs*, and then choose *MS-DOS* Prompt.

6. In the MS-DOS Prompt window, enter this command line: `Ping www.indstate.edu` and then click *OK*. In a few seconds you will see a message that gives the IP address of this host, along with the round-trip times it took for four packets to travel from your computer to the host and back. You should see output similar to below:

```
C:\WINDOWS>PING www.indstate.edu

Pinging baby.indstate.edu [139.102.70.207] with 32 bytes
of data:

Reply from 139.102.70.207: bytes=32 time=154ms TTL=62

Reply from 139.102.70.207: bytes=32 time=242ms TTL=62

Reply from 139.102.70.207: bytes=32 time=202ms TTL=62

Reply from 139.102.70.207: bytes=32 time=222ms TTL=62
```

7. Next type `Ping` followed by the address of a computer host within your organization. Note the difference in elapsed time from your host and from the Indiana State University campus host.

8. Type `Exit` and press *Enter* to close the MS-DOS Prompt window. Leave the PPP session connected.

## Using Internet Applications

The rest of this book will deal with how to use Windows Internet applications. To use one of the Internet application programs, click the *Start* button, select *Programs*, and select the appropriate icon. There are units in this textbook on electronic mail, news and discussion groups, FTP and TELNET, and the World Wide Web. In each case, make sure you have established an Internet connection before starting the software. Then when you start the Windows application for that service, it automatically communicates with the Winsock and TCP/IP software.

**NOTE** If you have a direct connection such as in an office or campus lab, you do *not* have to manually establish a PPP connection before running an Internet application.

## Ending a Dial-Up PPP Session

In most cases it is only necessary to terminate the dial-up connection in the dialing software. With the Windows 95 PPP connection, restore the *Connected To* dialog box and then click the *Disconnect* button. Appropriate commands will be sent to the modem and it will hang up the line. In some circumstances, the connection may be lost due to telephone line noise between the two modems. In this case, Windows 95 will offer to reconnect for you. See Figure 2.14.

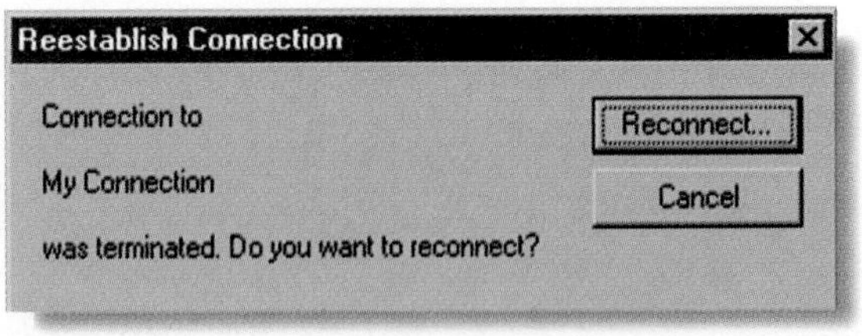

FIGURE 2.14
*Reestablish
Connection dialog
box*

**Reestablish Connection**    ☒

Connection to          [ Reconnect... ]

My Connection          [ Cancel ]

was terminated. Do you want to reconnect?

Most ISPs have a time limit for the connection. On our campus the time limit is two hours for the total connection time, and 10 minutes inactivity time.

**GUIDED ACTIVITY**

## 2.5  Ending a PPP Session in Windows 95

In this activity you will disconnect from the PPP connection.

1. We assume you are already connected to the Internet via a PPP connection. If you have not already performed Guided Activity 2.4, do so now.

2. Click on the *Connected To* icon in the Taskbar to restore its window. Note the information in the box about your connection speed and duration of the session.

**CHECKPOINT 2E**  How can you tell how many bytes have been transferred so far in the PPP session?

**HINT**  *If the Connected To icon does not appear in your taskbar, you are probably using the OEM version of Windows 95. Locate the modem icon in the tray area of the taskbar. Right-click the modem icon and select Status.*

◁ 🖳 11:48 AM  3. To terminate your PPP session, click the Disconnect button. You will not have a chance to override this command; so be sure you are ready to complete your session.

4. Repeat Guided Activity 2.4 if you wish to reconnect.

## Windows 95 Internet Software

Windows 95 is the newest version of Microsoft Windows that has replaced MS-DOS and Windows 3.1 and Windows for Workgroups. It comes with built-in TCP/IP and networking support, including PPP connections to dial-up services. Windows 95 also comes with the following character-based Internet programs to get you started. We will use GUI programs (defined on p. 70) for the rest of this book.

- Ping (to check the status of your Internet connection)
- FTP (to download and upload files)
- Telnet (to establish a remote terminal session)
- WinIPcfg (to display the TCP/IP configuration status while connected)
- Tracert (to display the names of intermediate routers between your PC and an Internet host)

Windows 95 now comes with a full-fledged World Wide Web browser called Internet Explorer. If your Windows 95 did not come with the Internet Explorer, you can download it free of charge from *http://www.microsoft.com/*. We discuss Web browsers in Units 4–5 and 9–9.

For more information about Windows 95, contact Microsoft. The Microsoft WWW home page address is *http://www.microsoft.com/*. There is a Windows 95 section with answers to frequently asked questions.

# SUMMARY

This unit contains a detailed discussion of the TCP/IP protocol, including IP addresses. The domain name server converts a name address into the 16-bit IP address. It is necessary to have a TCP/IP stack on your computer in order to connect to the Internet. In Windows, the Winsock software represents the TCP/IP stack.

There are three main ways to connect to the Internet. Direct connections are the fastest, using a dedicated connection to your school, campus, or office. Dial-up connections are the most common way to connect to the Internet, using a modem to connect to an Internet service provider. Shell accounts use a terminal connection to a text-based host.

The unit contains a step-by-step discussion of creating a dial-up connection in Windows 95 to an ISP. First add Dial-Up Networking, and then add the TCP/IP protocol. Next create a PPP connection to a specific ISP, and then use that connection to make the link. The unit includes a short demonstration of the Ping TCP/IP utility to test the connection and concludes with directions for disconnecting.

## Command Review

| | |
|---|---|
| Ping (MS-DOS) | Test the TCP/IP connection, returns IP address |
| Start→Programs | Launch a Windows program from the taskbar |
| Start→Settings→Control Panel | Open Windows Control Panel for making configuration changes |

## Vocabulary Exercise

*Write a short definition for each term in the following list.*

| | | |
|---|---|---|
| Asymmettric Digital Subscriber Line (ADSL) | Domain name server (DNS) | Ping |
| Authentication | Internet Protocol (IP) | Point to Point Protocol (PPP) |
| Chameleon Sampler | Internet service provider (ISP) | Routing |
| Dial-up connection | IP address | Serial Line Internet Protocol (SLIP) |
| Direct connection | ISDN | |

Shell account                Trumpet                V.34 (28.8 or 33.6 Kbps)
TCP/IP stack                 V9.0 (56 Kbps)         Web TV
Transmission Control         V.32bis (14.4 Kbps)    Winsock
   Protocol (TCP)

---

## Review Questions

1. Explain what is meant by TCP/IP protocol. Why is TCP/IP necessary to communicate with the Internet?

2. Describe the IP address format used with the Internet. Do you have to memorize IP addresses of the form 139.102.23.77?

3. How would you determine the IP address of the Web site at *http://www.nasa.gov*? Give the IP address.

4. Discuss the following methods to connect to the Internet. When is each type used?

    a. Direct network connection

    b. Dial-up connection to an Internet service provider

    c. Shell connection

5. What are SLIP and PPP?

6. Where can you find versions of TCP/IP software and other Internet applications?

7. What do the V.32bis and V.34 standards have to do with the Internet?

8. What is ISDN, and why would someone want to use it for connecting to the Internet? Are there faster ways to connect to the Internet?

9. List the steps to create a dial-up connection to the Internet, assuming that you are going through an Internet service provider.

10. What are some questions you should ask a prospective Internet service provider?

11. What is authentication?

12. What is Web TV, and why would someone want to purchase Web TV instead of a conventional computer to connect to the Internet?

---

## Exercises

1. If you have access to a dial-up Internet connection through your school, business, or local service provider, answer the following TCP/IP configuration questions:

    a. IP address

    b. Domain Name Server IP address

    c.  Domain

    d.  Type of connection (SLIP or PPP)

    e.  Phone number(s)

    f.  Modem protocols available (28.8k, 33.6k, 56k)

2.  What other services does your Internet service provider offer in addition to the basic Internet connection? List the setup fee and monthly charge for each service. Some examples include e-mail accounts, shell accounts, reserved line service, leased line service, and Web site hosting.

3.  Contact your local television cable company and determine if it offers cable modem data services. Find out what kind of cable modem is required for use with that system. Report on the monthly cost and connection speeds. If the cable operator does not offer cable modem service now, find out when they intend to offer that service.

4.  Using computer magazine ads and local computer stores, investigate modems that could be used with your computer. Prepare a comparison table that shows the characteristics for each modem. Consider such things as price, speed, type (internal, external, PCMCIA or PC Card), fax modem speed, special features, and included software utilities.

5.  Contact the local telephone provider in your community about ISDN. Gather statistics about available plans including installation fee, monthly cost, connection speeds (64 Kbps or 128 Kbps), and whether analog telephone service is available.

6.  Establish an Internet connection and use the Ping program to find the IP addresses for the following sites. Show the Internet address for each site you locate.

    a.  A school in your community

    b.  A national television network like MSNBC (*www.msnbc.com*)

    c.  A mail order computer company like Gateway 2000 (*www.gw2k.com*)

    d.  An automobile manufacturer like Lexus (*www.lexus.com*)

    e.  Purdue University (*www.purdue.edu*)

7.  Go to a local department or electronics store and investigate the Web TV devices that allow you to connect to the Internet and display the session through your television set. Your report should show the manufacturer name, model, cost, connection speed, and list important features. What additional functions does the device support?

## Internet Service Provider Study

In this project you are asked to prepare a report about Internet service providers in your community. Search through the local telephone directory, look in the newspapers, ask colleagues and instructors to come up with names of organizations that provide local Internet access. Your report should include:

- Name of the ISP

- Modem telephone number(s) for connection

- Voice telephone number for help, service, or billing questions

- Description of the basic Internet connection service offered and the monthly cost

- Web address for the ISP, if they have one

- Cost of extra services such as second e-mail account, Web server space

- Ratio of subscribers to incoming modem lines

- Special connection availability: 56K, ISDN

### PROJECT TEAM OPTION

Extend the ISP analysis to include regional and national ISPs such as AT&T WorldNet, IBM, Netcom, AOL, MCI, and Sprint. Table 2.2 (see page 17) includes a list of popular providers.

# Electronic Mail—The Basic Internet Tool

This unit introduces electronic mail—the basic Internet tool for sending messages to other users. Although your e-mail system may not match the ones illustrated here, you can draw enough conclusions to make efficient use of your particular system.

## Learning Objectives

At the completion of this unit, you should be able to

1. explain how electronic mail works,

2. discuss the advantages of using e-mail over other methods,

3. describe how e-mail addresses are constructed, including domain names,

4. open your e-mail program,

5. send an e-mail message,

6. read an incoming e-mail message,

7. send a message with an attachment,

8. send a message to a group,

9. forward an e-mail message,

10. use browser-based e-mail programs.

## Key Terms

*The following terms are introduced in this unit. Be sure you know what each of them means.*

Address book
Alias
Blind copy
Clipboard
Domain name
Electronic mail (e-mail)
E-mail signature
Emoticons
Eudora Light 3.0
Filters
Flame mail
HTML mail
Mail server
Mailbox or folder
Netiquette
Nickname
POPmail
Postmaster
Spamming
Trash

## Basics of Electronic Mail

Electronic mail, or e-mail, is a method to create and send messages electronically to one or more individuals. These messages are stored in the destination mailbox until the recipient is ready to read them. The two users do not have to be on the same network or type of computer—most e-mail systems can translate from one system to another.

## Similarities to Regular Mail

E-mail shares some similarities with regular or "snail" mail. With e-mail you must have an address for the recipient. You write the message and then "mail it" by using the Send command. The message is routed from your computer to the recipient's mailbox at the other end. Unlike regular mail, e-mail is usually delivered in a few minutes or less. The message will remain in the mailbox at the other end until the recipient reads it. Many mail systems allow the reader to store messages already read for future reference.

### E-MAIL MESSAGES

An e-mail message is a lot like a regular letter or memo. It contains a header with the recipient's address, the sender's address, the subject of the message, and the date and time when the message was sent. Following the header is the body or text of the message itself. Many users will add a signature block to the end of the message.

When you receive an e-mail message, there will probably be more things added to the header area, reflecting the handling of your message by the outgoing mail system and your own mailbox software. Figure 3.1 shows a typical e-mail message next to the mailboxes window. As new messages arrive, they are stored in the In mailbox, shown at the top. We will describe parts of this e-mail window later in the unit.

**FIGURE 3.1**
*E-mail message*

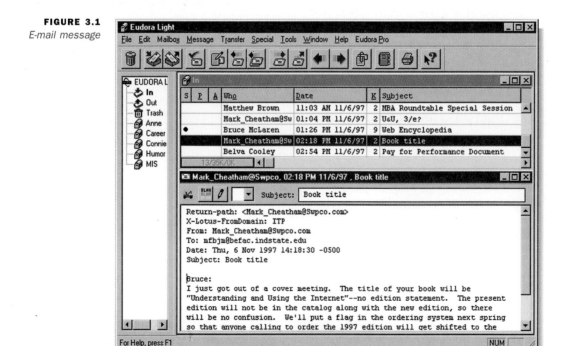

### POPMAIL SERVER

Most e-mail systems are built around users who are connected directly to the mail server, the computer that contains your electronic mailbox. When mail arrives for you, it is routed directly to your mailbox. You can then read that mail and reply as necessary. However, some e-mail users are not connected directly to the mail server and need to dial in with a modem to check their mail. A popular mail protocol called POPmail (post office protocol) was developed to enable a remote mail program to connect to the e-mail server and copy the mail messages to your computer. You don't have to remain on-line to the mail server to read messages and compose replies. When you are ready to send the messages, the POPmail program will reconnect to the mail server and upload the accumulated messages. Most of the examples in this chapter use Eudora Light 3.0, a popular POPmail program for Windows and Macintosh computers.

## Advantages of E-Mail

E-mail is very fast—mail is usually delivered immediately if the recipient's mail box is in the local area network, or up to a few minutes later to a remote location. E-mail is entirely electronic and doesn't require that paper copies of the message be created unless the recipient desires a printed version. Because the message is created electronically, you can use other computer tools such as a spell checker to improve the quality of the mail. Many systems provide electronic mail services at no cost to the sender or recipient; others may charge a nominal fee for low-volume usage. The Internet applies no charges to individual users; however, some Internet providers may add connection or per-message fees.

E-mail is convenient. When you are working on the computer and have a reason to communicate with someone else, it is easy and convenient to send an e-mail message. Of course, the person at the other end must have a mailbox account *and* must take the time to read your message. We still have a few staff members at our institution who choose not to use electronic mail!

With Windows or Macintosh software applications, it is easy to copy material from other documents to the Clipboard and insert it as part of an e-mail message. The reverse is also true: you can use the Clipboard to copy material from an incoming e-mail message into other messages and documents.

 **NOTE**  **A relatively new protocol, called MAPI, allows compatible applications programs to e-mail information *directly* from that program. A command like *File→Mail* or *File→Send To* in your application indicates that it supports MAPI.**

---

NET TIP

**Web Addresses**

Current links to most Web sites in this book can be found on the *Understanding & Using the Internet* Home Page. Choose **Resources** at **computered.swep.com**. Remember that a Web address may change at any time. An address given in this book as an example may no longer be valid. If this is so, either access the Home Page for the current link or do a search to find a similar site (see Unit 5 for a discussion of search methods).

## Disadvantages of E-Mail

E-mail works only if both parties agree to use it to communicate. If either party does not (or cannot) check the mailbox, communication does not take place. You might be in a location where it is difficult to use e-mail. On occasion some individuals send e-mail that they later regret sending; this is known as flame mail. You will find a section later in this unit that describes e-mail etiquette rules and covers the problems of flame mail and junk mail. Although most e-mail systems are compatible, some advanced e-mail programs add formatting codes that may confuse the receiver's e-mail client. Finally, some people have trouble getting attached files to pass properly between computers. There is a section about file attachments later in this unit.

## Mailbox Address

The mailbox address is based on a user name within the domain at a specific institution. For example, *mfbjm@befac.indstate.edu* is the author's e-mail address. *Mfbjm* is the individual user name; *befac* is the name of the network server that contains the mailbox for that user name; *indstate* is the name for Indiana State University; and *edu* represents an educational institution. *Indstate.edu* is called the domain name and is a unique name among all computers registered with the Internet.

Some organizations support the use of an e-mail alias. The alias is an easy-to-remember alternate address for an individual that may be easier to write. For example, my e-mail alias is *b-mclaren@indstate.edu*. If an organization assigns alias names in a consistent fashion, the alias may be easier to guess than a regular mailbox address. Some organizations allow the user to pick a tasteful alias. With an alias, the location of your specific mailbox can change but your e-mail address is constant, making it easier for people to send you e-mail.

### DOMAIN NAMES

In general, the last few characters of an address describe the type of organization for that mailbox. *Edu* means educational institution, most likely a four-year college or university. Not all schools use the *Edu* domain. *Com* stands for a commercial organization or business. *Gov* represents a government agency. *Mil* refers to military organizations. *Net* refers to network resources, or those who maintain the network. *Org* refers to other organizations.

NEW DOMAINS PROPOSED   Seven new top level domains have been proposed. If approved, they are expected to be available in spring 1998. *Firm* represents businesses or firms. *Store* reflects organizations that offer goods for sale. *Web* is for entities offering activities related to the World Wide Web. *Arts* is for entities emphasizing cultural and entertainment activities. *Rec* is for entities that offer recreational/entertainment activities. *Info* is for providers of information services. Finally, *Nom* is for those wishing individual or personal nomenclature.

Because the Internet has expanded to include global resources, a two-character code may be appended to the end of the address to represent the particular country of the organization. For example, *US* refers to the United States, *AU* to Australia, and so forth. A short list of international codes appears in Table 3.1. There are now over 240 international domain codes. See the Internet Assigned Numbers

| CODE | COUNTRY | CODE | COUNTRY |
|------|---------|------|---------|
| AU | Australia | KR | Korea (Republic) |
| BR | Brazil | RU | Russian Federation |
| CA | Canada | ES | Spain |
| FR | France | UK | United Kingdom |
| DE | Germany | US | United States |
| HK | Hong Kong | VA | Vatican City State |
| IL | Israel | ZW | Zimbabwe |
| JP | Japan | | |

**TABLE 3.1**
*Selected international domain codes*

Authority Web site at *http://www.iana.org/in-notes/iana/assignments/country-codes* for complete details.

**REGISTERING DOMAIN NAMES**   The InterNIC agency is responsible for registering *com*, *net*, *org*, and *edu* domain names. There is a $100 initial fee to register domain names for use (good for the first two calendar years) and a $50 annual fee thereafter to maintain the domain name. Domain names can be up to 26 characters long and cannot have any characters other than letters, numbers, and hyphens. InterNIC has a database server that will determine if a domain name is already registered under the name you want to register. For instance, I found that a marketing company in Toronto has already registered *mclaren.com* as a domain name.

If you are using an Internet service provider, its domain name is already registered; so you would not have to register your prefix to that domain name. For instance, suppose your ISP domain name was *abcd.com*. If your Internet location were *mclaren.abcd.com*, no further registration would be needed. For more information about registering domain names, see the Web site at *http://www.internic.net*. Web pages are discussed in Units 4–5 and 8–9 of this book.

Some individuals have purchased "rights" to well-known (but unused) domain names and have offered to sell those rights to the companies who want to develop an Internet presence under that domain name. The rights are good for two years and may be renewed. It would be wise for an organization to register its domain name now even if it is not yet ready to create a presence on the Internet.

**TIP**

To access the InterNIC domain registration database, use *http://rs.internic.net/cgi-bin/whois*. You can look up the owner of any registered domain name.

## SEARCHING FOR A MAILBOX ADDRESS

If you don't know the mailbox address of your recipient, there are several ways to learn it. The simplest is to ask the person. Many people now advertise their e-mail address in phone directories and on business cards. You could ask the person to send you an e-mail message (his or her mailbox address will be contained in that message). Many e-mail clients let you perform a search of the recipient's electronic directory. It is also possible to look up an e-mail address on the Internet using one of the World Wide Web search methods described in Unit 5.

Finally, and as a last resort, you could address the mail message to the Postmaster account, if the person teaches at or attends an educational institution. The postmaster account is usually maintained by someone who will attempt to look up the recipient's address and forward the mail to the recipient. For instance, to send mail to the postmaster at Indiana State University, you would address the message to *postmaster@indstate.edu.* You must, of course, know the domain name of the institution in order to use the latter option. The postmaster will usually send you an e-mail message with the correct address of your recipient.

# Using E-Mail

Before you can send or receive messages, you must have access to the e-mail system and have a mailbox account. In many systems, this step is automatic: when you are granted access to the system, your e-mail mailbox account also is established. Check with your instructor or system administrator if you are unsure of your mailbox status. It is likely that *your* e-mail system is different from the one pictured here, but nearly all of the basic principles still apply. Your instructor can fill in the gaps and inform you about any differences.

## Eudora Light 3.0

Eudora Light is the shareware version of the popular Eudora e-mail software. As mentioned in Unit 1, you can download a free copy of this software from Qualcomm Corporation. To download the compressed setup file, use your Web browser at the Eudora Web page at *http://www.eudora.com/.* As of this writing, the current release of Eudora Light is version 3.05.

*For the latest Eudora version information, see this textbook's Web page at* computered. swep.com. *It comes with hot links for Eudora Light and the other programs discussed in the book.*

Eudora Light comes with adequate built-in help, but no printed manual. You can download a copy of the 133-page manual in Adobe Acrobat (PDF) format (700K file) from the Eudora Web site and then print it on your own printer. Most users will not need the printed manual.

Eudora Light is a full-featured e-mail client that is easy to use and very popular. In fact, Eudora is the most popular e-mail program in use today. The remainder of this unit will demonstrate how to perform essential e-mail tasks using Eudora Light.

## Installing Eudora Light

**If your computer lab has already installed an e-mail client, you may skip this section.**

When you have finished downloading the Eudora Light setup program, run that program. It will automatically install itself and put Eudora Light on the Start button menu. When you run the program for the first time, it will display the configuration section. You can also use the *Tools → Options* command to display the configuration information. You can enter the configuration information for your name, mailbox address, and e-mail servers. This information will be provided by your instructor, system administrator, or ISP. Figure 3.2 shows the Eudora Light Options dialog box.

**FIGURE 3.2**
*Eudora Options dialog box*

# Creating a New Message

The procedure to send a message is simple.

- First, start the e-mail software.

- Then, specify that you want to send a message.

- You must supply the mailbox address of the recipient of the message and create an appropriate subject header for this message.

- Next, create the message by working with the message editor. Be sure to proofread your message before sending it out.

- Finally, send the message to its destination.

**CAUTION**   Most mail systems do not have a way to retrieve messages once they have been mailed; so think carefully about what you say *before* sending the message on its way. As in life, courtesy and politeness count on the Internet, too.

## GUIDED ACTIVITY

### 3.1  Creating a New Message

In this activity you will start the e-mail program and then create and send a short e-mail message. If you are not using Eudora, your instructor or system administrator may modify these instructions for your particular program.

1. If you have not already started your computer and begun Windows 95, do so now. Locate the icon for your e-mail program and double-click it to load that program. If you are using Eudora Light, look for a picture of a mailbox as the icon.

2. If you are using a dial-up connection to your ISP, make sure you are connected at this time. We will assume that you are now attached to the mail server's network.

3. Look for a button in the toolbar for creating a message. In Eudora, use the *Message → New Message* command (or press *Ctrl+N*) to create a new message. Figure 3.3 shows Eudora composition window with no information in it.

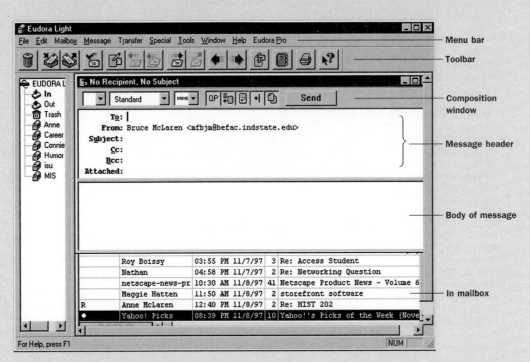

4. Notice that your name and user name have already been entered in the *From*: block of the message. Your instructor or system administrator will give you an e-mail address to use in the *To*: block. Enter that address now.

**CAUTION**    **Do NOT use *username@server* as the address.**

5. Press the *Tab* key to move to the *Subject*: block. Enter This is a Test as your subject. Some mail systems have you move from block to block in the header with the *Enter* key.

**Checkpoint 3A**    How do you move backward to a previous block in the header?

6. Press the *Tab* key to move past the Cc: and Bcc: boxes to get to the body section of the message. We'll cover these copy blocks later in the unit. Enter the message shown in Figure 3.4 or whatever your instructor asks you to do for this activity. Note that you can keep typing at the end of the line and your e-mail package will automatically wrap the text at the end of the line. You can use the arrow keys or the mouse to move the cursor to previous lines in order to correct errors. Remember to proofread your message and think twice about its appropriateness and tone.

7. When ready to send, click the Send button in the toolbar or use the *Message → Send* command for your mail program. Your message will be sent to the mail server to be forwarded to the recipient's mailbox.

8. Leave the e-mail program open because we will use it again shortly.

**FIGURE 3.4**
*Finished e-mail message*

Signature

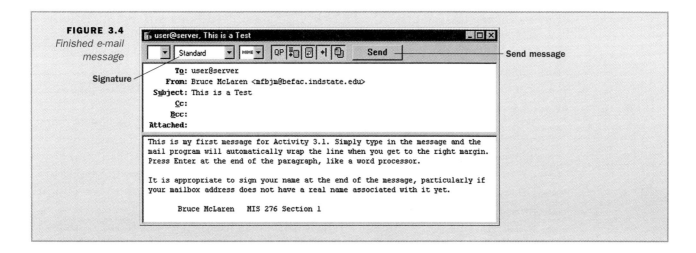

Send message

## SENDING MAIL TO OTHER SERVICES

You can send mail to individuals who have mailboxes on Prodigy, CompuServe, America Online, and others. You must know their user name on that service and then must append the domain name for each service. Table 3.2 shows the appropriate domain name for each service.

**TABLE 3.2**
*Internet addresses for selected organizations*

| SERVICE | MAILBOX ADDRESS |
| --- | --- |
| America Online | username@aol.com |
| CompuServe | nnnnn.nnnn@compuserve.com (username is nnnnn.nnnn) |
| Delphi | username@delphi.com |
| Genie | username@genie.geis.com |
| MCIMail | username(or number)@mcimail.com |
| Prodigy | username@prodigy.com |

## THE MESSAGE HEADER

The Eudora header consists of six parts. There are blocks for the recipient's e-mail address (To) and the sender's e-mail address (From). There is a block for the topic (Subject) of the message. You should choose something meaningful for the Subject block. There are blocks for addresses of people who should receive carbon copies (Cc) and blind carbon copies (Bcc). Blind copies are used when you don't want the recipient to know that you have sent a copy of that message to a particular individual. Finally, there is a block that lists any files you are sending along with the e-mail message (Attachments). Attachments are discussed later in this unit.

## EDITING THE MESSAGE

Most e-mail systems have a limited-feature word processor that can be used to create and edit the message. Simply begin typing on the first line and continue typing until you reach the end of the paragraph. The editor will wrap your message at the end of the line; so press the *Enter* key only at the end of a paragraph. Use the arrow keys or the mouse to move the cursor to different places in the message. Some e-mail systems use the *Ins* key to toggle between Insert and Typeover modes, just like a word processor. In Typeover mode, any new characters you type will replace existing characters in the message. Eudora Light uses the Ins key to toggle between Insert and Typeover mode.

You can learn the e-mail editor's keystroke commands for such things as delete a word, delete a line, and so forth. Eudora uses many of the same text editing shortcut commands as Microsoft Word. Delete and Backspace have the usual effects. *Ctrl+Delete* deletes the word to the right; *Ctrl+Backspace* deletes the word to the left. *Ctrl+Home* moves to the top of the message; *Ctrl+End* moves to the end of the message.

Some systems will automatically reformat lines for you as you insert or delete text, while others require that you issue the reformat command yourself. If you are using a Windows-based e-mail package, most of the usual Windows commands will work within the e-mail system. For example, you can use the Windows **Clipboard** to copy or cut text from one message and then paste it in the same or a different message. It is also possible to bring text into an e-mail message from another Windows document via the Clipboard.

## SENDING THE MESSAGE

Once you have finished editing the message, be sure to proofread it once more before sending it on its way. If your mail system has a spell checker, use it now. Also, beware of **flame mail**, or emotional messages that might have an unusually strong impact when read by the recipient. With the immediate response capability of electronic mail, we sometimes zip off a quick reply to stressful situations that can have an unintended effect. Our advice is to step back and count to ten before replying. If you were communicating in person, you would be forced to wait and might reconsider giving a brash reply.

## SENDING COPIES OF E-MAIL MESSAGES

You might want to make copies of your messages for yourself and others using the Cc: and Bcc: boxes. Most mail systems automatically keep a carbon copy of all outgoing messages. Eudora uses the Out mailbox for these messages. In fact, since your mailbox can rapidly fill with these copies, you should periodically empty your mailbox of unneeded messages (printing any you wish to save).

## SEND IMMEDIATELY OR PLACE IN QUEUE

Most POPmail packages, including Eudora, give you the opportunity to send your message immediately or place it in an outgoing mail queue. The latter method is helpful when you create mail messages off-line and then create a dial-up connection to the e-mail server and upload your messages from the mail queue. The Eudora *File → Save* command (or *Ctrl+S*) will place the current message in the Out mailbox, whereas the *Message → Send Immediately* command (or *Ctrl+E*) will send the message directly to the mail server. To have access to the full set of send options, hold down the *Shift* key when you click the Send button.

*You can change the* default *send type by using the* Tools → Options *command and then selecting the* Sending Mail *category. Remove the check from* Send Immediately, *and Eudora will change the Send button to the Queue button. You can reverse the change by putting the check back in the* Send Immediately *box.*

## Reading a Message

Once you load the e-mail software, it will prompt you if you have mail waiting to be read in your mailbox. Some mail systems (including Eudora) require you to enter a mail password before you can retrieve messages, demonstrated in the next Guided Activity. You can configure Eudora to "remember" your password so that you don't have to enter it each time. Be cautious with this setting, however; unscrupulous users that gain access to your mail account could send objectionable messages under your name.

Select the specific mail message from your mailbox, and open it. Some mail systems have several e-mail folders that can receive incoming mail, and your mail messages can be directed to a particular folder based upon the subject header using an e-mail filter, discussed later.

In Eudora, the In mailbox contains incoming messages. In other packages, new messages are automatically displayed. To read the message, choose it from the incoming mail messages by double-clicking its line. The message will be displayed in a window, as shown in Figure 3.1 earlier in this unit.

### OPTIONS FOR READ MESSAGES

After reading the message, you have several options: delete it, save it in a mailbox, forward or redirect it to another user's mailbox, or prepare a reply to the original sender. Most e-mail systems will let you leave the already read mail in the In mailbox. This is helpful if you want a reminder of that message to appear until you take some action and direct the message to another mailbox or another user.

### REPLYING TO A MESSAGE

Often you will reply to a message just read. To do so, highlight the mail message and use the *Message → Reply* command or click the Reply button in the toolbar. The e-mail system will open a new message window and place the address of the original sender in the To line, and your mailbox address in the From line. You can use the same subject or modify it and create your own subject. Then move to the editing window and create the reply. Most e-mail systems will copy all of the text from the original message, placing a > or other character before each line to signify it was part of the original message. You can respond to individual parts of the message or delete other parts that are not relevant to your reply.

**One caution is in order for replying to a message when it was originally sent to a group of recipients. Do you want your reply to go just to the original sender or to the entire group? Most e-mail systems let you choose All or Sender. Some people have been embarrassed to find that a reply intended only for the eyes of the original sender was circulated to all recipients!**

### PRINTING A MESSAGE

It is easy to print a message with Eudora and other e-mail systems. Select the message, and then use the *File → Print* command. Like Eudora, some mail systems also have a Print button in the toolbar that you can use. You can choose which pages to print (default is all pages) and some other printer options.

Eudora will print a special header and footer in bold for each page of the message. The sender's name, date, time, and subject appear in the header, while the recipient's address and page number appear in the footer. Like Eudora, some Windows mail systems let you choose options such as the font, page margins, and print quality. Use the *Tools → Options → Fonts* command to select the screen and printer fonts for your messages.

### FORWARDING A MESSAGE

To forward an existing message to another user, highlight that message in the mailbox and choose the *Message → Forward* command or click the *Forward* button in the toolbar. Eudora will open a message window with the contents of that message. You should enter the address of the person to whom you are sending the message and can make changes or comments as needed to the body of the message. Click the *Send* button or press *Ctrl+E* to forward the message.

Some systems allow you to auto-forward all messages to another e-mail address. This is useful if you have several user names but would like to check mail at only one address. Eudora Light does not support this feature.

### REDIRECTING A MESSAGE

Eudora offers another option for sending an existing message to another user. Redirect is similar to forward but places the original sender's e-mail address in the *From* block, adding <By way of> your e-mail address. Redirect does not place > before the lines of the original message. You can add additional comments in the message if you wish before sending the redirected message.

### DELETING A MESSAGE

To delete a message in Eudora, select the message and then click the **Trash** can icon in the toolbar, use the *Message → Delete* command, or use *Ctrl+D*. Your message will be copied to the Trash mailbox folder. Then you must use the *Empty Trash* command from the *Special* menu in the menu bar to remove the message completely. Like the Windows 95 Recycling Bin and the Macintosh trash can, this two-step process allows you to retrieve a "deleted" message from Trash before it is gone completely. Most users appreciate the value of this extra step.

## GUIDED ACTIVITY

## 3.2    Reading a Mail Message

In this activity you will open a received mail message and read its contents. You will create a reply and print the original message.

1. Make sure that your mail program is loaded and running and that you are connected to the Internet or your LAN.

2. Some mail systems can be configured to check your mailbox automatically when you open the mail reader. We will assume that you must do this step manually. If you are using Eudora, click the *Check Mail* button in the toolbar, or issue the *File → Check Mail* command, or press *Ctrl+M*. Eudora will ask you to enter your mail password, as shown in Figure 3.5. Your password displays as asterisks (*****) so that others cannot learn your password and use your account in an unethical manner.

**FIGURE 3.5**
*Enter Password dialog box*

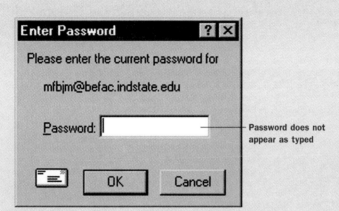

Enter Password

Please enter the current password for

mfbjm@befac.indstate.edu

Password: 

Password does not appear as typed

OK     Cancel

3. Your mail program will check for new mail and copy any messages to your In mailbox. Eudora displays those unread messages with a large bullet next to the message in the status area. To read a message, double-click it in the *In mailbox* window. Eudora will display the message in a message window. If necessary, use the mouse to resize the window to display the message in its original width. If the message is longer than one screen, Eudora will display a vertical scroll bar at the right side of the window that can be used to scroll through the message.

**Checkpoint 3B** How would you resize the window to display a wider message?

4. Click the *Reply* button of your e-mail system to create a reply to this message. In Eudora the menu bar command is *Message → Reply* or *Ctrl+R*. Eudora will display the original message with a > character in front of each line. You can edit the original message as needed and add your own reply comments. When finished, click the *Send* button or issue the appropriate command for your mailer or mail software.

5. Finally, you'll print the original message. First, highlight the message in the *In mailbox* window, or open the message. The Eudora menu bar command to print is *File → Print* (*Ctrl+P*); you can specify a certain page range or just click OK at the *Print* dialog box that appears next.

6. If finished with the original message, close its window by clicking the *Close* box in the upper-right corner or using the *File → Close* command. Leave the e-mail program open.

# Using Special E-Mail Features

Many e-mail packages support such features as group mailings, attaching document files to the message, and multiple mailboxes. You can request confirmation
that your mail has been delivered and opened by the recipient.

## ADDRESS BOOK

You can use the address book feature to create a nickname for a user that is easier
than typing in his or her full e-mail address. In the *To* block, simply type in the
nickname and Eudora will substitute the full e-mail address from the address book
when the message is sent. You can also click the *To* button in the Address Book dialog box to open a new message. Figure 3.6 shows the Eudora Address Book dialog box.

**FIGURE 3.6**
*Eudora Address
Book dialog box*

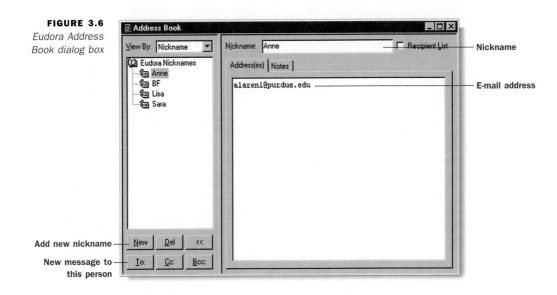

Use the *Tools → Address Book* (or *Ctrl+L*) command to open the address book.
In the Address Book dialog box, click the *New* button to create a new nickname,
and then list the e-mail addresses of all the users in that group, separated by commas. When finished, close the Nicknames box. When you want to send a message
to that group, just enter the nickname for the individual in the *To* block.

You can also define a set of user mailboxes as a mail group and then send the
same message to each member of that group with one mailing. Although each e-
mail package has its own commands, follow these basic steps. Create the mailing
group by giving it a name, and then list the mailbox address of each member of
that group. Save the group list. When you create a new message, specify the group
nickname in the To box instead of an individual name. When you send the message, it will automatically be delivered to all members of the group.

## SEARCH DIRECTORY

If you don't know the address of your recipient, you could search the electronic directory at the recipient's institution. The Eudora command is *Tools → Directory Ser-*

*vices* (or *Ctrl+L*). This feature works best at your own institution where the name of the electronic phonebook is known. Figure 3.7 shows the Directory Services dialog box with two matches for the search text. Click the *Ph* (*Phone*) button to search for names that match the search text. Click the *Server* button to get a list of available electronic directories. Other Web-based search methods are covered in Unit 5.

**FIGURE 3.7**
*Eudora Directory Services dialog box*

Click here to list phone servers

Search text

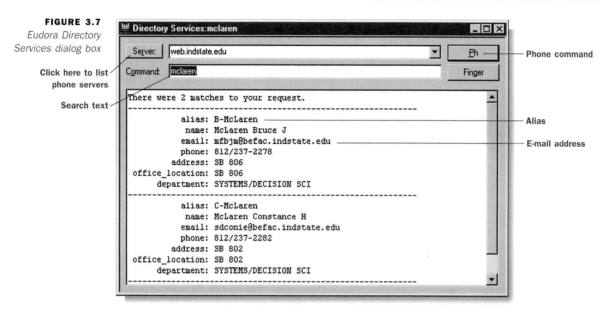

Phone command

Alias

E-mail address

## ATTACH DOCUMENT FILE

Most e-mail systems have the capability to append other information to the message. The document could be a word processing file, a graphic image, or a program file. Suppose you want to send a copy of a word processing file to a colleague. Create the new mail message as usual, and then attach a file to the message. In Eudora click the *Attach File* button in the toolbar, or use the *Message →️ Attach File* command. Your e-mail package will ask you the name of the file and may allow you to specify the encoding type. Eudora Light provides for the MIME and BinHex encoding methods; Eudora Pro also supports Uuencoded attachments.

When you send the message, the attached document is carried along. At the destination, the recipient will be told that the message has an attachment when the message is read. The recipient can save the file on a disk or view it immediately (if it's a document) or use the program or utility file. By default, Eudora saves the attachments in the Attach folder found in the main Eudora folder. You can change the location for attachments in the *Tools →️ Options* menu.

Since some mail systems have difficulty in handling different kinds of document files, you should ask your instructor what sorts of documents can be interchanged. For example, our campus e-mail system can handle nearly all kinds of document files so long as they are between the same kind of computer; when we try to attach a nontext file for transfer between an IBM-compatible PC and a UNIX computer, however, the information is frequently lost.

## DELIVERY NOTIFICATION

At times you would like to know when your mail message has been delivered and read by the recipient. You can request that the recipient's mail system send return notification. This feature will only function if you are sending a message to a mail server that supports delivery notification. When outgoing mail is handed off to another mail system, your delivery notification might indicate only that the message left your mail system, not that the recipient actually read it. Eudora does not support delivery notification.

### PRIORITY MESSAGE

It is possible on some e-mail systems to assign a "High" priority to an important message so that it stands out from other unread messages. On such systems, the mail message usually appears in a different color in the incoming mail box. In Eudora, click on the Priority button in the message toolbar to select a priority level. Eudora maintains five priority levels, from Lowest to Highest.

When you send the message with a different priority, it will show up as such in the recipient's mailbox. Take care not to abuse the High or Highest priority; remember the boy who cried "Wolf"!

### CANCEL MESSAGE

Few systems let you cancel a message that has already been sent. This feature, although rare, can be particularly useful when you have sent a message in error, or when a hasty response was shot back when a more deliberate response would have been more effective. The Cancel feature is not available with Eudora.

### MAILBOX FOLDERS

Most systems let you set up a **mailbox** or **folder** system whereby messages are stored according to their content. It is a convenient way to organize messages. Standard Eudora mailboxes include:

- *In* mailbox where incoming messages are placed

- *Out* mailbox where copies of messages you have sent are maintained

- *Trash* mailbox for messages you no longer want to keep

Suppose you are working on two projects and have exchanged e-mail messages with several users. You might want to file the replies in a mailbox associated with each project. That way, in the future you can more easily refer to messages about that project.

Most people have difficulty finding a particular mail message when many have been saved in the in basket. It makes good sense to organize your messages, particularly when you may have hundreds saved. Most mail systems allow you to create hierarchical groups of mailboxes, similar to the subdirectory or folder system on a hard drive. Thinking about a useful structure early on will save you grief later as your messages multiply.

### CREATING A MAILBOX

To create a mailbox in Eudora, use the *Mailbox → New* command, and then enter the mailbox name. If you want the mailbox to be stored as a separate Windows 95 folder, click that box. Click OK to create the mailbox. The current mailbox names are displayed in the mailbox window at the left side of the Eudora window. You can drag the borders of the mailbox window to change its size.

### TRANSFERRING A MESSAGE TO A MAILBOX

**TIP**

Use this technique to transfer a message from the Trash mailbox to another mailbox.

You can transfer a message to a mailbox by selecting that message and then using the Transfer command from the menu bar. Slide the cursor down to the desired mailbox, and then click its name. Eudora will move your message from its current mailbox to the selected mailbox. If a mailbox contains an unread message, Eudora displays the mailbox name in bold.

### MESSAGE SIGNATURES

Most e-mail systems let you create a personal **e-mail signature** that is automatically added to the end of outgoing messages, saving you time. Rather than resembling your written signature for checks or correspondence, the e-mail signature contains your name and address and anything else that you believe your recipients would benefit from having. Many people include telephone numbers and Web home page addresses. Although some people add clever sayings and quotations to their signature block, the added length makes it a little more difficult to read and reply to the message.

To create or edit a signature in Eudora, use the *Tools → Signature* command. Enter the characters you would like to see in your signature, and then close the Signature dialog box. Eudora will save your signature in a text file called Signature.txt stored in the Sigs folder within the Eudora folder. This signature text will be added to the end of all outgoing messages unless you turn off the signature by using the Signature button in the composition window, as previously shown in Figure 3.4.

### DIGITAL SIGNATURES

Some individuals want e-mail messages that can be authenticated as coming from the designated sender. Some e-mail systems allow you to add a digital signature to the message that is almost impossible to reproduce by anyone other than the authentic sender. Some e-mail systems let you encrypt the message so that it travels through the Internet in coded form. The recipient must have the key to decrypt the message. You will read more about encryption in the Electronic Commerce section in Unit 9.

### MESSAGE FILTERS

Some e-mail systems provide for **filters** that let you specify which messages you want to read, or *don't* want to read. You can provide e-mail addresses for the filter, or specify subjects that you want filtered. You can use filters to direct incoming e-mail into particular mailboxes by subject or sender. That way you can read new mail according to its subject and by priority. Unfortunately, some people misuse e-mail to harass or otherwise bother individuals. You can filter mail from these individuals into the Trash mailbox.

Eudora Light supports use of e-mail filters through the *Tools → Filters* command. The Filters window is shown in Figure 3.8. You can specify the content of

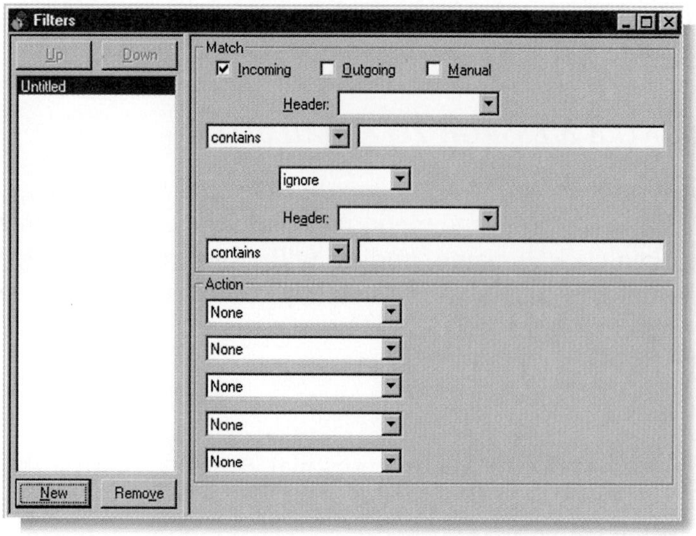

**FIGURE 3.8**
*Eudora Filters window*

any of the header blocks (To, From, Subject, and so forth) and give the filter condition (contains, doesn't contain, starts with, ends with, and so forth.) The action section lets you specify what to do when a message that matches that condition, including open, copy to, and transfer to another mailbox.

## SPELLING CHECK

Many e-mail systems employ a spelling checker, similar to a word processing system. E-mail users tend to make more on-line typos and spelling errors than they would in a word processing document. If your e-mail package has a spell checker, use it! Most require that you manually invoke the spell checker.

If you don't have a spell checker, proofread carefully before you send the message. While Eudora Light does not come with a spell checker, you may be able to purchase an add-on spell checker through its Web site at *http://www.eudora.com*. Eudora Pro does have a built-in spell checker.

## GUIDED ACTIVITY

# 3.3  Using Special E-Mail Features

In this activity you will create a Eudora nickname for a favorite recipient. You will send a message to that person and attach a short file to it. You will also prepare a signature for your messages. Your e-mail system may be different from this one.

1.  If not already open, open Eudora Light or your own e-mail client now.

2.  In Eudora use the *Tools → Nicknames* (*Ctrl+L*) command to create a nickname. Click the *New* button to add a new name. Figure 3.9 shows the Address Book with nicknames on the left and the e-mail addresses on the right, along with the New Nickname dialog box.

**FIGURE 3.9**
*Address Book window*

Nickname

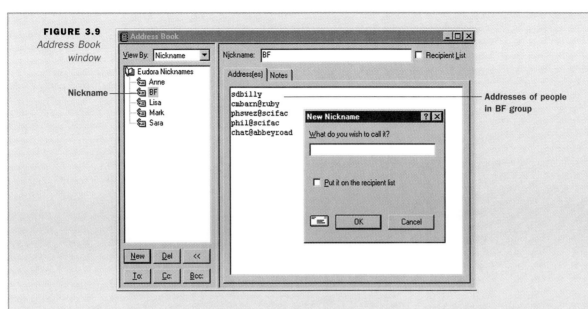

Addresses of people in BF group

3. Type a short (but polite) nickname for your instructor in the box, and then click OK.

4. Click anywhere in the Address box, and then type in the full e-mail address of your instructor. When finished, click *Close* to close the Nicknames window. When asked if you want to Save or Discard, choose *Save.*

5. Click the New Message button or use the *Ctrl+N* command to create a new message. In the *To* box, type the nickname for your instructor. When Eudora sends the message, it will automatically substitute the e-mail address you keyed into the Nicknames window.

6. Send yourself a copy of this message by placing your own e-mail name in the Cc box.

**Checkpoint 3C**    How could you make it easier to put your own e-mail address in the Cc box?

7. Write a short message to your instructor explaining what you have done in this activity. Do *not* send the message yet.

8. Use the *Tools → Signature* command to open the Signature block in Eudora. Type in your name, address, and local telephone number. This information will be added to the end of all outgoing e-mail messages. Figure 3.10 shows the author's signature block.

**FIGURE 3.10**
*Author's e-mail signature*

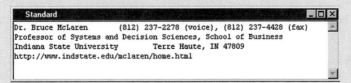

```
Standard                                                          _ □ ×
Dr. Bruce McLaren       (812) 237-2278 (voice), (812) 237-4428 (fax)
Professor of Systems and Decision Sciences, School of Business
Indiana State University        Terre Haute, IN 47809
http://www.indstate.edu/mclaren/home.html
```

9. Click the *Close* box to close the Signature window. Click the *Save* button so that your signature is saved.

**Checkpoint 3D**    How could you tell if your signature is being added correctly to an e-mail message?

10. Use the *Message → Attach File (Ctrl+H)* command to open the Attach Document window as shown in Figure 3.11. Select a folder and a file to attach to this message. For example, use a short word processing file that you have already created. If you can't think of a file, use c:\autoexec.bat from your computer. Click *Open* to select the file and close the Attach Document window.

**FIGURE 3.11**
*Attach File dialog box*

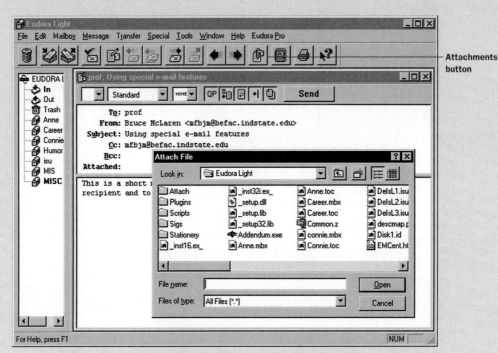

11. Now click the *Send* button to send your message and its attached file to the recipient. When the recipient receives your e-mail message, he or she will be notified that there is an attachment. They can decide whether to save the attachment as a file on their own computer.

12. Close Eudora.

## Netiquette—Internet Etiquette

To make better use of e-mail, we advise that you observe a few common-sense "rules of the road" in your own messages. We refer to these suggestions as **netiquette**.

■ Identify yourself in the message. Fill in your personal name in the mail configuration so that your name appears with your e-mail address in the From message header block.

■ Avoid inflammatory or intimidating statements that invite flame mail in return. Consider your response carefully before snapping off something you'll be sorry about later.

- Use ordinary capitalization—ALL CAPS is equivalent to "shouting" in e-mail!

- Read your mail promptly. Most senders expect that their messages are read as soon as received.

- Use emoticons when appropriate. Emoticons are described in the next section.

- Keep message length to a minimum, particularly when sending to a group or attaching a file. Remember that most users must pay for their connect time.

- Do repeat portions of your sender's message if you are replying to something they said. That way the recipient will have a context for your reply.

- Minimize the number of people to whom you send copies of messages. Most users are busy and don't have the time to read messages that are not relevant to them. Sending many copies of one message is called spamming.

 **NOTE** **An infamous spamming incident occurred in 1994 when an Arizona law firm sent thousands of messages offering their immigration services to discussion and news groups. Some estimate that up to 20 percent of the e-mail at AOL is junk e-mail.**

## INTERNET EMOTICONS

The whimsical images known as Internet emoticons are a set of symbols that denote some sort of emotion when viewed sideways. Because they can be created with any keyboard, they are a popular add-on for e-mail messages. Most Internet veterans advise that you use them sparingly, if you want to project professionalism. Remember that it is much more difficult to communicate subtle meanings with an e-mail message than with a phone call or face-to-face meeting. This is a good reason to use emoticons and abbreviations such as BTW (by the way), FYI (for your information), and IMHO (in my honest/humble opinion).

Some typical emoticons are shown below.

| | | | |
|---|---|---|---|
| :-) | smile or grin | :-( | frown or anger |
| ;-) | wink or light sarcasm | :-D | shock or surprise |
| :-1 | indifference | :-/ | perplexed |

## Net Ethics       *E-Mail Privacy*

E-mail is *not* the same as U.S. mail when it comes to privacy. Although it is forbidden to read other people's postal mail, electronic mail is not protected. In fact, the e-mail an employee of an organization receives is considered the property of the organization. Is it ethical for someone else to read your e-mail without your knowledge? If you happen to make a derogatory but private e-mail comment about company policies or an individual in the organization, can you be held accountable? If you accidentally send a sensitive message to the *wrong* e-mail address in your organization, should you be held responsible?

# Other E-Mail Packages

Eudora Light is the number one e-mail package in use today. The Windows 3.1, Windows 95, and Macintosh versions of Eudora Light are virtually identical. It is shareware software, so the price is right. Although Eudora Light contains all the basic e-mail services and many of the advanced ones, other POPmail packages are available.

## Eudora Pro

Eudora Pro is the commercial version of Eudora and sells for less than $90. Educational discounts are available for registered students, staff, and faculty of qualified institutions. Eudora Pro shares most of the same interface features of Eudora Light and remains remarkably easy to use. Eudora Pro adds the following features:

- Enhanced message filters to automatically identify and file incoming mail messages.

- Built-in spell checker to find typos. (You do have to remember to use it, though!)

- Character formatting such as bold, italic, underline, and variable font size. (You must read the message in a compatible e-mail client for these features to work properly.)

- Uuencoding and uudecoding support for attachments exchanged with other platforms.

- Customizable address book with entries for e-mail address, street address, and voice and fax telephone numbers.

- Support for multiple e-mail accounts within the same Eudora client.

- Attachments can be easily forwarded and redirected.

- Return receipt request can be made to cooperating mail servers at the destination end.

- 200-page user manual and glossy quick-reference guide with single-user licenses.

- 90 days' free technical support (no support is available for Eudora Light.)

Eudora Pro can be purchased directly over the Internet at *http://www.eudora.com* or from resellers. When you install it, Eudora Pro will automatically pick up your Eudora Light mailboxes, signature files, and address book entries.

## Pegasus (Pmail)

Pegasus mail is the other well-known shareware e-mail system that is available for multiple platforms. Pegasus mail versions are available for DOS, Windows 3.1, Windows 95, and Macintosh. Originally designed for Novell NetWare networks, Pmail is now available for dial-up POPmail systems, too. Pmail offers most of the same features as Eudora Pro but lacks a few items. The Pegasus user interface is shown in Figure 3.12.

**FIGURE 3.12**

*Pegasus e-mail interface*

## Commercial E-Mail Packages

Some schools and businesses use commercial e-mail packages such as Microsoft Mail, MS Exchange, and Lotus cc:Mail. These are fine packages that carry full features and a hefty price. They are designed to work with a local area network but usually allow POPmail access from dial-up users. Some of the advanced features of the commercial e-mail clients are *not* generally available when messages are read on another brand of e-mail client.

## Web Browser E-Mail Support

Many Web browsers now offer e-mail support from within the browser itself. Netscape and Internet Explorer (version 3.0 and later) offer sophisticated e-mail functions, including attachments and address books. Web browser e-mail was originally developed to complement newsreader capability. Many users will be able to use the Web browser for most or all of their e-mail needs.

### NETSCAPE COMMUNICATOR

Figure 3.13 shows the Netscape Messenger In box and the contents of one e-mail message. Messenger is part of Netscape Communicator 4.0, a suite of Internet products including the Navigator Web browser, the Composer Web document editor, and other modules. Messenger is a full-function program that provides access both to e-mail and to news groups, discussed in Unit 6. Messenger supports HTML mail, which allows rich formatting and images within messages using HTML formatting commands.

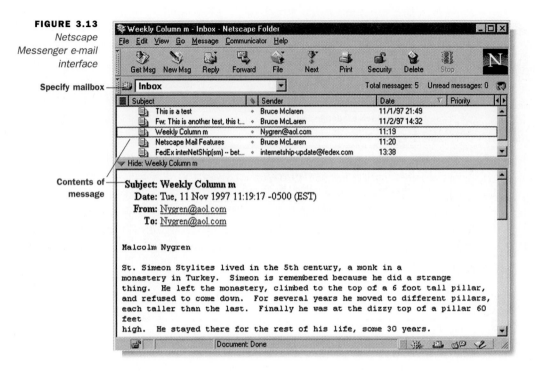

The Messenger composition window is shown in Figure 3.14. Note that the formatting toolbar just below the Subject line permits choice of font, character formatting, bullet and number lists, indenting, and alignment. The last icon permits the sender to insert hyperlinks and graphic images. Messenger is part of the Netscape Communicator Standard Edition. To configure Messenger for your e-mail address

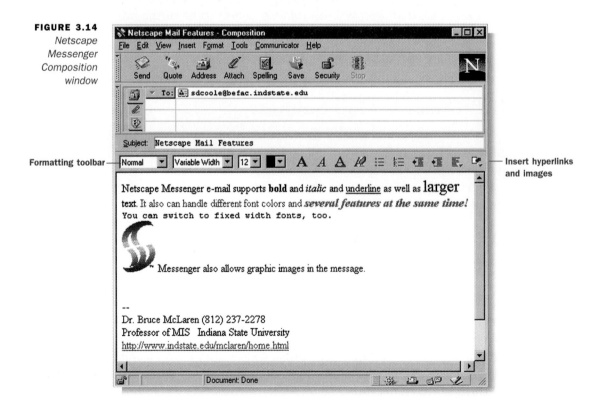

and mail server, use the Netscape *Edit → Preferences* command and select the *Mail & Groups* category. The Identity and Mail Server categories contain boxes for your personal information. Netscape permits information about multiple users to be stored in user profiles.

### MICROSOFT INTERNET EXPLORER

Figure 3.15 shows the MS Outlook Express e-mail window. Outlook Express is the e-mail client included with Microsoft's Internet Explorer 4.0 and replaces the Internet Mail program packaged with earlier versions of Internet Explorer. Like Netscape Messenger, Outlook Express is a full-featured e-mail client that also supports HTML mail. Unlike Messenger, upon installation Outlook Express detects the mailboxes in Eudora Pro e-mail client and offers to convert the mailboxes and the messages in them to Outlook Express format.

**FIGURE 3.15**
*Outlook Express e-mail window*

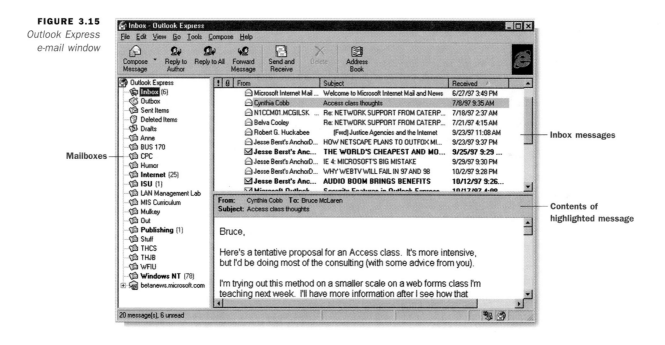

Figure 3.16 shows the Outlook Express composition window. It provides most of the same formatting features as Netscape Messenger. When you click the small arrow next to the Compose Message button (or use the *Compose → New Message Using* command), you will see several colorful templates known as stationery. These HTML files resemble stationery patterns that you would see on paper and dress up the message.

To configure Outlook Express with your e-mail information, use the *Tools → Accounts* command. Highlight the appropriate e-mail account, and then click the *Properties* button and fill in the server name, your mailbox address, and your personal name in the dialog box.

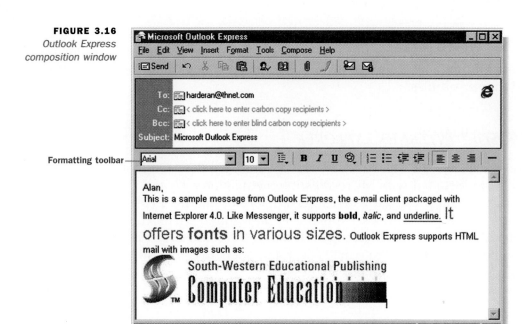

Formatting toolbar

# SUMMARY

Electronic mail is the most common application used on the Internet. E-mail is fast, inexpensive, and can be a very effective way to communicate with one or more users. Each user must have a mailbox address of the form *username@server.domainname*. The domain name of the organization must be registered with interNIC.

Eudora Light is the freeware version of Eudora. An e-mail message is created in a composition window similar to a word processor. When finished, the user sends the message to the mail server, which forwards it along to the correct mailbox. When you check your mail, the messages are sent to the In box mail folder where each can be read. You can reply to the message, print a copy, transfer it to another mailbox, forward it to another user, or delete the message.

Most e-mail systems support an address book for frequent recipients. You can attach a file to the message to be sent to the destination. Some e-mail systems provide for notification that a message has been delivered and read. Many users create a signature file for personal information such as name, address, home page address, and phone numbers. The signature information is automatically added to the end of outgoing messages. You should spell check messages before sending them.

Eudora Pro is the commercial version of Eudora. Pegasus mail is another shareware product. Both Netscape Communicator and Internet Explorer come with HTML mail clients that provide a rich environment of formatted messages with embedded images.

Netiquette is etiquette for the Internet. Avoid sending inflammatory statements, known as flame mail. Emoticons help convey subtle meaning that might not be evident from the text of the message. Read your mail promptly. When replying to a message, include portions of the original message.

## Command Review (Eudora Light)

| | |
|---|---|
| File → Check Mail (Ctrl+M) | Check for new mail |
| File → Print (Ctrl+P) | Print a message |
| File → Save (Ctrl+S) | Save a message in Out mailbox to be sent later |
| Help → Topics | Bring up Eudora help screen |
| Mailbox → New | Create a new mailbox |
| Message → Attach File (Ctrl+H) | Attach file to e-mail message |
| Message → Delete (Ctrl+D) | Delete the current message—send to Trash mailbox |
| Message → Forward | Forward a message |
| Message → New Message (Ctrl+N) | Create a new message |
| Message → Redirect | Redirect a message |
| Message → Reply (Ctrl+R) | Reply to a message |
| Priority button | Set message priority (Lowest ... Normal ... Highest) |
| Send (Queue) button | Send mail message (immediately or to Out queue) |
| Signature button | Add or inhibit the signature from this message |
| Tab (Shift+Tab) | Advance to the next (previous) block in header |
| Tools → Address Book (Ctrl+L) | Create an e-mail entry for an individual or group |
| Tools → Directory Services | Search an electronic phonebook |
| Tools → Filters | Create an e-mail filter |
| Tools → Options | Set configuration for e-mail address, personal name |
| Tools → Signature | Create or modify an e-mail signature |
| Transfer → <mailbox name> | Move current message to specified mailbox |

## Vocabulary Exercise

*Write a short definition for each term in the following list.*

| | | |
|---|---|---|
| Address Book | Emoticons | Netiquette |
| Alias | Eudora Light 3.0 | Nickname |
| Blind copy | Filters | POPmail |
| Clipboard | Flame mail | Postmaster |
| Domain name | HTML mail | Spamming |
| Electronic mail (e-mail) | Mail server | Trash |
| E-mail signature | Mailbox or folder | |

## Review Questions

1. Describe electronic mail and explain how it differs from regular mail.

2. What are the advantages and disadvantages of using e-mail as compared to other ways of communicating?

3. Discuss the purpose of the following parts of an e-mail message header.

   a. To:

   b. Subject:

   c. Cc:

   d. Bcc:

   e. Attachments:

4. How does POPmail allow you to check your mail from a remote location?

5. Discuss the purpose of each of the following domain suffixes.

   a. Edu

   b. Net

   c. Mil

   d. Gov

   e. Com

6. How would you identify the country associated with an e-mail address?

7. Discuss the following e-mail terms.

   a. flame mail

   b. message priority

   c. mailbox folder

   d. message signature

   e. message filter

8. Suppose you have a word processing file that you would like to send to another user over the Internet. Discuss ways to do this.

9. What is an emoticon, and how can it be used with e-mail?

10. How would you forward a message to another user?

11. How would you send the same message to a group?

12. How do you create a Eudora nickname for a frequent e-mail recipient?

## Exercises

1. Obtain your personal e-mail user name and practice using the e-mail software. Learn the commands for reading new mail and sending mail. If available, personalize your e-mail by assigning your real name to your account. (*Hint:* In Eudora Light, use the *Tools → Options* command to assign your real name.)

2. Send an e-mail message to yourself. Print a copy of that message when you receive it.

3. Send an e-mail message to your instructor with a copy to yourself. Print a copy of the message. In that message explain the advantages of using e-mail.

4. Explore your e-mail software and determine whether it supports the following functions. Write down the commands to accomplish each task.

   a. e-mail mailboxes

   b. forward mail

   c. auto-forward incoming mail to a different user name

   d. assign message priority

   e. delivery notification

   f. signature

   g. message filter

   h. cancel a mail message

5. Mail a message to a group. If available, create a mailing group rather than listing e-mail addresses in the To: block of the header. What are the commands to create a mail group?

6. Find out the e-mail address of a friend or relative at another campus, and then send a message to that person. Ask them to send a reply, and then print out the original message and the reply.

7. Send a text file as an attachment to a person at another location. If you cannot locate a text file to send, use the Windows Notepad to create a simple text file that contains the text of this exercise.

8. Add your personal identity information and e-mail servers to your Web browser's e-mail client, and then send a message to yourself or a friend. Take advantage of the browser's formatting capabilities to select different font sizes, bold and italic, and font color. What happens when you open that formatted message in a "regular" e-mail client?

# E-Mail Implementation and Use

In this project you are asked to prepare a report on the use of electronic mail in your school or organization. Research the use of e-mail in the organization, including the type(s) of e-mail clients used. Find out how e-mail addresses are created in your organization, and how they are publicized (e.g., phone book, Web page, searchable electronic directory, etc.) Consider the following questions as you do your research:

- How are people trained in the use of e-mail?

- What proportion of the organization's members actually use e-mail on a daily basis?

- Is access limited to a direct connection within the organization or can participants dial up and connect through a modem?

- What kinds of e-mail uses are most valued?

- Do individuals attach files to their e-mail messages?

- What is the maximum number of messages that can be saved?

- Do individuals prefer to use e-mail, voice mail, or telephone?

- What *additional* applications could be accomplished in e-mail that would benefit your organization? Be prepared to interview several users about this issue.

## *PROJECT TEAM OPTION*

Prepare a one-page quick reference card that describes the most important functions of your organization's e-mail system. Your quick reference card should give the commands or buttons that accomplish each function. Format the quick reference card appropriately for easy reference. If you do not have an organization-wide e-mail system, use Eudora Light as described in this unit.

# Hypertext and the World Wide Web

In this unit you will learn about the World Wide Web and how multimedia information can be displayed in hypertext fashion. We cover popular viewers including Netscape Communicator and Internet Explorer and give numerous examples of information found on the Web.

## Learning Objectives

At the completion of this unit, you should be able to

1. explain the origin of the World Wide Web,

2. use hypertext links in Web pages,

3. list the kinds of documents that are available on the Web,

4. describe the basic features of Web browsers,

5. start your Web browser,

6. retrieve information by clicking on hypertext links,

7. print a hypertext page,

8. use the bookmark feature to save favorite sites,

9. find information by searching the Web document.

## Key Terms

*The following terms are introduced in this unit. Be sure you know what each of them means.*

Bookmark
Browser
Cache
Favorite
Form
Graphic Image File (GIF)
Graphical User Interface (GUI)
Home page
Hyperlinks
Hypertext
HyperText Markup Language (HTML)
HyperText Transfer Protocol (HTTP)
Index.html
In-line image
Internet Explorer (IE)
JPEG
Link
Lynx
Netscape Navigator
Page
Plug-in
Quick menu
Uniform Resource Locator (URL)
Viewer
World Wide Web (WWW or the Web)

# *The World Wide Web*

The **World Wide Web** (**WWW** or **the Web**) refers to that portion of the Internet that is organized in hypertext format. This format links information to hot links within menus, making it much easier for users to locate that information. The Web is the most popular and fastest growing segment of the Internet. Most organizations planning for a presence on the Internet are implementing it on the Web.

## Origin of the World Wide Web

The Web began in Switzerland at CERN, the European institute that performs research into high-energy particle physics. Researchers at CERN designed the Web to share information about their research and work with other researchers. It soon became obvious that the Web was superior to Gopher for distributing information, and it has become the dominant way to access the Internet.

## The Hypertext Concept

**Hypertext** refers to documents where related resources are linked together. As you view the document, certain parts (words and phrases) are highlighted. If you click on a highlighted phrase in a hypertext document, the viewer will immediately jump to and display related information about that phrase. Documents are displayed as **pages**, one at a time. A page is usually larger than one screen, but only the information from one page can be sent over the Internet at a time, making transmission of information seem faster.

A well organized hypertext document can help the reader find desired information. The top of the document might contain an index with linked section headings. If you click on a section heading, you would go directly to that part of the document without scrolling manually. The end of each page could contain more hypertext links that let you go back to the top of the document or to another page.

Hypertext documents can also be organized in layers of detail. If most readers are thought to want the overview level of detail, the document is written to that perspective. Those who wish more detail can click on links to detailed explanation pages. Another clever alternative is to provide a graphical image, a map, for example. The reader can click on a portion of the map to receive information about items linked to that location.

---

NET TIP
**Web Addresses**

Current links to most Web sites in this book can be found on the *Understanding & Using the Internet* Home Page. Choose **Resources** at **computered.swep.com**. Remember that a Web address may change at any time. An address given in this book as an example may no longer be valid. If this is so, either access the Home Page for the current link or do a search to find a similar site (see Unit 5 for a discussion of search methods).

## Multimedia Resources

You can use the World Wide Web to access all kinds of information from the Internet. You can view text, pictures, sound, video, and animation. It has become the most popular way to view information on the Internet. Although somewhat complicated for those who create multimedia pages, the Web is quite simple for the user. Simply click on a highlighted link and the object is retrieved and displayed automatically. One pitfall of using multimedia is that although text displays very quickly, other objects take more time. Animation and video images require a significant amount of time to retrieve and display. This is particularly important if you are connected to the Internet with a telephone connection at 28.8 Kbps, the most common speed. Those who have a direct connection at several million bits per second will still experience a noticeable delay when viewing multimedia objects from the Web.

## Basic Web Services

Several document protocols are available through Netscape, Internet Explorer, and most other Web browsers. The type of service is denoted by the protocol portion of the URL address. Hypertext formatted documents with multimedia contents use the *http:* protocol in the URL. Gopher services use *gopher:* as the protocol. FTP services use *ftp:* as the protocol. Telnet services use *telnet:* as the protocol. Network news services use *news:* as the protocol. Files with hypertext commands that are loaded from the local disk drive instead of the Web use the *file:* protocol. Table 4.1 gives examples of URL addresses for different services supported by Web browsers.

**TABLE 4.1**
*Basic Web services*

| TYPE | URL ADDRESS | MEANING |
|---|---|---|
| HTTP | *http://www.whitehouse.gov* | President Clinton and Vice President Gore |
| Gopher | *gopher://gopher.nd.edu* | Notre Dame Gopher Server |
| FTP | *ftp://ftp.netscape.com/* | FTP file location of Netscape Navigator |
| Telnet | *telnet://ssinfo.purdue.edu* | Telnet location of Purdue University student services |
| News | *news://news.indstate.edu* | News server at ISU |
| File | *file:///ex1.htm* | File on hard drive containing HTML commands |

# *WWW Browsers*

Web client programs, called browsers, present a menu of information resources for a particular Web site. Links are highlighted, usually with an underline and a different color such as blue or red. One important difference between a Web browser and a Gopher client is the former's ability to display information graphically.

# GUI Browsers

Most Web browsers are designed for graphical user interface (GUI) systems such as Windows, Macintosh, and X-Windows (the UNIX graphical interface.) Although they are very different platforms, most browsers present a consistent user interface across platforms. You can generalize use of different browsers on the same platform as well.

## MOSAIC

The Web browser that launched the hypertext movement is called NCSA Mosaic. Mosaic was developed at the National Center for Supercomputer Applications at the University of Illinois in the late 1980s and early 1990s. Mosaic has been licensed to several companies for commercial development and resale, but a version is available for educational users on many FTP sites. (For examples of FTP sites, see the home page for this text at *computered.swep.com*.)

## NETSCAPE NAVIGATOR

Although Mosaic represented an important step in Web access, some of its developers split from the university and formed their own company. Their Web browser is called Netscape Navigator, or Netscape for short. Netscape has become the leading Web browser in a very short time, holding a 60 percent market share. Figure 4.1 shows the Netscape home page Web site.

Like Mosaic, Netscape is available on the Netscape Communications Corporation home page at no cost. The rest of this unit and the following one will deal with Netscape's latest version called Communicator. Communicator is a suite of

**FIGURE 4.1**
*Netscape Web site*

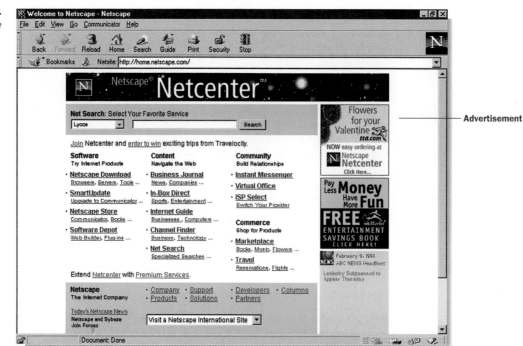

Advertisement

useful Web tools, including Navigator. Netscape Communicator Standard Edition is also free. Table 4.2 shows the Communicator tools and their purpose.

TABLE 4.2

*Netscape Communicator tools*

| TOOL | PURPOSE |
|------|---------|
| Navigator | Web browser and interface to the other tools |
| Messenger | E-mail client for sending, receiving, and sorting e-mail messages |
| Composer | Web page editing tool for creating HTML documents |
| Collabra | News group tool that helps you participate in discussion groups |
| Conference | Allows remote users to work together |

Because Netscape Communicator users spent most of their time in the Navigator browser, for the remainder of this unit Netscape will refer to Netscape Navigator. Where necessary, the term Communicator is used to refer to the entire suite of tools.

### MICROSOFT INTERNET EXPLORER

Microsoft's Internet Explorer (IE) is the only major competitor to Netscape Navigator. Internet Explorer has the power of Microsoft behind it. Microsoft's goal is to dominate the Internet market like it has the markets for operating systems and applications software. In late fall 1997, Microsoft introduced version 4.0 of Internet Explorer that is comparable to Netscape Communicator 4.0. Internet Explorer is available at no cost from Microsoft's Web site. It also is included in later releases of Windows 95. Figure 4.2 shows the Internet Explorer 4.0 interface at the Microsoft home page.

**FIGURE 4.2**

*Internet Explorer 4.0 interface*

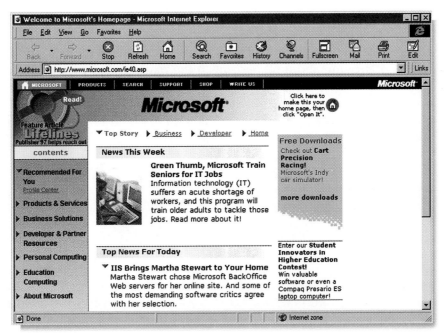

Internet Explorer also was originally based on the Mosaic browser. The competition between Netscape and Microsoft is healthy, but may result in incompatibilities with some documents. (See the Net Ethics sidebar below.) However, the Internet Explorer commands are *very* similar to Netscape Navigator commands. Someone familiar with one browser will have little trouble switching to the other product. While most of this unit deals with Netscape, Internet Explorer features are also described. There is a comparison table for commands from each browser at the end of this unit.

### OTHER GUI BROWSERS

Other browsers are available, but most of them are, like Netscape and Internet Explorer, based on Mosaic. Each of the "Big Three" commercial information services (CompuServe, America Online, and Prodigy) has its own browser. Companies selling Internet suites may package their own browser. It seems unlikely that many of these browsers will continue to be marketed.

## Text-Based Browsers: Lynx

Some Web software is available for text-only systems. The best known of these is called **Lynx** and works with DOS and UNIX systems. Although more limited than the GUI clients, text-based browsers have the advantage of being much faster because they do not have to receive graphical images before you can work with a menu at a Web site. There is a version of Lynx available for VT100-compatible terminal users. Lynx can be found on many FTP sites. (For an example of Lynx, see the home page for this text by visiting Resources at *computered.swep.com*.) It is also possible to Telnet to a UNIX site and run Lynx from that server via Telnet, although this is very slow.

## *Using a Browser to Explore the WWW*

Netscape is the most popular Web browser for the Windows and Macintosh platforms, occupying about 60 percent of the market. It is easy to use and simple to install under Windows. Likewise, Microsoft's Internet Explorer is frequently found on computers that run Microsoft Office 95 and Microsoft Office 97. Although the United States Justice Department has issued a temporary injunction against Microsoft at this writing, Internet Explorer is likely to be an integral part of Windows 98.

### Net Ethics    *Browser Competition*

Because of the strong competition between Netscape Communications and Microsoft for browser supremacy, each has been accused of creating internal features that prevent the user with one browser from taking advantage of some capabilities of Web pages designed for the other browser. Do you think it is appropriate for Web developers to take advantage of these differences so that you must have a particular Web browser to use that site?

Although we will assume that you have already installed your browser, in case you have to reinstall it, use the Run command in the Start button menu and specify the installation file on your hard drive. This setup program will lead you through the installation process. For Netscape Communicator it might be something like cb32e404.exe for the 32 bit version 4.04. For Internet Explorer, it might be ie4setup.exe. If you have installed your browser under Windows 95 or Windows NT, you should be able to uninstall it later by using the Add/Remove Programs icon in the Control Panel.

## Starting Your Browser

During the installation process, your browser will install itself in the Start button menu and should leave a shortcut icon on your desktop. To start Netscape, use the Start button menu, click *Programs*, and then select *Netscape Navigator* in the Netscape Communicator program group, or double-click the Netscape Navigator icon on your desktop. To start Internet Explorer from the Start button, click *Programs*, and then select *Internet Explorer* in the Internet Explorer program group, or double-click the Internet Explorer icon on your desktop.

*Some users will right-drag the Web browser shortcut to the Start button menu so that it appears on the first menu panel, above Programs.*

Because your browser requires a TCP/IP connection, it will check for a current TCP/IP session. If it doesn't find one and you are using dial-up networking, your browser will bring up the PPP Connect To dialog box and wait for you to initiate the connection. It is possible to bring up your browser *without* the TCP/IP connection if you want to display a Web page contained in a file on your disk.

After loading, your browser will display the default home page. Most organizations will set their own Web site as the default home page, as shown in Figure 4.3 for Indiana State University. If you have just installed Netscape on your machine, it will default to the Netscape home page. Internet Explorer defaults to the Microsoft home page. You can override the default home page, as described later in this unit.

**FIGURE 4.3**
*Indiana State University home page*

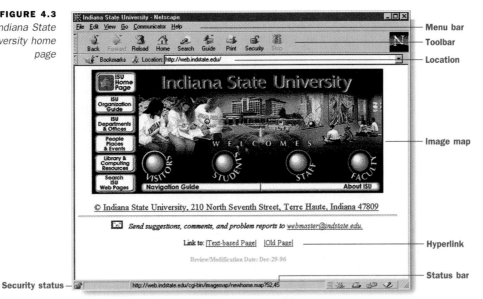

## The Main Browser Window

Figure 4.3 shows the standard configuration for the Windows 95 version of Netscape. Like other Windows applications, Netscape features a standard menu bar with toolbar buttons just beneath it for frequently used commands. The Location block just beneath the toolbar shows the Internet address of the particular document being displayed and can be used to enter another address. The symbolic Netscape N at the right side of the window is animated to indicate when something is being retrieved: you'll see meteors flashing by the N in that window.

The large window in the middle of the screen displays the Web document, in this case the official home page at Indiana State University. A home page is the top-level menu document for a particular Web site. It contains jumping-off points, in this case the 12 buttons embedded in the graphic image on the screen. At the bottom of the page is the status bar. The status bar provides messages about the information being transferred. At the far right is a progress bar that fills with color as a document is being retrieved. The padlock at the lower left indicates whether security has been implemented for this page: an open lock means that transactions are sent across the Internet as plain text, whereas a closed lock indicates that transmissions are encoded for privacy. We'll discuss security issues in a later unit.

**Hyperlinks** represent addresses for other Internet resources and usually appear underlined and in blue. When you click on a hyperlink, your browser will open the document found in that hyperlink. You'll have a chance to try a hyperlink in the next Guided Activity.

## Uniform Resource Locator (URL)

The **Uniform Resource Locator** or **URL** is an address for an Internet resource. The URL for Figure 4.3 is *http://web.indstate.edu/*. We'll discuss each part of this URL.

- *http:* stands for **HyperText Transfer Protocol (HTTP)**, the rules used to create hypertext pages on the Web. We will discuss hypertext documents in more detail later in this unit. Other protocols such as FTP, Telnet, News, and Gopher also are available through Netscape. In all cases, follow the protocol type with the specific Internet address of the desired resource.

- *//web.indstate.edu* is the domain address for one Web server at Indiana State University. Many home pages on the Web begin with the initials *www*. If you know the domain name for a particular institution, you might type its address into the Location text box to see if it has a home page. See the home page for this text at *computered.swep.com* for more examples of home pages.

- The next item in an URL is the path to the specific page. If you were to click on the "Library & Computing Resources" section of the main menu graphic, shown in Figure 4.3, the resulting URL would be *http://web.indstate.edu/libcomp/*. In this page the path is */libcomp/*, referring to the Library and Computing folder. When no HTML file name is shown at the end of the URL, as is the case here, then the Web server searches for the default HTML file called **index.html** in that folder.

**TIP**

Today's browsers do not require you to enter the http:// portion of the URL. Thus for this URL, you could have just entered *web. indstate.edu.*

## GUIDED ACTIVITY

# 4.1    Using Netscape Navigator

In this activity you will start Netscape (or your own Web browser) and look at several Web pages.

1. If you have not already started Windows, do so now. If you are using a dial-up connection, start it now and connect with your Internet service provider.

2. Locate the Netscape icon (or the icon for your Web browser) and double-click it to start the browser. It should come up in a few seconds and display your default home page.

3. If you selected the Netscape home page, it might look like Figure 4.1. Otherwise, your own home page will be pictured.

4. If you are using Netscape, click the *Location:* box (or use the *File→Open Page* command) to select a different page. At the Open Page prompt or in the Location box enter:

   `http://www.whitehouse.gov`

**Checkpoint 4A**    What does http: mean in the Location box?

5. After a few seconds, Netscape will retrieve the home page for the White House, as shown in Figure 4.4. The graphic image may not fit on one screen; so you might have to use the scroll bars to view the entire image.

6. To see what is new, click on the *What's New* hyperlink in the middle-right area of the White House page. After a few moments you will see a list of new

**FIGURE 4.4**
*White House home page*

**Back button**

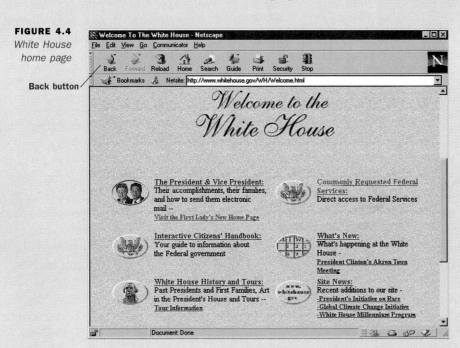

items available through the White House Web site, including recent presidential speeches or initiatives.

7.  Return to the main White House page by clicking the *Back* button in the toolbar. If your Web browser is equipped for sound, you can listen to the President's radio speeches by clicking on The Virtual Library link and following the menu choices.

 **NOTE** **Most Web browsers (including Netscape Navigator version 3.0 and above) are able to play back the sound found in the .AU files containing audio speech. If your browser cannot handle sound files, I recommend that you upgrade to a later version.**

8.  We will continue with more Netscape operations in the next activity, so leave it open for now.

## Retrieving Information with Netscape

When you start up Netscape, it will display the default home page. If you are at school or an office, your browser will probably have this already configured. If you have installed your own copy of Netscape, it is initially configured to display the Netscape home page, as pictured in Figure 4.1. In either event, you will notice that information appears in fonts of different sizes and colors. Some text may be underlined and represents a link to an Internet resource. In other cases, there may be an image with graphical "buttons" for you to click. The ISU home page of Figure 4.3 shows an image map with 12 rectangular and round buttons for you to click.

As you move the mouse pointer to a link, Netscape will display its URL address in the status bar area at the very bottom of the screen. If you are pointing to an image map, the status bar will display the name of the image map and the $x,y$ coordinates within that image. Try it with the ISU home page.

### FOLLOWING A LINK

To retrieve information from the Web, find the hyperlink line in the current page and click on it. The default display option is to show the hypertext links in color (blue or purple) and underlined. Netscape shows new links in blue and displays links you have followed previously in purple. You can control how long previously visited links are displayed in purple. The default for Netscape Navigator is 30 days; setting this box to zero means visited links will always be remembered. This feature saves you from inadvertently going down the same path twice.

After you click on a hyperlink or button, Netscape will attempt to decode the URL address and get the corresponding IP address from your domain name server. For example, if you enter *http://www.hp.com* as the URL, the DNS would convert that to Hewlett-Packard's IP address of [192.151.11.10]. When it has the IP address, Netscape will request that the information from that page be sent over the Internet to your computer. Unlike some other applications, the Web does *not* require a continuous connection to the server of the page you required. It will send you the page and then disconnect you from that Web server.

**TIP**

Netscape Navigator version 4.0 and later "remembers" previously visited site URLs and will automatically fill in the Location box as you enter a URL. Not only does this save time, but it also prevents errors.

**TIP**

With Communicator, if you click and hold down the Back button, you'll get the same list of sites you have visited during this Netscape session. Click one to go directly to that site. With Internet Explorer, click the small down arrow to the right of the Back button to get the site list.

Most Web browsers use a disk cache to maintain graphic images of previously visited sites. Thus it will not take as long to retrieve an image from that site in future visits. You can determine how much of your disk drive to use for the cache—more space allocated to the cache will enable graphical pages to be loaded much quicker *after* they have already been visited once. This setting is found in the *Edit→Preferences→Advanced→Cache* command. My computer allocates 15 MB of disk space to the cache.

### OPENING A SPECIFIC URL LOCATION

As mentioned in the previous Guided Activity, use the *File→Open Page* command (or click the *Location* box in the Location toolbar) to open a specific Web site. For Internet Explorer use the *File→Open* command or click the *Address:* box in the toolbar. You must have the complete URL location address for the site, and it is easy to mistype part of this address. A list of representative Web sites and their addresses can be found on this text's home page by visiting Resources at *computered. swep.com.* (The period at the end of the address is *not* part of the URL.)

### VIEWING PREVIOUS PAGES

Your browser has two buttons in the toolbar for viewing pages previously viewed during this session. The Back button (or *Go→Back* from the menu bar) will take you backward to the immediately previous page. The Forward button (or *Go→Forward* from the menu bar) will reverse that command, taking you forward in the list. You can also right-click the browser window and select *Back* or *Forward* from that menu.

The Go menu will also display most of the sites you have visited during this browser session. Click *Go*, and then select the page you want to jump to. Because your browser keeps information from these pages in the memory cache, they will display very quickly.

### WEB FORMS

Forms are documents that let you enter information into a message and send that message elsewhere on the Web. Your browser can handle forms automatically. When you access a page that calls for some response, such as creating an e-mail message or searching for specific information, a form is used. Figure 4.5 shows an example of an order form within Netscape. As you fill in information, use the *Tab* key to move to the next field and *Shift+Tab* to move to a previous field. Typically, the designer of the page will have included a Send button that you can click to cause the completed form message to be forwarded.

### TROUBLESHOOTING A BAD CONNECTION

Occasionally your browser will inform you that it cannot retrieve the page. We always recommend that users try the same command again. There are several reasons why you might not be served the Web page you requested:

■  The domain name server cannot decode the address: try again.

**FIGURE 4.5**
*Netscape order
form*

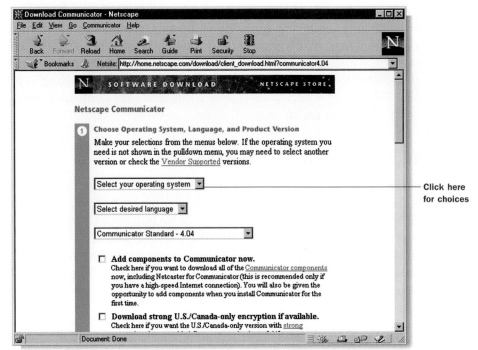

- The server may be too busy to acknowledge your request: try again.

- The server may be down temporarily: try again.

- The Internet is too busy and your request times out: try again.

- The address is incorrect: be sure you entered it correctly.

- The address has changed (many sites will leave a forwarding address).

- You may not have permission to open that page.

> **CAUTION**    **In any event, if you do get an error message that you can replicate, write down its contents precisely to show your instructor or lab assistant. Make sure you copy down the URL location of the site you were trying to reach.**

### CHANGING YOUR DEFAULT HOME PAGE

To change the default Netscape home page, use the *Edit→Preferences→Navigator* command and enter the URL in the Home Page box, as shown in Figure 4.6. If the current page is the home page, click the *Use Current Page* button to save time. The next time you start Netscape or click the Home button, the new selection will take effect. In the same dialog box you can choose how long visited pages remain in your history list. The default is 30 days. Visited links are highlighted in an alternate color for the same time.

In Internet Explorer you can change the default home page with the *View→Internet Options* command. It is found in the opening screen in the General tab, as shown in Figure 4.7. You will return to this dialog box later in the unit for other configuration changes.

**FIGURE 4.6**

*Netscape Navigator Preferences dialog box*

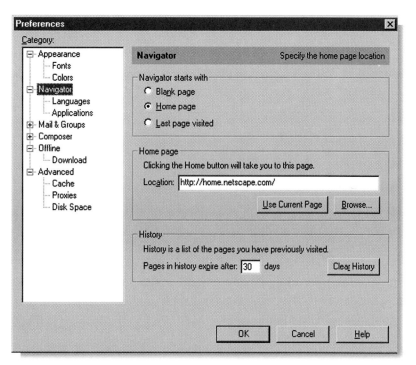

**FIGURE 4.7**

*Internet Explorer Internet Options dialog box*

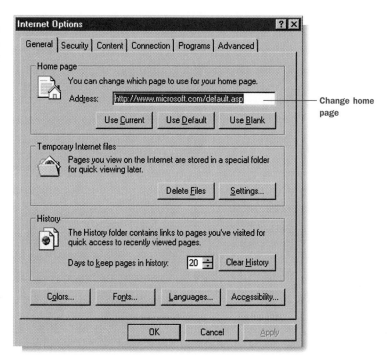

Change home page

# Interrupting a Web Page

If you entered the wrong URL, or the current page is taking too long, or there are errors, you may get impatient waiting for the page to appear. You can interrupt the transfer of a Web page by clicking the Stop button in the toolbar, or by pressing the *Esc* key. Your browser will display whatever has been transferred so far in the session.

Your browser will transfer the text portions of the Web page first and then the graphic images. Some images are large and take a long time to load, especially if you don't have a direct connection. Pressing the Stop button will display the received portion of the page and might allow you to select the next link. If you interrupt a graphic image as it is being transferred, it will be partially saved in the disk cache; the next time you visit that site, your browser will download the unsaved portion of the image. This is a new feature with Netscape Communicator and saves considerable time with graphics-intensive sites.

## Reloading a Web Page

If something goes wrong with the display of a page, you can click Netscape's *Reload* button, or use the *View→Reload* command or its shortcut, *Ctrl+R*. Netscape will request that the Web page be retransmitted. With Internet Explorer click the *Refresh* button, or use the *View→Refresh* command.

One use for reloading a page occurs when you are developing your own Web pages, discussed in Unit 8. After you make a change to the HTML document and save it on the disk drive (or send it via FTP to the Web server), use the Reload button to load the new version.

## Getting Help

Each time you highlight a menu bar command, the status bar will give you a one-sentence description of that command. You can learn about various commands by selecting a menu item and then moving the cursor to read the help from the status bar. Netscape also uses tooltips—move the cursor onto a button for a moment, and Netscape will display a phrase that describes that button.

Many Netscape users will find that the most common operations are available with the browser's toolbar buttons. These will display with text and pictures. In case your copy of Netscape doesn't show the toolbar buttons, use the *View→Show Navigation* Toolbar command to turn it on. If you would like to display the pictures along with text in the toolbar, use Netscape's *Edit→Preferences→Appearance* command and make that selection.

Many dialog boxes have a Help button for assistance with choices in that box. Choosing the Help button brings up a hyperlinked Help window. From there you can scroll the contents window at the left side, or use the Index button and search for help by keyword. The Find button will search through the actual help display on the right side. You will want to maximize the Help window to see more of it at one time.

For general help, press the *F1* function key or use the *Help→Help Contents* command in Netscape. Figure 4.8 shows the Netscape NetHelp window.

More extensive help is available in the Netscape *Help→Handbook* menu bar. Unfortunately, this is online help, so you must be connected to the Internet in order to retrieve the help document from the Netscape Web server. A printed manual comes with the commercial version of Netscape Navigator if you choose to purchase it.

In Internet Explorer, get help by pressing *F1* or using the *Help→Contents* and *Index* command. A similar hyperlinked help window appears in which you can select the desired help topic in the left pane and see the help in the right pane. Figure 4.9 shows the Internet Explorer help window.

FIGURE 4.8
*Netscape NetHelp
window*

Contents —

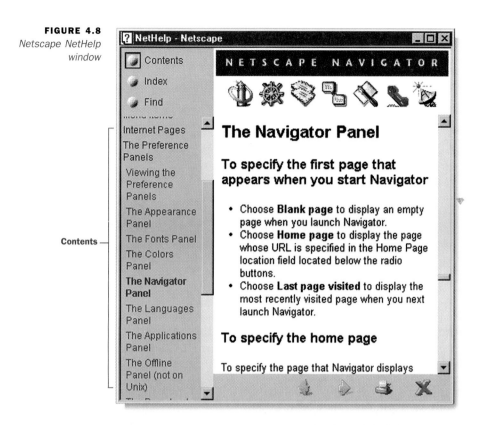

FIGURE 4.9
*Internet Explorer
Help window*

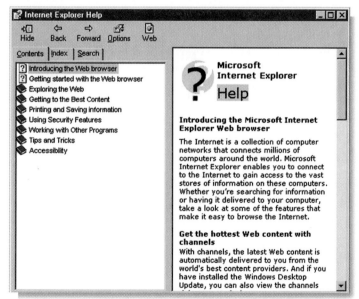

# Printing a Web Page

Because your Web browser uses the default Windows printer driver, a printer set up for Windows should be able to print Web documents. To print a page, click the Print button in the toolbar or use the *File→Print* command. At the Netscape Print dialog box shown in Figure 4.10 you can specify the print range (defaults to All pages), number of copies, and the print resolution. Most users will simply click OK to begin printing. The Internet Explorer Print dialog box is similar.

**FIGURE 4.10**
*Netscape Print
dialog box*

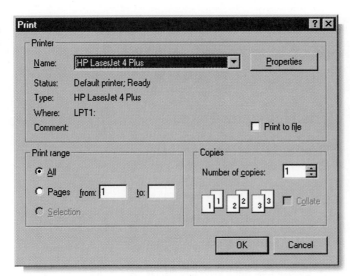

**NOTE** **If you click the Print button in Internet Explorer, the entire document is printed without displaying the Print dialog box. This is similar to the Print button's function in Microsoft Office.**

Keep in mind that many Web pages are essentially graphic images and may not look as good on a low-resolution monochrome printer as they do on your monitor. If you have a color printer such as an ink jet, printed images should look very good.

**TIP**

If there are many pages in the current Web document, use Netscape's *File→Print Preview* command instead and scroll through the preview. Then print only those pages that are of interest to you by specifying their page numbers in the Print dialog box. Internet Explorer does not have a Print preview feature.

## Using the Find Command for the Current Page

Although most Web pages are relatively short and are subdivided into sections, some are very long, making it difficult to search manually for a particular keyword. You can scroll up and down in the current page with the vertical scroll bar, just like any other Windows document. Most Web browsers allow the use of the *PageUp* and *PageDn* keys provided the focus is in the browser window and not the Location box.

You can use the *Edit→Find* (or *Ctrl+F*) command to locate keywords in the *current* Web page. You'll be asked to enter the keyword string in the Find What text box, and select the search direction, as shown in Figure 4.11. Click the Find button and your browser will search from that point in the desired direction. If a match is found, it will move the pointer to the next point at which the keywords are found and highlight the keyword on the screen. The Find command can help with large or complex Web pages. Note that Find may not discover keywords that reside in forms. The Netscape Find box is similar but lacks the Match whole word only option.

**FIGURE 4.11**
*Internet Explorer
Find dialog box*

# Using Bookmarks and Favorites

Because bookmarks are so easy to use, we recommend that you add your favorite places to the bookmarks or favorites feature of your Web browser. With a bookmark you don't have to memorize a particular location's URL; you just click on it. You can organize your bookmarks in hierarchical fashion and edit the sequence of pages in the bookmarks list. In Netscape the bookmark feature is called a bookmark, while Internet Explorer uses Favorites to describe bookmarks. They are essentially identical.

## JUMPING TO A BOOKMARK LOCATION

To jump to a page in your bookmarks list, click the *Bookmarks* button in the toolbar, then click the bookmark item of interest. Netscape will fetch the indicated page. Figure 4.12 shows a portion of the author's set of Netscape bookmark locations. Notice that some of the bookmarks are folders—click on the folder to display its individual bookmarks. Folders can contain folders.

**FIGURE 4.12**
*Netscape Bookmarks list*

Bookmark button

Bookmark folder

Individual bookmark

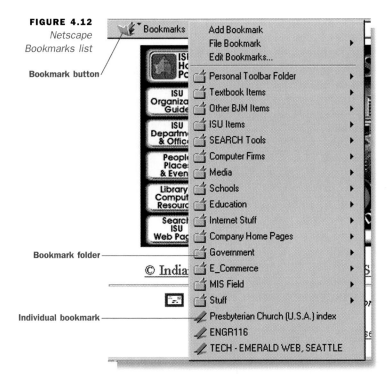

If you have more bookmark items than will display on one screen, then open the Bookmarks window and choose the *Edit Bookmarks* command. You can scroll down to view the full list. Double-click the selected item, and Netscape will load that document.

With Internet Explorer, click the *Favorites* button to open the Favorites panel at the left side of the browser window, shown in Figure 4.13. To open any item in the favorites list, simply click it. Notice that the highlighted favorites are organized in a folder called ISU Items. You can drag items from one place to another in your favorites list.

FIGURE 4.13
Internet Explorer
Favorites panel

Favorites panel —

ISU Items folder —

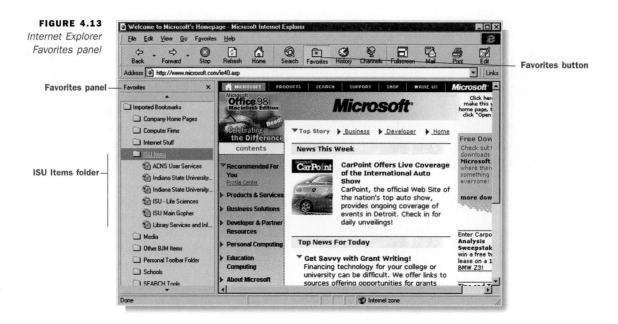

Favorites button

## ADDING A LOCATION TO THE BOOKMARK LIST

To add a location to your bookmark list, first jump to that Web page. In Netscape click the *Bookmarks* button and select the *Add Bookmark* command. The location and description of that location will be placed at the bottom of your bookmark list. In Internet Explorer use the *Favorites→Add to Favorites* command to add the current page to the Favorites list. Internet Explorer maintains bookmarks in alphabetical order in the favorites list.

## EDITING A BOOKMARK IN NETSCAPE

In Netscape click the *Bookmarks* button, and then use the *Edit Bookmarks* command to open the Bookmarks window. Figure 4.14 shows this dialog box for the author's personal home page. Use the *Edit→Bookmark Properties* command to bring up the Properties of a selected bookmark item. In this properties dialog box (see Figure 4.15) you can see the Internet location of each page, when you last visited that page, the date it was added, and room for a description of the item.

FIGURE 4.14
Netscape
Bookmarks dialog
box

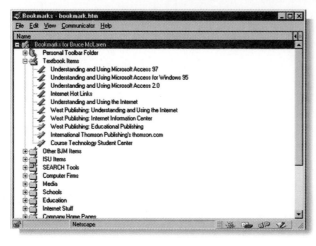

**FIGURE 4.15**

*Netscape Bookmark Properties dialog box*

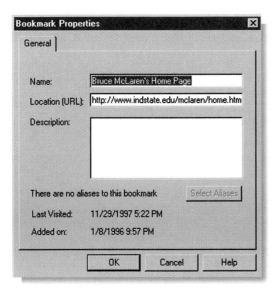

To change the position of an item in the bookmark list, drag that item to move the selected bookmark item up or down to the desired location. Netscape will display a dark line to indicate where the bookmark would be moved. The Windows Clipboard can also be used to move multiple bookmark items. Select them by *Ctrl* clicking each one, and then use *Edit→Cut*. Select the bookmark line that the moved items are to follow, and then use *Edit→Paste* to add them to the list.

You can insert horizontal divider lines between groups of similar items. Select the bookmark item that the line should follow, and then use the *File→New Separator* command. You can remove a bookmark permanently by first selecting it and then using the *Edit→Delete* command. We'll demonstrate using the bookmark feature in the next Guided Activity.

## GUIDED ACTIVITY

## 4.2   Using the Netscape Bookmark Feature

In this activity you will add some sites to the bookmark list and then use the bookmark list to go to those sites.

1. Start Netscape as usual, and go to the ISU home page at *http://web.indstate.edu/*.

2. Click the *Bookmarks* menu bar and choose the *Add Bookmark* command to add this site to your bookmark list.

3. Open the CNN home page at *http://www.cnn.com/*. Add this site to your bookmark list.

4. Add the following sites to your bookmark list: *http://www.whitehouse.gov/* and *http://www.netscape.com/*.

5.  Next use the *Bookmarks→Edit Bookmarks* command to open the bookmarks window.

6.  Drag the Whitehouse site to the top of the list. Drag the CNN site to the bottom of the list.

7.  Highlight the CNN site line, then use the *File→New Separator* command to place a horizontal line above the CNN line.

 **Checkpoint 4B**   What is the sequence of sites within your bookmark list?

8.  Click the Close button to close the Bookmarks window.

9.  Click the Bookmarks menu bar, and then click on the CNN line. Netscape should open that site immediately. Practice by clicking on the other sites.

10.  Open the bookmark list, and then highlight the CNN item. Use the *Edit→Bookmark Properties* command to place a short phrase in its description box.

11.  Click *OK* to close the Properties window, and then close the Bookmarks window. Leave Netscape open for now.

## EDITING FAVORITES WITH INTERNET EXPLORER

Choose the *Favorites→Organize Favorites* command to open the Organize favorites dialog box shown in Figure 4.16. Favorites is actually a folder within the Windows folder on your hard drive. Notice that it contains other folders (such as My Documents) that appear in Microsoft Office as well as Web documents.

To change the properties of a favorite item, right-click it and choose *Properties*. Figure 4.17 shows the Internet Shortcut tab of the Properties dialog box. You can change the target URL for this site. Internet Explorer also can notify you when the contents of this favorite have changed in the Subscription tab of this dialog box.

**FIGURE 4.16**
*Internet Explorer
Organize Favorites
dialog box*

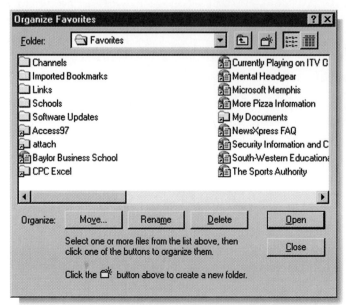

**FIGURE 4.17**
*Internet Explorer*
*Favorites Properties*
*dialog box*

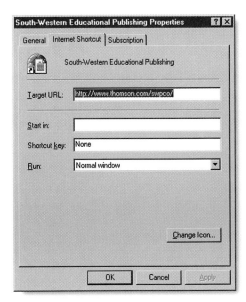

You can receive an optional e-mail message or Internet Explorer can put a red dot next to the item in the Favorites list.

Click the yellow *New Folder* button in the toolbar to create a new Favorites folder, and then drag other favorite items to the folder. When you open the Favorites panel in Internet Explorer, folders and individual items are displayed in alphabetical order. You can remove a favorite permanently by right-clicking it and selecting *Delete.*

# Advanced Browser Operations

## The Netscape Quick Menu

You can click the right mouse button in Netscape Navigator to reveal the quick menu, also known as the popup menu. The quick menu contains useful menu options for the selected object that you can select without going through the menu bar or the toolbar. Figure 4.18 shows the Netscape quick menu for an image super-

**FIGURE 4.18**
*Netscape quick*
*menu*

**Right-click here**

**Quick menu**
**for image**

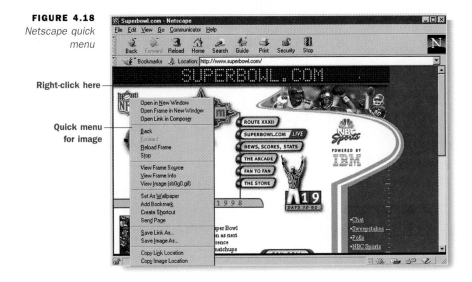

imposed on the NBC Super Bowl home page. The NFL logo image is also a link to the NFL home page.

The quick menu has these choices:

- Open in a new window, or open this page in Composer, the Web page editor.

- Back and Forward, allowing you to move to previous pages displayed during the current Web session. If you are viewing a Web page with frames (discussed later in this unit), you can also go back within the frame. You can also reload this page.

- View the source HTML code or view the image, in this case the NFL logo file called sb0g0.gif. This option will not be present if you do not right-click an image.

- Add this page to the Bookmarks list, and create an Internet shortcut on the desktop: double-click that shortcut and Netscape will load, opening the current location.

- Save the link to the NFL home page or copy the link to the Windows Clipboard. If you do not right-click a link, this option will not appear.

- Save the actual image on your hard drive or copy the image to the Windows Clipboard. If you do not right-click an image, this option will not appear.

## The Internet Explorer Quick Menu

Like Netscape Navigator, Internet Explorer also comes with a quick menu. The Super Bowl home page is shown in Figure 4.19; right-click the NFL logo to display the quick menu. Many of the same choices are available with Internet Explorer, in-

**FIGURE 4.19**
*Internet Explorer quick menu*

cluding saving the image on your hard drive or Clipboard, opening the link in another window, or adding the page to Favorites.

## Saving Web Pages

You can save the contents of a Web page as a file on your disk drive in the original HTML source. HTML stands for HyperText Markup Language, the set of formatting commands used in Web documents to indicate special effects on that page. Use the *File→Save As* (or *Ctrl+S*) command to save the current page as a disk file. Netscape will use the .html extension for the file name, while Internet Explorer uses .htm as the extension. We will cover creating home pages and HTML files in Unit 8.

## Retrieving a Saved Web Page File

You can retrieve a Web page that has been saved as a file with the *File→Open Page* (or *Ctrl+O*) command in Netscape, and *File→Open* in Internet Explorer. Instead of retrieving that page from the original Web server, it is fetched from your disk drive. Your browser might hang up if there are calls on that page to the original server. Many people use the *File→Open* feature when testing a new home page offline from the Internet.

## Viewing and Saving a Graphic Image

One of the advantages of working with Netscape is its built-in ability to display in-line images automatically. An in-line image is a graphic displayed next to text. You can turn off the automatic display of in-line images in Netscape with the *Edit→Preferences→Advance* command and remove the check in front of Automatically Load Images. In Internet Explorer you can do the same thing with the *View→Internet Options→Advanced* command; remove the check in front of Display Pictures. This may have the effect of speeding up display of graphical pages. Most users will not want to change from the automatic setting.

If the page contains references to external graphic files, Netscape is also able to display them in a separate window if they use the graphical image file or GIF (pronounced like "gift" without the T) or JPEG (pronounced "jay-peg") file formats. Most images found on the Web use one of these two formats, with JPEG files being more compressed and thus quicker to download.

You can save a favorite graphic image from a Web page you have retrieved. Right-click the image to bring up the quick menu, and then choose the *Save Image As* or *Save Picture As* command. Specify the disk location, the file type, and then click Save. You can view the image separately in a graphics program, or even include the image in your own Web pages.

CAUTION  **Many graphic images that appear in Web documents are copyrighted and cannot be stored or used in any other application. Check with the owner before you use any images! Visit the Web site for the ten common myths about copyrighted material on the Web. The URL for this site can be found in the textbook home page at** *http://computered.swep.com* **by selecting the Resources link.**

**GUIDED ACTIVITY**

## 4.3    Viewing and Saving a Graphic Image

In this activity you will open Disney's Web site, review its policy about use of images, and download an image from its Web server.

1.  Start Windows and load Netscape or your own Web browser.

2.  Open the Web site at *http://www.disney.com/* and scroll to the bottom of the home page.

3.  Click on the link to review the legal restrictions and terms of use policy. Note the restriction for personal, noncommercial use on any single computer and the requirement that Disney's copyright notice be displayed whenever any copyrighted material is displayed.

**Checkpoint 4C**    How would you print a copy of the legal restrictions notice?

4.  Click the Back button to go back to the home page.

5.  Right-click any one of the Disney images on the opening page.

6.  From the quick menu, select *Save Image As* (Netscape) or *Save Picture As* (Internet Explorer). Use the name disney.jpg or whatever name is used in the home page, and then save it on your own disk.

7.  Repeat this process with the textbook's home page at *http://computered.swep.com*. Save a copy of the computer collage art image found there on your own disk.

8.  Leave your browser open for now.

## Retrieving and Playing Multimedia Files

Moving images and sound clip files can also be received by Netscape and may require suitable helper applications to play. To hear the sound, you must have a compatible sound card with speakers or headphones. The standard PC speaker may play distorted sound if you have the appropriate driver.

Sound and other multimedia files can be very large. A one-minute sound file could easily be 1 MB in size or larger; so caution is suggested before you download a file with a slow Internet connection. Multimedia files that you download with Netscape are stored in the cache folder that Netscape sets up. When they finish playing, you can play them again by looking in that folder. Internet Explorer will ask you whether you want to save the downloaded file or open it when it finishes loading. If you choose the latter, you will not be able to use it later without downloading it again, but you do save disk space.

Later versions of Netscape Navigator and Internet Explorer come with built-in multimedia players, also known as **viewers** or **plug-ins**. Both browsers have the following built-in viewers:

- play music and voice files (.AU and .WAV file extensions)

- play embedded video files (.AVI)

- video support for .QT and .MOV file extensions

- telephone-like support over the Internet

Other applications must be installed externally to your browser in order to be played. Most viewers can be installed automatically by your browser. When you encounter an item that your browser cannot handle, it may ask your permission to download a viewer for that application. Typically the download takes only a few minutes, and you must restart your browser after the download is complete.

## GUIDED ACTIVITY

## 4.4    Playing a Multimedia File

In this activity you will return to the Disney home page and access a multimedia audio file. If you do not have audio playback capabilities on the computer you are using, skip this activity. Remember to follow Disney's restrictions and use policy.

1. Open your browser and return to the Disney home page at *http://www.disney.com*. Access the Walt Disney Records link.

2. At the Disney Records page, click the *Sound Tracks* link in the upper-left corner of the page.

3. Select one of the titles such as *Beauty and the Beast*. The mix of sound tracks will probably change over time, typical of most Web sites.

4. Scroll down in the Beauty and the Beast page until you see the list of tracks. Notice that several tracks can be downloaded for the Mac or Windows. Select one of the tracks that matches your computer and click its link, as shown in Figure 4.20. The *Beauty and the Beast* .AU file of track 9 is 865 KB and represents about 40 seconds of music.

 **NOTE**   **Your browser may ask you whether you want to open this file or save it to disk. For this activity, select *Open This File*.**

5. When the file completes its download, it will begin playing automatically. It could take as long as ten minutes to download the entire file if you have a modem connection to the Internet. You can adjust the volume or work with the other controls in the audio player window. Figure 4.21 shows the Netscape audio player with similar controls.

6. When the sound ends, you can play it again or close the player window.

**Checkpoint 4D**   How would you download this file if you intend to play it again?

7. Downloading film clips from the Disney site will be used as an exercise. Leave your browser open for now.

**FIGURE 4.20**
*Internet Explorer audio player*

**FIGURE 4.21**
*Netscape audio player*

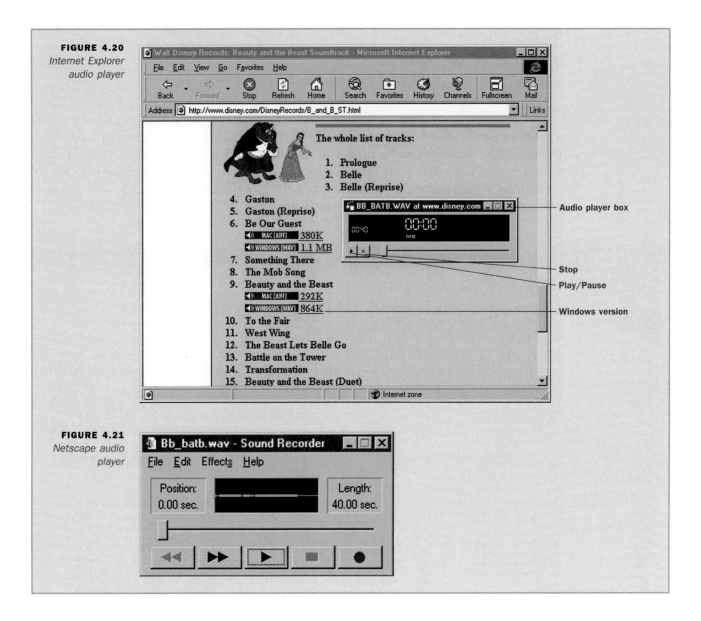

# SUMMARY

This unit presents a comprehensive overview of the World Wide Web and provides detailed instructions on using the two most popular browsers, Netscape Communicator and Internet Explorer. Hypertext refers to documents where related resources are linked together, allowing you to jump from one spot to another and back. Hyperlinks may be underlined, graphical buttons, or areas in an image.

The URL is the Internet address of a document and contains information about the location of that document. You can type the URL into the Location or Address block, or use the *File→Open* menu bar command. You can save the URL of frequently viewed sites in your bookmark or favorites list. When the browser opens, it displays the default home page. You can change the default home page. You can print the current page, or even save it to your own disk drive.

## Command Review (Netscape and Internet Explorer)

| Command | Netscape Communicator | Internet Explorer |
| --- | --- | --- |
| Enter an URL | Location: box<br>File→Open Page (Ctrl+O) | Address: box<br>File→Open (Ctrl+O) |
| Go to Home Page | Home<br>Go→Home | Home<br>Go→Home Page |
| Back, Forward | Back, Forward buttons<br>Go→Back<br>Alt+LeftArrow,<br>Alt+RightArrow | Back, Forward buttons<br>Go→Back<br>Alt+LeftArrow,<br>Alt+RightArrow |
| Stop | Stop or Esc | Stop or Esc |
| Retransmit Page | Reload button<br>View→Reload (Ctrl+R) | Refresh button<br>View→Refresh (Ctrl+R) |
| Print document | Print button<br>File→Print and<br>File→Print Preview | Print button (no print menu)<br>File→Print |
| Bookmarks | Bookmarks button | Favorites button |
| Add to bookmarks | Bookmarks,<br>Add Bookmark | Favorites, Add to Favorites |
| Search | Search button | Search button |
| Find item | Edit→Find in Page (Ctrl+F) | Edit→Find on this Page (Ctrl+F) |
| Change configuration | Edit→Preferences | View→Internet Options |
| Components | Toolbar (Navigator,<br>Messenger, Collabra,<br>Composer) | Toolbar (Outlook Express,<br>Web Editor, Channels) |

## Vocabulary Exercise

*Write a short definition for each term on the following list.*

Bookmark
Browser
Cache
Favorite
Form
Graphic Image File (GIF)

Graphical User Interface (GUI)
Home page
Hyperlinks
Hypertext
HyperText Markup Language (HTML)

HyperText Transfer Protocol (HTTP)
Index.html
In-line image
Internet Explorer (IE)
JPEG
Link

| Lynx | Quick menu | Viewer |
|---|---|---|
| Netscape Navigator | Uniform Resource Loca- | World Wide Web |
| Page | tor (URL) | (WWW) |
| Plug-in | | |

## Review Questions

1. What is the World Wide Web?

2. Explain the concept of hypertext.

3. What types of multimedia information can be viewed from Web documents?

4. What are Internet Explorer and Netscape Communicator?

5. Explain the following World Wide Web terms.

   a. home page

   b. URL

   c. HTTP

   d. link

   e. .GIF file

6. Explain how bookmarks or favorites can be used in your browser. Explain how to customize your bookmarks or favorites list.

7. What Web protocols or services are available through your browser? Briefly define the use of each protocol.

8. Explain how to play a multimedia file through your browser.

## Exercises

*You should use your own Web browser for these exercises. Keep in mind that the World Wide Web is constantly changing, and that information may appear in different formats and in different places over time. For the latest updates, see the textbook home page at* http://computered.swep.com *and select the* Resources *link.*

1. Use your Web browser to access your school or organization home page. Make a list of the important things that appear on the opening page.

2. Use your Web browser to access the home pages for the following sites. Print a copy of the home page for each site. Make a note of the important items on each opening page.

   a. *http://www.microsoft.com/*

   b. *http://www.cbs.com/*

   c. *http://home.netscape.com/*

   d. *http://www.ge.com/*

   e. *http://www.yahoo.com/*

3. Access the ISU home page at *http://web.indstate.edu/* and access the People, Places, & Events section. Click the ISU PhoneBook link, and then look up the title and e-mail address of John Moore.

4. Go to the White House Web site at *http://www.whitehouse.gov*. Prepare a list of the information available from the opening page of this comprehensive site.

5. Connect to the Library of Congress home page at *http://www.loc.gov* and answer the following questions.

   a. List the options shown in the opening image map. Give a brief description of the services available with each choice.

   b. What does the "link to text only button" link in the upper right corner do?

   c. List the first five current electronic exhibits available in the Library of Congress.

   d. What is THOMAS? What kinds of services are available there?

   e. Describe the purpose of *Civilization* magazine.

6. Open the CNN Web site at *http://cnn.com* and print out the contents of the opening home page.

7. Visit the Disney Web site at *http://www.disney.com/* and access the Disney World home page. Go to the Disney Institute section and answer the following questions from that section:

   a. Where is it located?

   b. What is the purpose of the Disney Institute?

   c. List at least three programs the Disney Institute offers.

   d. What accommodations are available at the Disney Institute?

## Automobile Configuration Web Site

Suppose you are in the market for a new car. Several automobile manufacturers have home pages with elaborate specifications and feature lists. You can even configure a vehicle with the precise model, colors, and options. Many companies allow you to order brochures, locate dealers, and so forth. Visit the Dodge Web site at *http://www.4adodge.com* (or the Web site of another vehicle that you are interested in) and list the major services found at that site.

Select a car from the lineup of vehicles, and choose the model and desired features. Then print the configuration and the resulting price.

### *PROJECT TEAM OPTION*

Select at least five automobile manufacturer Web sites and prepare a comparison table for the contents of those Web sites. Be sure to include ease-of-use as one of the criteria that you place in the table. Which Web site does your team prefer and why? Be sure to include the URL address for each of the Web sites. Format your comparison table for ease of understanding.

# UNIT 5

# Searching for Information on the Web

This unit demonstrates techniques for finding information on the Web using Netscape Navigator and Internet Explorer. It includes instructions on using the major search tools—such as Yahoo and Lycos—to find Web sites, and gives tips for successful searching. The unit also covers use of electronic telephone directories for business and personal information searches.

## Learning Objectives

At the completion of this unit, you should be able to

1. access the search tools from Netscape and Internet Explorer,

2. browse through the predefined categories in Yahoo and Lycos,

3. perform a simple text search using Yahoo and Lycos,

4. use options to perform a complex search,

5. locate the phone number and address of an individual by searching an electronic telephone directory,

6. locate an e-mail address and other personal information,

7. find a map for a geographic location,

8. search through indexes for specific information sources,

9. search for a job on the Internet.

## Key Terms

*The following terms are introduced in this unit. Be sure you know what each of them means.*

AltaVista
Bigfoot
Boolean searching
hit
HotBot
Infoseek
Lycos
miss
Online Career Center
search tool
simple search
Yahoo

# Types of Searches

You know that there's an incredible amount of information on the Internet, but *finding* the correct information can be a challenge. You can divide into four categories the types of information available through various search tools:

1. Web site URLs

2. Personal and business information (e-mail address, phone number, street address, home page URL)

3. Other information (news groups, discussion groups, maps, and so forth)

4. Contents of a particular Web site made available by an internal search method.

Search tools provide a way to find information from the Web. They store this information in databases that you can access from your Web browser.

# Search Tool Basics

In most instances, the user brings up the search tool's Web site in a browser and then searches through the database of Web sites and other information to find the desired information. The search engine makes navigating through the database simple. Table 5.1 gives the names and URL addresses for the popular search tools. The following section will explain how information gets into the database of search tools like Yahoo, Lycos, and Infoseek. Then, you will learn how to use the search tools.

**TABLE 5.1**
*Internet search
tools*

| NAME | URL ADDRESS |
| --- | --- |
| AltaVista | http://www.altavista.com |
| Excite | http://www.excite.com |
| HotBot | http://www.hotbot.com |
| Infoseek | http://www.infoseek.com |
| Lycos | http://www.lycos.com |
| PlanetSearch | http://www.planetsearch.com |
| ProFusion | http://www.profusion.com |
| WebCrawler | http://www.webcrawler.com |
| Yahoo! | http://www.yahoo.com |

NET TIP

**Web Addresses**

Current links to most Web sites in this book can be found on the *Understanding & Using the Internet* Home Page. Choose **Resources** at **computered.swep.com**. Remember that a Web address may change at any time. An address given in this book as an example may no longer be valid. If this is so, either access the Home Page for the current link or do a search to find a similar site.

**TIP**

To see if a particu-
lar URL is already
in the Yahoo data-
base, search for
that URL.

# Building the Database

Most search tools constantly scan the Web to analyze Web sites and add them to the database. These automated search tools look for keywords in the site title, first page, and in the document header area that is known as *metatext*. When you create your home page, pay special attention to the fields such as description, keywords, and so forth. Select phrases that would be a likely match to the search criteria that a user might input.

Individuals and organizations can also submit their own Web pages to the search tools for inclusion in the database. This can be done manually by following the appropriate *Add URL* link from the search tool Web site, or by using a program or service to submit the URL automatically. Most of the sites at Yahoo, the most frequently visited Web site, were added in this manner. The AltaVista and HotBot search engines look at every document found on the Web.

# Running a Net Search from Your Browser

Both Netscape Communicator and Internet Explorer now come with a Search button. Click the Search button to bring up a Web site with links to several search tools in different categories. Netscape's list highlights four search tools at the top of the site, including Lycos, Yahoo, Excite, and Infoseek. Twenty-two search tools appear in the lower section of the page. You can get help on using any of these tools from the same search page.

When you open Internet Explorer's net search page, one of the search tools opens in a vertical panel at the left edge of the browser window. You can also request a list of search engines from this panel, displaying links to 15 more search tools, along with the ability to permanently add your own favorite search engine to the list. To close this vertical panel, click the Search button in Internet Explorer again.

Of course, you can also open the search tool directly from the Location or Address box by typing in its URL, or add favorite search tool URLs to your bookmarks or favorites list.

# Browsing the Category Index

The most straightforward way to find information is to browse through the search tool's category index, similar to following a book's table of contents. In this case, the search tool has already organized the information by subject category. You will find similar Web sites grouped together. Most of the general-purpose search tools offer a category index, usually with more than a dozen main subjects.

### YAHOO SUBJECT CATEGORIES

Yahoo offers 14 categories in its main browsing index, as shown in Figure 5.1. Yahoo is found at *http://www.yahoo.com* in North America. Yahoo is also available in 11 other countries.

Yahoo has 14 main categories on its opening page, from Arts & Humanities to Society & Culture. Minor category topics appear in a smaller type size beneath the major category. For instance, within Education are Universities, K–12, and College Entrance.

Click any category link to display the subcategories beneath that topic. Figure 5.2 shows the subcategories within the Education top category on Yahoo. At the

FIGURE 5.1
*Yahoo search tool*

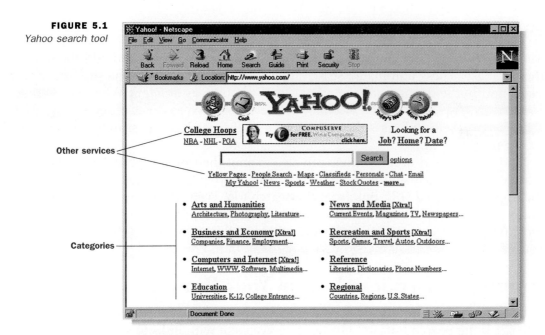

FIGURE 5.2
*Yahoo Education subcategories*

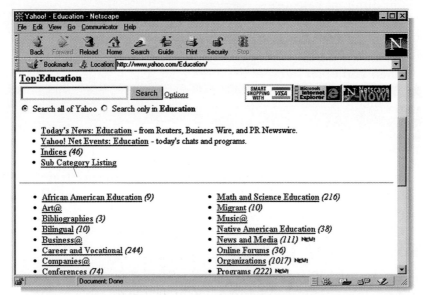

top of that page is a search block, explained in the next section; links to current news about education; a list of scheduled chat sessions about education; and a set of sites that give other education links. At the bottom of the window are the individual subcategories with the number of entries in each shown in parentheses. Click one of these subcategory links to display individual sites. Categories that end with an "@" sign appear in more than one place in the Yahoo database; clicking on that heading will take you to the primary location.

Yahoo frequently presents lower-level results in two groups, categories and individual sites. For instance, Figure 5.3 shows a portion of the items in the Math and Science Education subcategory. The top items represent additional Yahoo "sub-subcategories," while the bottom group contains individual Web sites that fit within this subcategory. The following Guided Activity will give you a chance to try Yahoo yourself.

**FIGURE 5.3**
*Yahoo Math and Science Education sites*

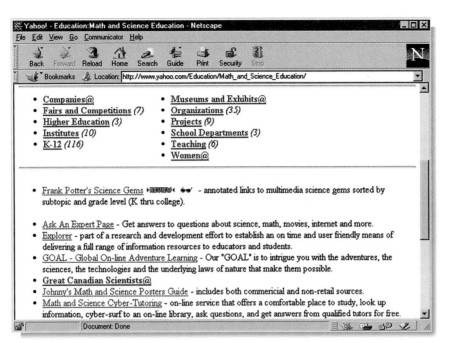

## GUIDED ACTIVITY

# 5.1

## Using Yahoo's Category Database

In this activity you will browse the Yahoo subject category database to find information about on-line newspapers.

1. If you are not already in Windows 95, open it now. Connect to your Internet Service Provider and open your Web browser.

2. Click the Location box in your browser (or click the Address box in Internet Explorer) and connect to the Yahoo Web site at *http://www.yahoo.com*. Although you should see a screen similar to Figure 5.1, remember that Web sites are dynamic and content is constantly changing.

**Checkpoint 5A** What other ways can you open a Web site?

3. Select *Newspapers* under the *News and Media* link.

4. Scroll down and select the *Los Angeles Times* link. You should see the daily electronic front page of this newspaper similar to Figure 5.4. Remember that your screen will not look exactly like this one.

5. Select one of the story links and click on it. Note the search tools at the top and bottom of the story Web page. We'll discuss search tools within Web sites later in this unit.

6. When you are finished reading the story, use the Back button to return to the Yahoo home page. Leave your browser open.

**FIGURE 5.4**
Los Angeles Times
*electronic front
page*

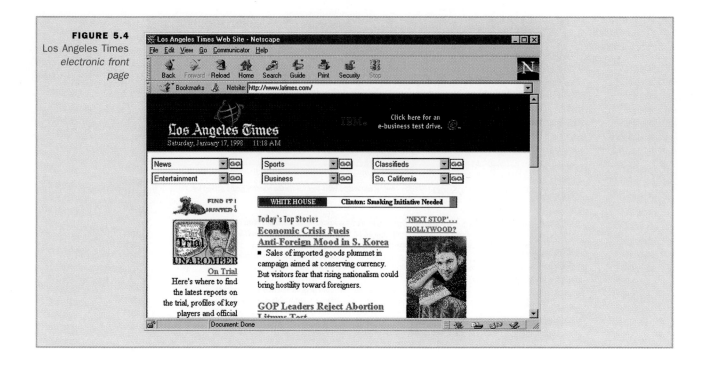

## LYCOS SUBJECT CATEGORIES

The other popular search site is **Lycos**, found at *http://www.lycos.com.* Its home
page is shown in Figure 5.5 in the Internet Explorer browser. *Note:* You can access
this and other search tools with any browser. The Lycos Web guides consist of 22
subject categories that are similar to Yahoo's.

**FIGURE 5.5**
*Lycos home page*

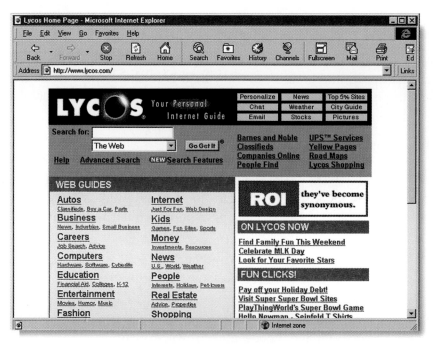

Click on a Web guide category to bring up the subcategories within that subject. Figure 5.6 shows the Money subcategory. The sub-subcategory entries are shown at the top of the screen, while specific sites with an abstract of the contents appear below. There are links to Lycos resource guides on the right side. Through these resource guides, Lycos provides more editorial content than Yahoo.

**FIGURE 5.6**
*Lycos Money subcategory*

## OTHER YAHOO SERVICES

Yahoo provides additional services as part of the main search page. You will find college and pro sports scores with top news stories. There are links to news stories, stock quotes, maps, and personal search facilities. The following Guided Activity will show you how to use the Yahoo maps facility.

## GUIDED ACTIVITY

# 5.2   Using the Yahoo Maps Facility

In this activity you will use the Yahoo Maps to display a map of the White House in Washington, D.C.

1. Make sure you have initiated a connection to the Internet and have started your Web browser.

2. Enter the Yahoo URL—*http://www.yahoo.com.* Click the *Maps* link just below the search box. Refer to Figure 5.1 if you have trouble locating the *Maps* link.

3. At the next screen, enter the street address for the White House. The address is `Pennsylvania Ave NW & New York Ave NW`, and the city information is `Washington, DC 20501-0005`. Click the MapIt! button.

**NOTE** **I was unable to get the proper map White House location by using 1600 Pennsylvania Ave as the address. If Yahoo displays the White House address without drawing the map, click the** *Use this address* **link to see the map.**

4. In a few seconds Yahoo should draw the map as shown in Figure 5.7.

**FIGURE 5.7**
*White House area map*

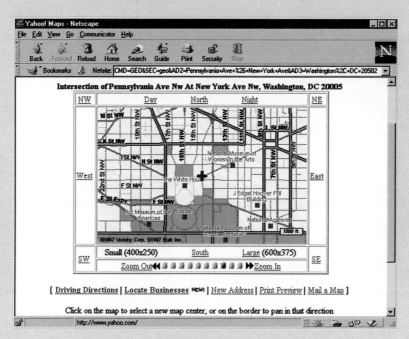

5. You can zoom in on parts of the map by clicking the Zoom In button at the bottom of the map. To move the center of the map, click on the map where you would like the new center to be. To print a copy, click the browser's Print button.

**Checkpoint 5B** How would you use the other underlined links around the edge of the map?

6. Leave your browser open for now.

### OTHER LYCOS CATEGORIES

Like Yahoo, Lycos offers maps, news, and other miscellaneous information. There are links to the Barnes and Noble on-line bookstore and UPS. Lycos also is available in different European countries, as shown near the bottom of the Lycos home page. The Lycos Spain home page is shown in Figure 5.8.

# Searching the Web Directly

Although the Yahoo and Lycos subject indexes are convenient to use, sometimes you need to go directly to the database and provide your own search terms. The

**FIGURE 5.8**
*Lycos Spain home page*

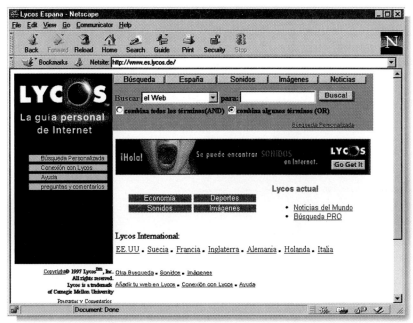

search tools will scan the millions of listings and return those that meet your criteria. The better your search criteria, the more likely you will find useful sites in the list of hits. This section will show you how to take advantage of the tools.

## BASIC SEARCH PROCEDURE

A simple search means that you type a single keyword into the search box and then click the Search button. Unless you specify otherwise, the Yahoo search engine will search categories, titles, and comments that contain your keyword. The search engine will return a list of sites that meet your criteria. The list is *usually* sorted in descending order by probability that the site fits your criteria. Thus, a site in the lower section of the list is less likely to be useful. For example, when searching for the word *Pentium* in Yahoo, there were nine Yahoo category matches and 235 site matches. The category list refers to existing Yahoo subject categories described earlier in this unit. Click on the link to go directly to that site.

Sites that are useful to you are called hits. Frequently the search engine will return many Web site references that match your criteria but that are not useful. These sites are called misses. To refine your search, modify the criteria in the search box and run the search again. Advanced search options are described in the next section.

Although each search tool offers its own set of options, most offer the ability to specify more than one keyword as search criteria. For example, if you search with the phrase *high school*, the search engine will return documents that contain both the words high and school, but not necessarily together. In Yahoo, this criterion represents 1,086 categories and 8,678 sites. For example, you might return a site that refers to the highest score in that elementary school. Both Yahoo and Lycos now default to requiring that all of the words in the search criteria match your results.

If you enclose your keywords in double quotes, the search engine will look for those words as a single phrase. Thus, when you specify *"high school"* as the criterion, only documents that contain those two words together will be shown. With this criterion, Yahoo will list 194 categories and 2,877 sites.

The general rule for doing searches is to start with a broad criteria, and then narrow it down as you explore the information. For example, you can specify that any of the words must appear and then move toward requiring that all of the words appear. If you start with a restrictive search, you might end up with just a few hits.

## GUIDED ACTIVITY

## 5.3    Doing a Net Search

In this activity you will enter the criteria in a search engine and find Web sites that match your criteria. In this case you are looking for sites about waffles.

1.  Make sure that you are connected to the Internet and start your browser.

2.  Open the Yahoo home page at *http://www.yahoo.com*.

3.  In the search block, type `waffles` and click the *Search* button.

4.  Notice that Yahoo displays a maple syrup advertisement that pertains to your criteria along with the category and site matches, as shown in Figure 5.9. When you run this, the advertisement is likely to be different.

FIGURE 5.9
*Yahoo search results for waffles*

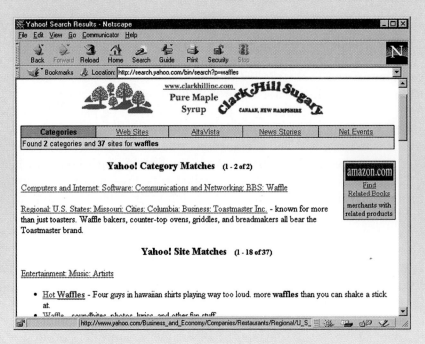

5.  Scroll through the list of sites and note those that are not related to waffles as a food. This time there were sites about a physician, a singing group, and a college publication by the same name.

**6.** Select one food-related site and click its link to display the contents.

**Checkpoint 5C**   Describe the different ways you can get back to the original Yahoo home page.

**7.** Leave your browser open. You will use it in the next Guided Activity.

## ADVANCED YAHOO SEARCH OPTIONS

In addition to the phrase search with double quotes, Yahoo offers more advanced search options. Click *options* to see these choices.

- You can indicate a required word in Yahoo by preceding it with a + sign; a − in front of a word means that it must *not* be found in any of the search results.

- By preceding a search word with **t:** you are restricting the search results to document titles; by preceding a search word with **u:** you are restricting the search to document URLs only. If neither appears, Yahoo will search titles, URLs, and the body of Web sites.

- Attaching an * to the end of a word acts as a wild card criterion—anything that begins with the criterion is acceptable. For instance, In* will accept any site that begins with In.

- The Yahoo search options page also lets you restrict the search to documents that are not older than a particular date. The current default is three years.

- Use the help located on the Yahoo search page to learn how to use the advanced search options.

## ADVANCED LYCOS SEARCH OPTIONS

In addition to supporting phrase searching with double quotes, Lycos offers additional advanced search options. Click the *Advanced Search* link to see these options.

- Next to the Search criteria box is a "For drop-down" box. Here you can specify that you are searching for any of the words or all of the words.

- Lycos also allows you to specify a non-exact match for your search criteria. You can pick from *strong match, close match, near match,* and *good match* as qualifiers for the "All the words" option.

- Lycos and Yahoo support **Boolean searching** where the words AND, OR, and NOT can be used to qualify the search criteria. This is similar to the use of + and − in Yahoo. You can also use the words ADJ (next to each other, as in "adjacent"), NEAR (terms must appear within 25 words of one another), and FAR (terms must appear at least 25 words away from each other) in these searches.

- You can choose how to display the result of the search—the default is to display detailed descriptions which include the link, the title, and a short paragraph from the first page of each site that matches.

- In general, use the help available from the Lycos search page to help you use these advanced search options.

**GUIDED ACTIVITY**

## 5.4 Using Advanced Search Methods

In this activity you will use the Yahoo advanced search tools to locate sites dealing with Windows NT.

1.  Make sure that you are connected to the Internet and your browser is started.

2.  Open the Yahoo home page at *http://www.yahoo.com*.

3.  In the search box enter Windows and click the Search button. Notice the number of entries in the search results that don't match Windows NT. At the time of this writing, there were 71 categories and 6,460 sites.

4.  Scroll to the bottom of the search results page and replace the search text with "Windows NT". Click Search.

**Checkpoint 5D**    What is the difference between Windows NT and "Windows NT" as search criteria?

5.  The resulting list will be much smaller. At this writing it consisted of six Yahoo categories and 894 sites, still a very large number. Leave the browser open for use in the next activity.

# *Finding Directory Information*

It is very useful to be able to look up directory information such as addresses, telephone numbers, and e-mail addresses on the Web. Several specialized search tools are available for you to search. Some use electronic versions of the telephone "white pages" or "yellow pages" you already use, while others represent a database of information that individuals have submitted. The latter would only contain *your* information if you have sent it to the search tool. Most of these tools send you an e-mail message to confirm that the submitted information is correct.

## Searching for E-Mail and Street Addresses

Bigfoot contains databases for e-mail addresses, home pages, white pages, and links to yellow pages with business information. To use Bigfoot to find an e-mail address, you need only specify the name of the individual. Anyone who matches that name will be displayed. Optionally, you can specify the city and state of the individual in an advanced search. Yellow pages searches actually go through the telephone company's own on-line directory. You will learn how to use Bigfoot in the following Guided Activity.

**GUIDED ACTIVITY**

## 5.5    Searching for E-Mail and Street Addresses

The following activity will demonstrate how to use Bigfoot to locate the e-mail and street addresses of an individual and the street address of a business.

1.  Make sure that you are connected to the Internet and that your browser is started.

**Checkpoint 5E**  How can you tell whether you are connected to the Internet, and how long you have been connected, if you are using dial-up networking?

2.  Open the Bigfoot home page found at *http://www.bigfoot.com*. See Figure 5.10.

**FIGURE 5.10**
*Bigfoot personal
search page*

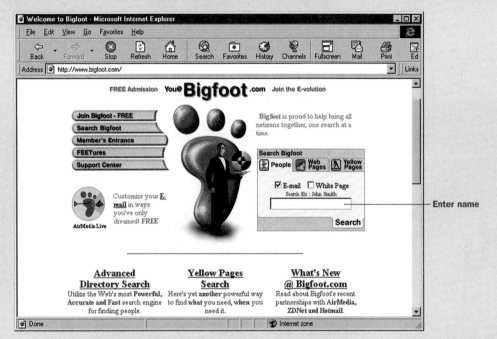

3.  In the upper-right corner, enter your personal name (as in John Smith) in the Search Bigfoot box. Click both the E-mail and White Page boxes, and then click Search.

4.  The top portion of the search results will list several e-mail addresses, one of which may be yours. The lower portion lists names, addresses, telephone numbers, and city information for several individuals. If you are listed, click the *View Map* link to see a map of your home address.

5.  Click the Back button to return to the Bigfoot home page.

6.  Scroll down the page, and click the *Yellow Pages Search* link in the middle of the page to open the business search window.

7.  You should see a United States Yellow Pages map as shown in Figure 5.11. Click the state where you would locate a business. In this example we'll click on Indiana (IN in the green section).

**FIGURE 5.11**
*Bigfoot Yellow
Pages map*

8.  Next, Bigfoot will display a Web form for you to fill in the category or business name, the city, and the state. In this example we'll select Union Hospital for the business name, Terre Haute for the city, and Indiana for the state. Click on Find.

9.  In this search Bigfoot found 12 instances of various Union Hospital clinics and services. You can click the *Map* link to display a map, or get driving directions by clicking the *Directions* link.

10. Leave your browser open for now.

Table 5.2 shows other search tools that provide directory information about individuals and businesses. They are essentially similar to Bigfoot. For most, your White Pages information is obtained automatically, while information about e-mail address and personal home page URL must be submitted by you. Internet Address Finder and WhoWhere provide information in English and other languages.

**Net Ethics**      *Personal Privacy*

With the availability of Web search tools, your e-mail address, street address, telephone number, and even a map to your home are available on-line. Do you think it is appropriate for this information to be given out freely? Are there ways to protect your privacy with paper directories? Should these methods be extended to the Internet?

**TABLE 5.2**
*Personal and business directory search tools*

| TOOL | URL ADDRESS | TYPE |
|---|---|---|
| AT&T | *http://www.att.com/directory* | Toll-free and residential numbers |
| Bigfoot | *http://www.bigfoot.com* | E-mail, White and Yellow Pages |
| Four11 | *http://www.four11.com* | E-mail and White Pages |
| HotBot | *http://www.hotbot.com* | E-mail, White and Yellow Pages, news groups |
| Internet Address Finder | *http://www.iaf.net/* | White Pages |
| Switchboard | *http://www.switchboard.com* | E-mail, White and Yellow Pages |
| WhoWhere | *http://www.whowhere.com* | E-mail, White and Yellow Pages |
| Yahoo People Search | *http://yahoo.four11.com* | E-mail and White Pages |

# Other Search Tools

In the last unit you learned about using the Find command to locate information in the current document. Use *Edit→Find* (Ctrl+F) in Netscape and Internet Explorer to move to the next occurrence of a particular string in the current page. This can be helpful in a large Web page.

## Embedded Search Tools

Many comprehensive Web sites come with an embedded search tool for locating information within that site. These tools work much like the general-purpose search engines described earlier in this unit, but they examine only the contents of that Web site, not the entire Internet. Enter keywords and click the Search button to find specific information.

The Microsoft home page is one of the better-designed Web sites. The toolbar at the top of all pages includes links to the Microsoft home page, products, search, support, shop, and write us. Its search facility is shown in Figure 5.12. Although you can limit your search to specific categories, the default is to search all of *www.microsoft.com*. Search tips also appear on the same screen, making it easy for a user to prepare the correct search criteria.

UPS and Federal Express both offer on-line package tracking services to customers. If you know the airbill or tracking number, you can find out within seconds whether the package has been delivered. Figure 5.13 shows the UPS tracking results for a package that was delivered to my door about one hour ago.

## Personalized Searching

Many of the popular search tools allow you to customize them for your particular needs. That means you can "preload" the criteria so that news and Web sites that interest you are automatically saved on your computer. These tools are constantly scanning the Web to find information that is of use to you. Thus, when you want

**FIGURE 5.12**
*Microsoft search page*

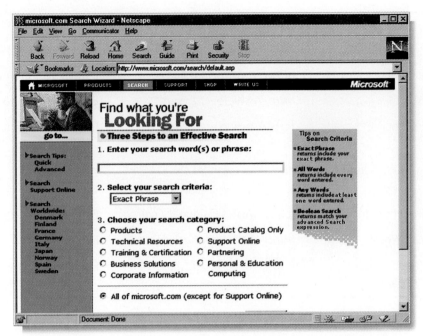

**FIGURE 5.13**
*UPS tracking results*

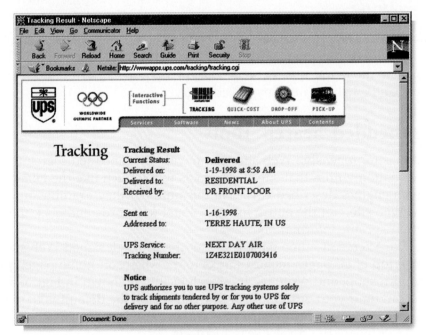

to look for that information, it is already available on your desktop. Some search tools, like Infoseek, attach themselves to your browser's push channels for easier access. Some search tools will even send you an e-mail message when the content of your favorite site has changed.

# Specialty Search Engines

You can find search tools on the Web that specialize in finding information about a single subject such as Star Trek (James Kirk Search Engine). Some search tools focus on a particular country, cataloging sites found in that country. Other search sites specialize in maintaining links to sites in education, mathematics, and so forth. Try searching Yahoo for *Search* to get a comprehensive list.

## Searching for News Groups

Although most of this unit has focused on Web sites and e-mail addresses, you may want to find news and discussion groups that pertain to a particular category. (News and discussion groups are covered in more detail in Unit 6 of this book.) Infoseek is one of those tools that has a news group button in the search box, as shown in Figure 5.14. Enter the name or subject for the news group, make sure the News Group button is pushed, and click the Seek button in Infoseek. Other search engines may also contain databases for news groups.

**FIGURE 5.14**

*Infoseek news group search page*

News group search

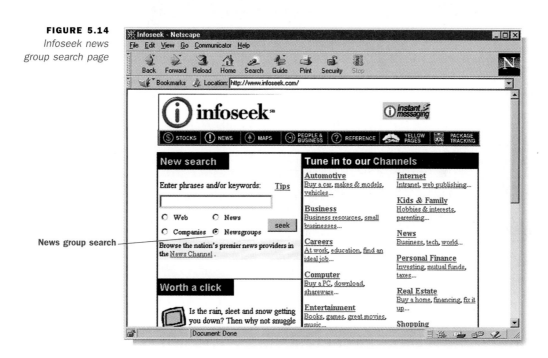

## Meta Search Tools

These search sites submit your search criteria to several search engines simultaneously, providing the results in a comprehensive fashion. These tools include MetaCrawler at *http://www.metacrawler.com* and ProFusion at *http://www.profusion.com*. Searching is free at ProFusion for now, but you must register first. Results are formatted so that only unique items appear. For instance, I searched ProFusion for *sun-dried tomatoes* and chose the three fastest search engines. I selected Excite, Infoseek, and Magellan and retrieved 36 unique items. Try this exercise on your computer.

## Searching for Jobs

Many have found that job searches on the Web have simplified the process. The job hunter can find lists of jobs, and employers can find résumés of prospective employees. Some companies have a permanent link to employment opportunities on their home page. For example, see the Wal-Mart home page for links to career opportunities (*http://www.wal-mart.com*) and even a way to submit your résumé electronically.

The **Online Career Center** Web site at *http://www.occ.com* contains information about searching for a job on the Web and links to available positions at participating companies. For example, State Farm Insurance Company listed information systems opportunities near the center of Figure 5.15. You can post your résumé there at no charge. OCC accepts plain text résumés or HTML résumés that display as Web pages.

**FIGURE 5.15**
*Online Career Center home page*

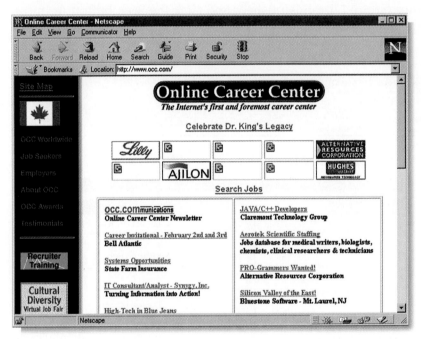

There are numerous other on-line job services, including comprehensive sites to help prepare you for the job search before you start searching for positions. You will be exploring on-line job search tools in the project at the end of this unit.

# SUMMARY

This unit presents techniques for searching the Web. It includes browsing through precompiled databases that are organized by category and subcategory, as well as free searches using search criteria. Yahoo and Lycos are two very popular search sites. Both offer browsing as well as free searches using keywords.

The Yahoo and Lycos search engines permit you to be more explicit with criteria, including use of multiple-word phrases (enclosed in double quotes) and Boolean searching with the qualifiers AND, OR, and NOT. Other advanced search features include NEAR and being able to specify the age of an included site. Some search engines let you choose the format and level of detail of the search results.

You can also search for personal and business information on the Web. You can find out e-mail addresses, telephone numbers, addresses, and related personal information. Some of the search sites offer maps that you can print for addresses you have located. You can find information about careers and job listings on the Internet.

Finally, many comprehensive Web sites contain internal search engines that help you locate information within that Web site. This includes tracking searches where you locate information about express package deliveries.

## Vocabulary Exercise

*Write a short definition for each term in the following list.*

| | | |
|---|---|---|
| AltaVista | HotBot | Online Career Center |
| Bigfoot | Infoseek | search tool |
| Boolean searching | Lycos | simple search |
| hit | miss | Yahoo |

## Review Questions

1. How would you initiate a net search from your browser? List at least three different ways.

2. What is the difference between *browsing* a search catalog and using a *direct* search tool?

3. How does information get into the search engine databases?

4. Explain the difference between these search criteria: *apple sauce*, *"apple sauce,"* and *apple AND sauce*.

5. List the Yahoo services that are available from the opening page of the Web site.

6. What is meant by the phrase *Boolean searching*?

7. In Yahoo how would you restrict the search to document titles only?

8. How would you find someone's e-mail address on the Web without asking them?

9. Explain how to add your own e-mail address to a search engine like Bigfoot, WhoWhere, and Internet Address Finder.

10. What is meant by the term *Yellow Pages search*? What information would you expect to find there?

11. What is an embedded search tool, and why would you want to have one in a large Web site with multiple pages?

12. How would you search for a job on the Internet?

## Exercises

*You should use your own Web browser for these exercises. Keep in mind that the World Wide Web is constantly changing and that information may appear in different formats and in different places over time. For the latest updates, see the textbook home page at* http://computered.swep.com *and select the* Resources *link.*

1. Open Yahoo and select the News and Media Link. Choose Television, and look for commercial stations in your area. Write down each station's call sign and the URL, along with a short description of the services found at that home page.

2. Use the Yahoo direct search method to locate the Web site of your favorite local radio or television station. Print the first page of the opening home page for that station.

3. Use the Yahoo or Lycos map service to print a copy of your own street map. Use your home, school, or office street address.

4. Search for information about David Letterman's Top Ten List.

5. Search for information about college scholarships and financial aid.

6. Add your own name and your *permanent* e-mail address to the Internet Address Finder service at *http://www.iaf.net*. Then, search for yourself and print out a copy of the resulting information.

7. Locate the URL for a Web site that matches each of the following subjects or items.

   a. A site that contains the printed works on-line of William Shakespeare.

   b. Technical support for a SoundBlaster sound card from Creative Labs, Inc.

   c. An official site for the Indianapolis 500 motor speedway. From this site, find the winners from 1940, 1960, and 1980.

   d. The on-line version of the *Washington Post*.

   e. Soft drink manufacturers.

8. Find the street address and telephone number for each of the following businesses using an on-line Yellow Pages search engine.

   a. A restaurant in Honolulu, Hawaii

   b. A physician in Terre Haute, Indiana

   c. A travel agency in Hartford, Connecticut

   d. A used auto dealer in Boise, Idaho

   e. A Dairy Queen restaurant in West Lafayette, Indiana

9. Use the ProFusion search tool to locate information about sun-dried tomatoes. Print the first page of the results from this search. Compare that page to the first page of the search results from Yahoo alone using the same criteria.

10. Use a search tool to locate information about Shreve Hall at Purdue University. Give the name of the person after which the hall was named, and explain why the person was important. Provide the URL of the document that contains this information.

## Searching for a Job On-line

Suppose you are searching for a job as a computer programmer or systems analyst. Search the Web to find at least five relevant job openings in those fields in your geographic area. List the job title, company, location, and any relevant information about that position. You might start with the Online Career Center site, but don't limit yourself to just one site, particularly if you do not live in the United States.

### PROJECT TEAM OPTION

Prepare a report about searching for a job on-line using information from the Internet itself. Your report should include a list of at least six sites (with URLs) that provide job searching capabilities. Discuss how to add your résumé to on-line applicant databases.

# UNIT 6

# Discussion Groups: News Groups and Mailing Lists

One of the Internet's most often referenced features is its news and discussion groups—or computer bulletin boards—covering nearly any subject imaginable. Available with a phone call or e-mail, computer bulletin boards offer a way to post messages and replies to those messages. The Internet provides a forum for thousands of news and discussion groups, and that number is growing every day.

## Learning Objectives

At the completion of this unit, you should be able to

1. explain what discussion groups are,

2. know the difference between news groups and Listserv mailing lists,

3. access a news group and read postings,

4. create a response to a news group posting,

5. join a mailing list discussion group,

6. unsubscribe from a mailing list.

## Key Terms

*The following terms are introduced in this unit. Be sure you know what each of them means.*

Archive
Article
Digest
Discussion group
Frequently Asked Question (FAQ)
Listserv group
Lurking
Mailing list
Moderated (list or group)
Net News Transport Protocol (NNTP)
Network news
Newbie
News group
Newsrc file
Newsreader
News Xpress newsreader
Post
Subscribe
Thread
Timed out
Unsubscribe
Usenet news

## Network News

The Internet brings people together in **discussion groups** to share opinions and ideas. These individuals share some common interest. The discussion group provides a forum for individuals to **post** messages or articles that are (or should be) relevant to the group. All members of the discussion group can view messages that are posted to the group. The term **network news** describes these groups as well as the procedure for organizing and distributing the messages in the group.

# News Groups

A **news group** represents a broad collection of articles about a particular subject. The **article** could be an e-mail message or a multimedia object such as an image, a sound, or a video. The group begins when someone starts it by posting a question in the group. Other users read the question and prepare responses, often asking new questions in the process. You can follow the trail of messages and replies to a specific question, also known as a **thread**.

Your news server is "fed" updated copies of postings from other news servers attached to the Internet. The news feeds are done automatically using the Internet itself, based on the arrangements your system administrators have made with other organizations.

There are thousands of different news groups, with more being started each day. The name of the group is important because it acts as advertising for the contents of that group. You may join news groups that seem appropriate for your interests.

To help guide users to the many news groups available, name categories were developed. For example, you might notice a group called *comp.databases.ms-access*. This group deals with issues relating to the computer database called Microsoft Access. The first word in the group represents the kind of information maintained there. Table 6.1 lists the **Usenet news** categories and one other popular category that is not considered part of Usenet. Usenet represents a set of news groups of general interest.

There are other categories that are not part of the official Usenet hierarchy. For instance, *k12* addresses issues dealing with education in grades K–12, *ieee* includes discussions related to the Institute of Electronic and Electrical Engineers, and *biz* refers to business issues. At Indiana State University, *is* refers to internal news groups that are specific to ISU. Your organization may have its own news groups.

# Newsreader Software

To read news you must have a **newsreader** program. The newsreader allows you to subscribe to certain news groups, scan through lists of postings in these groups, and download and display the contents of specific postings. Although each is slightly different, all newsreaders share certain characteristics that are described below. The **News Xpress newsreader** profiled in this book is shareware that is available via FTP from the Internet. News Xpress is a popular NNTP newsreader that works under Windows. **NNTP** stands for **Net News Transport Protocol**, used to transfer news articles between computers on the Internet.

---

NET TIP
**Web Addresses**

Current links to most Web sites in this book can be found on the *Understanding & Using the Internet* Home Page. Choose **Resources** at **computered.swep.com**. Remember that a Web address may change at any time. An address given in this book as an example may no longer be valid. If this is so, either access the Home Page for the current link or do a search to find a similar site (see Unit 5 for a discussion of search methods).

**TABLE 6.1**
*Usenet news categories*

| CATEGORY | DESCRIPTION |
|---|---|
| alt | Deals with "alternative" ways of looking at things. Some of the news groups here are quite unusual while others deal with conventional topics. This group is not one of the seven Usenet categories but is included because many important topics begin here before migrating to one of the other official categories. |
| comp | Includes all types of computer topics, from operating systems to individual software packages to peripheral devices to computer folklore. |
| misc | As it sounds, this is a miscellaneous category for groups that don't easily fit into any other category. There are groups in this category dealing with items for sale, stock market investing, and a listing of job offerings. |
| news | This category refers to the news network and news group information. When you join Usenet news for the first time, you may be automatically added to the groups *news.announce.newgroups*, *news.announce.newusers*, and *news.newusers.questions*. These groups contain answers to newcomers' frequently asked questions. |
| rec | This category contains information about recreational activities, games, and the arts. It includes groups about topics like stamp collecting, wines, chess, video games, classical music, and sports. |
| sci | This category includes items about scientific subjects, including research and applications. For example, you would find groups about archaeology, the Hubble space telescope, image processing, economics, and manufacturing in this category. |
| soc | The final category includes groups that discuss social issues such as the Celtic culture and many of the countries of the world. This category also includes groups for genealogy, religion, politics, and veterans' affairs. |

 **NOTE** **You can download this shareware program from the Internet at *ftp://ftp.malch.com/nx201.zip*. It must be expanded and the files placed in a folder. Then add a shortcut to Nx.exe to your Start button menu or desktop. For more details about downloading files via FTP, see Unit 7.**

When you start News Xpress for the first time, you may be asked to establish the news server configuration and enter your personal e-mail information. Your instructor or computer center assistant can provide this information. Use the *File→Options* command to bring up the tabbed Options dialog box. Figure 6.1 shows the Options dialog box with the Servers sheet present. The ISU news server is called *news.indstate.edu*; your server will be different. Include your user name and password if your news server requires that information. The Personal Information tab contains your personal name, e-mail address, e-mail server, and so forth. If you are using News Xpress in a computer lab, the configuration probably is already set.

**FIGURE 6.1**
*Options dialog box—servers and directory information*

Enter your own ———
news server

Enter your own ———
e-mail server

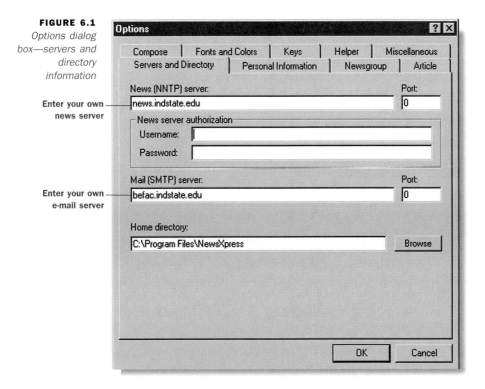

## CONNECTING TO THE NEWS SERVER

Use the *File→Connect* command (or *Ctrl+O*) to open a connection to your news server. News Xpress can be configured to connect automatically at startup with the *File→Options→Newsgroup* command. After connecting to your news server, News Xpress will show you a tabbed dialog box with the names of the subscribed groups, as shown in Figure 6.2. If the toolbar is not present, use the *View→Toolbars→Main* command to turn it on.

**FIGURE 6.2**
*Main News Xpress window*

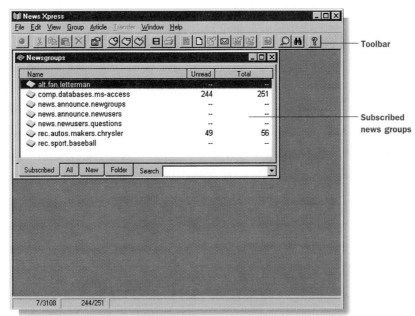

———— Toolbar

———— Subscribed
news groups

You may be asked whether you want to download the current complete set of news groups. Our campus news server contains more than 3,100 news groups, and this process takes a few minutes. The next time you start News Xpress, you will not have to download the list again unless you want to refresh it with any new groups that may have appeared since the last time you created the list.

**NOTE**   **If your news server is busy, you may see a message like "Could not resolve Host." Wait a few moments, then try again. If the busy condition persists, double-check the server configuration information. You may need to try again later when there is less traffic.**

## SUBSCRIBING TO A NEWS GROUP

Before you can examine the postings in a particular group, you must subscribe to that group. The newsreader will show you the set of all available news groups at your institution, and you select or subscribe to those in which you are interested. Your school may have preselected news groups, but you should be able to select additional groups through this process. Click on the All tab to display the complete set of news group names as shown in Figure 6.3. There are four ways to select a news group in News Xpress:

- Click the round button at the beginning of that line (converting it into a tilted rectangle that resembles a book).

- Use the Subscribe button in the toolbar.

- Use the *Group→Subscribe* command.

- Right-click the group and select Subscribe (first make sure the right mouse button is set for Track menu in the *File→Options→Miscellaneous* menu).

**FIGURE 6.3**
*List of all news groups*

Subscribe button ——

Unsubscribe button ——

Status bar ——

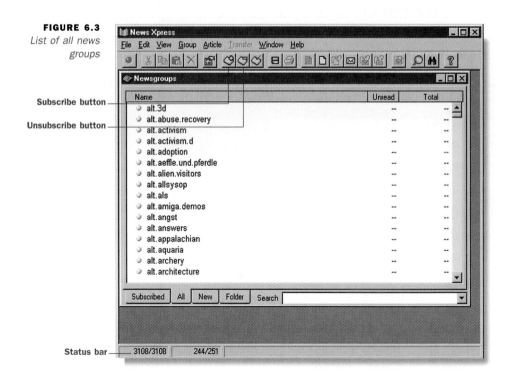

When you are finished, click the Subscribed tab and the newsreader will display a list of the subscribed groups. A group with an entry in the "Unread" column means that there are new articles in that group that have appeared since the last time you started News Xpress. The total number of articles in that news group also appears.

The Web site associated with this book contains a directory of some of the more popular news groups arranged alphabetically within main categories. The *news.lists* and *news.groups* groups contain listings of many of the mailing lists and news groups currently available. Subscribe to these, and then search for lists and groups that interest you. Some Web search services like Yahoo and Lycos also give references to relevant news groups. Web searches are described in Unit 5.

## *SEARCHING FOR PARTICULAR NEWS GROUPS*

News Xpress has a Search box in the main window that lets you select news groups by category. Click the *All* tab, then make an entry in the Search box. Only news groups that match that search string will be displayed. Suppose you want to see any news groups containing the text *comp.* Enter `comp.` in the Search box, and 855 news groups (out of the original 3,108) will be displayed. You'll see that some of the matching groups contain *comp.* in the middle of the name, not just at the beginning.

## *SELECTING A NEWS GROUP*

From the newsreader you can select a particular group for examination. Click the *Subscribed* tab in the News Xpress window to see the list of subscribed groups. Double-click the desired news group. After a few moments the newsreader will retrieve the current set of postings for that group. Most newsreaders remember which postings you already have read within each subscribed group and will not display those again. If you uncheck "Skip old articles" in the News Xpress *File→Options→Article* menu under Options, old articles will appear.

**News Xpress will let you open a news group from the *All* tab, even if you have not subscribed to that group.**

After you choose a group, you will see a list of the current articles in that group, as shown in Figure 6.4. The subject header, size (lines), the posting date, and the name of the contributor of the article appear for each article in the list. Remember that to save time, only the header information has been retrieved from the news server, not the article itself.

**For large news groups, it could take several minutes to retrieve all of the headers for the postings in that group. The News Xpress status bar shows the progress of retrieving the headers.**

The symbol in front of each line gives information about that article. A white document symbol indicates that this is a new article, while a gray document symbol means you already have read it. A folder symbol means the article is the beginning of a thread of related articles. A yellow folder indicates unread responses are contained, while a gray folder means you have read those responses.

Already read

Folder indicates
thread

Re: indicates reply
to previous posting

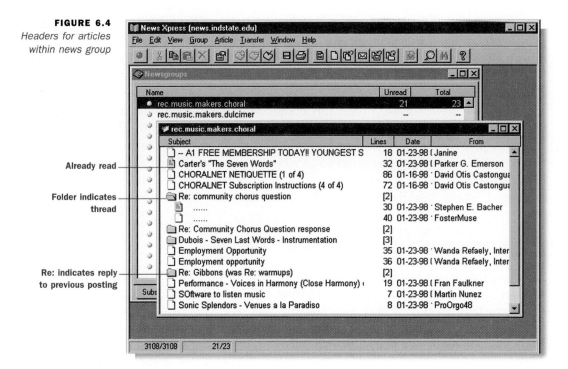

## EXPANDING THREADS

You can expand all threads with the *View→Expand/Collapse Threads* command, or the *Ctrl+Y* shortcut. When expanded, related articles are displayed beneath the header for that thread. You can expand a single thread by double-clicking it. The number of articles contained within a thread is shown in square brackets in the Size column; thus [4] means there are four articles in that thread. If Re: (from the Latin *in re*, meaning "with regard to") appears at the beginning of the subject line, that article is a reply to a previous posting.

## READING AN ARTICLE

Once you have found an article of interest, choose it by double-clicking anywhere on its line. News Xpress will open another window, fetch the article for you, and display it in a window. Larger postings will take longer to retrieve, especially if you are using a modem instead of a direct Internet connection.

When the beginning of the article has been retrieved, it will be displayed in the window. You can begin reading the article even while the newsreader is continuing to retrieve the rest of the text. Figure 6.5 shows a sample article. Notice that the article resembles an e-mail message with the header information at the top. If the article is a reply to a previous posting, News Xpress will display the text of the previous article in blue and place a greater-than symbol (>) in front of each line from the original posting. You can change these settings in the *File→Options→ Fonts and Colors* window.

The arrows in the view toolbar at the top of the article window allow you to quickly move to the previous or next article. That way you can scan through the messages quickly without closing each one. If your computer doesn't display the view toolbar, use the *View→Toolbars* command and put a check in front of *View*.

**FIGURE 6.5**
*Article window from previous news group*

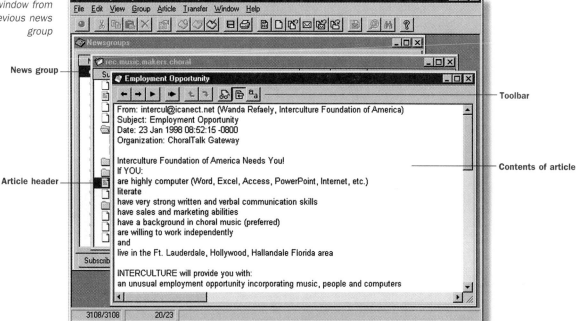

News group

Article header

Toolbar

Contents of article

**TIP**

Move the mouse cursor over each button in the News Xpress toolbar; after about one-half second, your computer will display a short description of the purpose of that button as a tooltip.

## *SAVING OR PRINTING AN ARTICLE*

When in the article window, you can use the *File→Save* command to save the article to your disk as a text (*.txt*) file in the default directory. In News Xpress you can also click the diskette button in the toolbar to accomplish this task. In some cases it may be possible to retrieve a read article from the news server again if you haven't made a copy of it, but articles are removed after a short time if space is at a premium. (Space is always at a premium in computer systems!)

Use the *File→Print* command to create a printed copy of the article, or click the printer button in the toolbar. The process is virtually identical to printing an e-mail message. The printed output will contain the article header at the top, and then the content of the message.

## GUIDED ACTIVITY

## 6.1  Joining a News Group

In this activity you will subscribe to a news group and read an article. In the next activity you will prepare a response for that article.

1.  Start Windows and open News Xpress or your own newsreader client. Make sure you have an Internet connection.

2.  Use the *File→Connect* command to establish a link to your news server. Your newsreader may be configured to do this automatically.

3.  Click the *All* tab to see a list of all news groups.

4. Next, scroll through the list until you find *rec.sport.baseball* and click it once to select it. If that group is not present, select another group that your news server provides.

5. Use the *Group→Subscribe* command to add that group to your list of news groups.

6. Now double-click the *rec.sport.baseball* line to retrieve the article headers posted in that group. You should see a list similar to Figure 6.4 shown earlier in this unit.

7. Select one of the articles and double-click its header. The contents of that posting will appear in a window on your screen and is shown in Figure 6.6. Leave your newsreader open for now.

**Checkpoint 6A**    Why will your list of articles in this group change each time you connect to the news server?

**FIGURE 6.6**
*Contents of baseball posting*

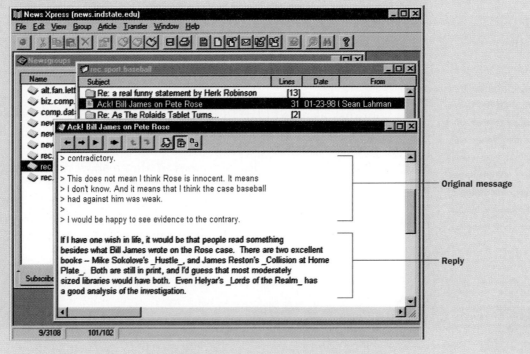

## RESPONDING TO AN ARTICLE

Most of the postings you read will be just that—items to read. Occasionally, you may want to reply to the sender of the article. You can do that by creating a private e-mail message for the sender, or by posting another article yourself to the entire news group. Of course, if you send a private mail message, only the recipient sees your comments.

**SENDING E-MAIL WITHIN NEWS XPRESS** One useful feature of the News Xpress newsreader is that it contains a simple e-mail facility so that you can create an e-mail message without having to leave the newsreader itself. Of course, if you are using Windows, it is easy to have an e-mail package like Eudora running in another application window and then simply jump to it to create the message.

It is helpful to copy a portion of the original posting into the message so that the recipient of your message knows what you are talking about. News Xpress automatically places the contents of the previous message in the reply. You can edit out any parts that are not relevant. If your news reader does not copy the original message, use the mouse to highlight the portion of the message you want to copy, and then use the *Edit→Copy* command in News Xpress to place the contents in the Clipboard. Then use the *Edit→Paste* command to paste the original message into your reply.

Next, use the *Article→Reply* command to start the e-mail process. Typically, you will have to enter the mailbox address and subject of the e-mail message manually. News Xpress automatically places the contents of the previous message in the reply. Add your own comments, and then carefully reread the message before you send it (both for spelling and for taste or tone). Use the *File→Send* command to send the reply.

Note that News Xpress may not automatically send each mail message. You can create your mail replies off-line, saving telephone connection charges. Outgoing e-mail messages are placed in the Outbox folder. When finished creating all your mail messages, click the Folder tab in the main News Xpress window. Double-click the Outbox folder, and then use the *File→Send* (or *Ctrl+E*) command from the main News Xpress window to send all of the mail messages through the Internet.

The first time the author tried this feature the e-mail could not be sent because the dial-up connection had **timed out**. Because nothing was sent over the PPP connection for ten minutes while the article was read and the e-mail reply created, the connection hung up. However, you can usually redial, establish the connection, and pick up where you left off without losing your work. Your ISP will have its own restrictions on dial-up account inactivity for time-outs.

**POSTING A REPLY TO AN ARTICLE** If you believe that the wider audience of the news group would benefit from your opinions, then you can create a reply to the original article. Use the *Article→Followup* command to create a follow-up article tied to the original article. This command produces a window similar to an e-mail window where you can add your own thoughts to the article. It automatically places all of the original posting into your response with greater-than signs (>) at the beginning of each line. You can edit out any of the original article that is not pertinent to your reply. Shorter messages tend to be read more carefully and more often.

When finished, use the *Post→Send* (or *Ctrl+S*) command to complete the response. As with the e-mail function of News Xpress, you can write your responses off-line, then send them all at one time, reducing your telephone connection costs if you are connected to a commercial service. From the main News Xpress window, first select the Outbox postings, and then use the *File→Send* (*Ctrl+E*) command to send all of the postings from this session. The next activity demonstrates a reply to a news group posting.

## GUIDED ACTIVITY

## 6.2   Replying to a News Group Posting

In this activity you will create a reply to a news group article.

1. You need to begin by retrieving a posting from a news group. Of course, *your* article will be different from the one shown here.

2. Use the *Article→Reply* command to create an e-mail response to your message. Unless you want to send a response to the original sender, readdress the response *to yourself*.

**Checkpoint 6B**   What other choices are available for responding to a news group posting?

3. Create your response. Note how News Xpress places ">" in front of the original posting within your message in Figure 6.7.

**FIGURE 6.7**

*E-mail reply to Fort Wayne baseball posting*

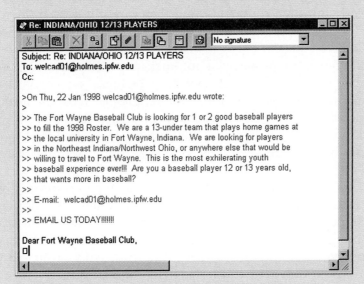

4. When finished, choose the *File→Send* command. News Xpress will post your response directly to the recipient's mailbox.

5. You may close the News Xpress newsreader.

### *SAVING AN ARTICLE IN A FOLDER*

News Xpress will let you save an article in a folder for future use, much like an e-mail system. In the main News Xpress window, click the Folder tab to display the folders. News Xpress comes with three standard folders:

- Copy-Self (for copies of postings you have created)

- Outbox (for outgoing postings)

- Trash (for deleted articles; Trash may be "dumped" when you leave News Xpress but you can change this setting in *File→Options→Miscellaneous* window).

You can use the *Transfer→New* command from the News Xpress menu bar to create a new folder and transfer the current article to that folder. The folder is actually saved in an archive file outside of News Xpress, in the default home directory. For example, you might want to create an archive of useful articles, save that archive, then transfer it via e-mail or another way to interested users.

## POSTING A NEW ARTICLE

You may want to assemble your courage and create an article with a new topic in an existing news group. Many Usenet news groups are moderated and your article will not appear automatically until it has been approved by the moderator. Articles for moderated lists may take as much as a day to appear, while postings to unmoderated lists might appear in less than an hour.

From the main News Xpress window, use the *Article→Post* command to create a new article that is not a response to another posting. News Xpress will open an editing window that closely resembles an e-mail window. You will be asked for the name of the news group and for an appropriate subject line. You will see the header information and can move the cursor beneath the header to create the text of your article.

You do not need to press the *Enter* key at the end of each line—News Xpress will wrap each line at the right margin. Proofread your article before sending it. Other readers tend to be critical of articles with simple mistakes in them. You might be branded as a newbie, or someone new to the Internet. (See the suggestions for news and discussion group etiquette at the end of this unit.)

When finished with your article, use the *File→Send* command (or *Ctrl+E*) to post the article to the Internet. As with replies and e-mail, your reply can be created off-line. To complete the posting, when back in the main News Xpress window, select the Outbox folder, and then use the *File→Send* command to send the queued postings on to the Internet.

## CREATING A NEW NEWS GROUP

As it turns out, creating a news group is one of the more democratic processes on the Internet. Before a new group can be created, you must create a proposal for the group and then have users vote on your idea. New news group proposals are listed in the *news.announce.newgroups* group under the RFD (Request for Discussion) label. It might sound easy, but in practice it is not that simple. Most users

### Net Ethics    *Spamming*

A few years ago a small law firm created a furor when it simultaneously sent a posting to hundreds of news groups offering its services to help aliens in the United States obtain a visa. Thousands of individuals had to spend time downloading these messages. Some users received multiple copies of the same message. At the time it was considered the Internet equivalent of junk mail. Do you think it is appropriate to use Internet resources to send out so-called "junk mail"? Have you received junk e-mail that you would rather have not had to deal with? Where do you draw the line between aggressive marketing and spamming?

can find an existing group to fit their needs. It is recommended that you piggyback your discussions on some existing group, possibly in the *alt* category, until the group is so large that it becomes evident that a separate group is needed.

### UNSUBSCRIBING TO A NEWS GROUP

Your newsreader software will provide a way to **unsubscribe** to a news group. With News Xpress, change to the Subscribed sheet, and then select one or more news groups. Use the *Group→Unsubscribe* command to unsubscribe from those groups. The book symbol at the beginning of each unsubscribed group will change to a small circle, indicating you no longer subscribe to that group.

You can also select a subscribed group, and then click the unsubscribe button in the toolbar. If the right mouse button is configured properly, you can also right-click the target news group, and then select Unsubscribe from the quick menu. Use the *File→Options→Miscellaneous* command to make sure the right mouse button is set to the Track menu choice.

### MANUALLY EDITING THE NEWSRC FILE (OPTIONAL)

You can manually edit the **newsrc file** which contains a list of all the news groups. Before editing the newsrc file, make a backup copy! The newsrc file lists the name of the news group, article numbers that you have read, and whether you have subscribed to that group.

Those groups that end with an exclamation point (!) are *not* subscribed to; remove the ! from the groups you wish to join. Add an exclamation point to the end of groups you wish to leave. To learn the location of your newsrc file, use the *File→Options* command in News Xpress, click the Servers and Directory tab, and note the Home directory location. You will find your newsrc file in that folder.

## Other Newsreader Software

Other shareware newsreader packages are available. Both the Netscape Communicator and Microsoft Internet Explorer Web browsers have newsreader capabilities built in. Figure 6.8 shows the Outlook Express newsreader window. The Netscape newsreader, called Collabra, is similar.

## *Listserv and Mailing List Discussion Groups*

**Listserv groups** combine elements of e-mail and Usenet news. After you formally join a Listserv group, the Listserv software automatically will send you an e-mail message containing postings to that group. Thus you do not have to go through a newsreader and request specific articles for review; they appear automatically in your e-mail in basket. Some people refer to Listserv discussion groups as automated **mailing list** systems. Figure 6.9 shows a sample e-mail posting.

The simplicity of the system may stimulate an enormous amount of e-mail traffic, depending on the activity level of the group. To reduce the number of individual messages, some Listserv groups send a **digest** of postings. A digest is a single e-mail message containing multiple postings and replies that were collected over a short period, often a week.

**FIGURE 6.8**
*Outlook Express
newsreader window*

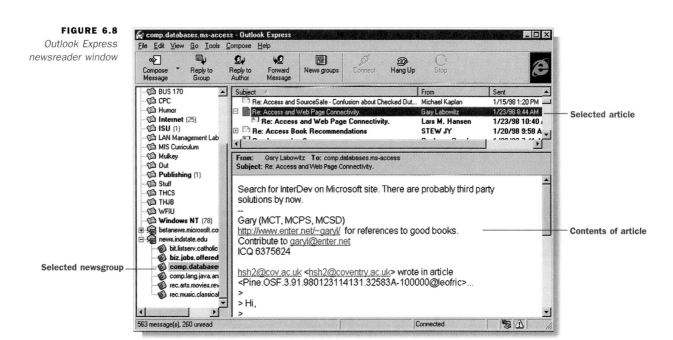

Selected article

Contents of article

Selected newsgroup

**FIGURE 6.9**
*Team Anchordesk
mailing list daily
message*

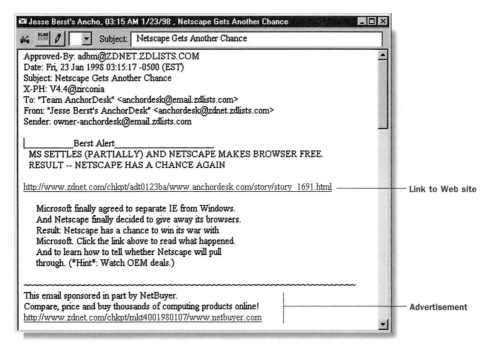

Link to Web site

Advertisement

While news groups allow you to make an individual response to the sender of a particular article, Listserv groups with human moderators don't automatically accept input from users. The moderator will read submissions, and possibly edit those that are appropriate before placing them into the group postings. If the e-mail addresses of contributors are included in their postings, you can create a separate reply directly to the user. Often an individual will request that replies be sent directly to them, not the entire Listserv group.

## Sending Instructions to the Listserv Group

Most Listserv servers automate administrative tasks associated with maintaining the group's membership list. You send a one-line e-mail message to the server with an instruction for the group as the message body. You can request help for the group, subscribe and unsubscribe to the group, get a list of available topics for the group, receive a list of available files, and receive a file from the group. We will discuss the methods for subscribing and unsubscribing to Listserv groups next.

**CAUTION**  If you have created a personal signature in your e-mail system, you should turn off the signature before sending a Listserv command. Because the signature text is added to the end of the message, the Listserv processor may try to interpret that text as a Listserv command and return a series of error messages. Some Listserv hosts let you use the end command (or one blank line) at the end of your Listserv message so that a trailing signature is not misinterpreted as a command.

## Subscribing to a Mailing List

You subscribe to a group by sending an e-mail requesting that your name be added to the group roster. For example, suppose you want to subscribe to the BIGTEN-L mailing list at Purdue University. This group explores issues associated with the Big Ten conference. First you must locate the exact name of the mailing list server, in this example *listserv@vm.cc.purdue.edu*. Send an e-mail message to this address, and place this one-line request in the body of the message:

```
SUBSCRIBE BIGTEN-L your-real-name
```

Be sure to substitute your real name (not your e-mail address) for the last item in the message. When you send the e-mail message it will cause the Listserv server to add your e-mail name and address to the mailing list for that group. You will receive a greeting from the group, and then automatically receive all of the communications for that group.

## Submitting a Posting to the Mailing List

When you are ready to submit something to the group, create an e-mail message. We advise that you carefully edit your message because many people will likely receive your posting. See the pointers on discussion group etiquette at the end of this unit.

There are usually *two* addresses associated with a mailing list. One address is for administrative tasks such as subscribing and unsubscribing to the Listserv group. The other address is where you send your postings. Check the discussion group's welcome message that you received when you subscribed, or read the fine print in the postings that appear. They will tell you the relevant e-mail addresses.

  Beware of something that I did by accident. I wanted to get a list of the available mailing list commands, so I sent an e-mail message containing help as the command. Unfortunately, instead of sending it to the administrator of the group, I used the group address and it went to all of the members of the group. I immediately received several concerned calls wondering if I really needed help!

## Unsubscribing to a Mailing List

If you no longer desire to be a member of a particular Listserv group, send another one-line e-mail message with the `unsubscribe` or `signoff` command. For example, if you want to remove yourself from the BIGTEN-L Listserv group, use the following command in the body of the message:

UNSUBSCRIBE BIGTEN-L

Some systems use the `signoff` command instead of `unsubscribe` to remove a name from the mailing list.

## Finding a Listserv Group

You can often find references to other Listserv groups in postings on news groups and on discussion groups. Some news groups have an equivalent discussion group that includes all of the postings on a weekly basis. Frequently updated lists of mailing lists are available on the Internet. On the Web, visit *http://www.yahoo.com/ Computers_and_Internet/Internet/Mailing_Lists/* for a catalog of publicly available mailing lists. Other good catalogs of publicly accessible mailing lists can be found at *http://www.neosoft.com/internet/paml* and *http://www.tile.net/tile/listserv/index.html*.

## GUIDED ACTIVITY

### 6.3  Joining a Listserv Group

In this activity you will join a Listserv mailing list group for Mike's Midnight Movie Reviews. Instructions are also provided for you to unsubscribe from this group.

1. Start Windows and open your e-mail client.

2. Create a new e-mail message. In Eudora this would be with the *Ctrl+N* command.

3. In the To box type `listproc@colossus.net`. Leave the Subject line blank.

4. In the body of your message type: SUBSCRIBE M3REVIEW

5. Turn off the Signature feature of your mailer, and then send the message.

**Checkpoint 6C**  Why do you turn off the Signature feature before sending the subscribe e-mail message?

6. You should receive another e-mail message notifying you that you have been added to the mailing list. Save that reply letter in an e-mail folder because it contains instructions about unsubscribing from the group. (*Hint:* Typically, you would create another e-mail message to the same address with UNSUBSCRIBE M3REVIEW <your e-mail address> as the message.) You should begin receiving e-mail messages about movie reviews from this mailing list.

**There also is a Web site for this movie review discussion group. Check out** *http://www.vidkraft.com/m3review* **for more details and past reviews.**

## Setting Up Your Own Mailing List

You can create a mailing list for a special topic and become its administrator. Doing so requires that you have access to a server with specialized software that enables it to become a Listserv host. For more information about Listserv groups, join one of the groups that deals with Listserv mailing lists such as *news.groups*.

We have a mailing list for adopters and users of this book at Indiana State University. The name for this group is InetBook-L. Send an e-mail message to *maiser@befac.indstate.edu* with the one-line message:

```
SUBSCRIBE  INETBOOK-L
```

For more information check the home page for this book under Resources at *http://computered.swep.com/*.

### DISTANCE EDUCATION AND DISCUSSION GROUPS

There has been considerable interest in distance education using the Internet rather than closed-circuit or broadcast television as the medium. One thought might be to set up live, on-line chat sessions (see Unit 9). However, that implies that users will be on-line at the same time, and that all have the technical capability for chat access.

A recent distance education conference for higher education pointed to the use of mailing lists, combined with Web pages. The instructor can post a message for the entire group by sending it to the mailing list. Individual students are able to post messages to the entire group, or send e-mail to a specific individual, such as the instructor.

One Midwest school was particularly successful in using archives of previous discussions that could be downloaded at any time. This school also kept records on *when* students sent messages to the Listserv. Messages were received at virtually every hour of the day and night. Ironically, one of the biggest dilemmas was whether to charge out-of-state tuition for Internet-based students who never stepped a foot on campus!

### SPECIAL MAILING LIST FEATURES

Each Listserv or mailing list software program will have its own set of features. Most permit you to receive a list of commands by sending an e-mail message to the Listserv processor with HELP as the message. Table 6.2 shows some of the available commands.

## News and Discussion Group Etiquette

Although we have given basic instructions for using news groups and discussion groups, the following pointers will make the procedure better for everyone.

- Before you submit an article, be sure to look for the frequently asked question (FAQ) list within the group. You might find that your question or comment already has been made and documented, and it would be inappropriate (and wasteful) to repeat that posting.

- Make sure that your comments are brief and to the point.

- Be certain that your posting is being sent to the appropriate group or list. Many groups have a FAQ guide to the news groups about a particular subject. For instance, the guide for Windows news groups explains the purpose of each group, including some in other news group areas.

- If your reply is quite specific, use an e-mail reply rather than posting to the entire group. That way, other group readers will not have to read something that is not germane to their interests.

- Lurking (reading without replying or posting anything yourself) is frowned on by some discussion groups. You aren t obligated to contribute to the group, but if you have something worthwhile to say, go ahead and post it.

- Follow the basic e-mail Netiquette suggestions made in Unit 3.

**TABLE 6.2**
*Common Listserv and mailing list commands*

| COMMAND | MEANING |
|---|---|
| *HELP* | Returns list of mailing list commands. |
| *FINGER <address>* | Returns information about user at this address. |
| *LIST* | Shows all the mailing lists available at this site. |
| *SUBSCRIBE <list-name>* | Subscribe to indicated mailing list. Also SUB. |
| *UNSUBSCRIBE <list-name>* | Unsubscribe from list. Also SIGNOFF and UNSUB. |
| *REVIEW <list-name>* | Give list of members of list. Also ENUMERATE. |
| *ADD <list-name> <address>* | Adds an address to list, used by moderator. |
| *REMOVE <list-name> <address>* | Removes an address from list, used by moderator. |
| *INDEX* | Asks mail server for list of files available at this site. |
| *SEND <filename>* | Asks mail server to send you a FAQ or archive file. |
| *END* | Terminates reading of mail server commands. Also EXIT. |

# SUMMARY

Discussion groups provide an electronic forum where individuals can have discussions about topics of common interest. News groups and mailing lists are examples of discussion groups. A news group is a collection of articles called postings about a single subject or theme. Postings are made to the news group through a newsreader client that is similar to an e-mail client. Internet users who have subscribed to a particular news group can connect to the news server and retrieve postings made to that group. If a member of the group does not check for new messages, there is no way those messages will be read by that member. Therefore, a news group requires active participation by each member.

News Xpress is a popular newsreader client. Available as shareware, it is fast and easy to learn. You see the list of all news groups as well as the ones to which you have subscribed. Double-click on a group to display its message headers. Double-click on a single message to display the message. Your newsreader keeps track of which messages you have already read. A user can send a reply back to the entire group or just to the original sender of the posting. The newsreader will display threads of messages and their replies.

Unlike news groups, mailing lists automatically mail out the postings to all the individuals who have subscribed to that group. They can retrieve and read the postings with their normal e-mail client program. Because all messages are delivered to the members via e-mail, it is more likely that a mailing list member will actually read a message. A mailing list requires only passive participation by each member. You can search for relevant news groups and mailing lists using Web search tools.

## Command Review

| | |
|---|---|
| Article → Post | Create a new posting for a news group. |
| Article → Reply | Create a private e-mail response to the originator of a posting. |
| Edit → Copy | Copy highlighted text to the Clipboard. |
| Edit → Paste | Take text from the Clipboard and paste it into the document. |
| File → Connect (*Ctrl+O*) | Connect to the news server. |
| File → Disconnect (*Ctrl+D*) | Disconnect from the news server. |
| File → Options | Call up the configuration menu for server, e-mail address. |
| File → Print | Print the current article. |
| File → Save (*Ctrl+S*) | Save current article on disk. |
| File → Send (*Ctrl+E*) | Send your reply over the Internet. |
| Group → Subscribe | Subscribe to selected news group. |
| Group → Unsubscribe | Unsubscribe from selected news group. |
| Transfer → New | Create a new folder and transfer selected article to it. |
| View → Expand/Collapse Threads (*Ctrl+Y*) | Expand or collapse threads of articles. |
| View → Toolbars | Turn on or off specified News Xpress toolbars. |

## Vocabulary Exercise

*Write a short definition for each term in the following list.*

| | | |
|---|---|---|
| Archive | Mailing list | Newsreader |
| Article | Moderated (list or group) | News Xpress newsreader |
| Digest | Net News Transport Pro- | Post |
| Discussion group | tocol (NNTP) | Subscribe |
| Frequently Asked Ques- | Network news | Thread |
| tion (FAQ) | Newbie | Timed out |
| Listserv group | News group | Unsubscribe |
| Lurking | Newsrc file | Usenet news |

## Review Questions

1. What is a discussion group?

2. Describe the types of articles that might be posted in each of these news group categories.

   a. alt            e. rec

   b. comp           f. sci

   c. misc           g. soc

   d. news

3. Explain how to accomplish the following news group functions with your own newsreader program.

   a. subscribe to a news group

   b. retrieve a list of articles within a news group

   c. read an article

   d. post a new article

   e. unsubscribe to a news group

4. After reading a news article, you would like to make a reply. Discuss the ways you can make that reply.

5. What is the meaning of a thread in a news group? How is that useful to you when you read messages posted to that group?

6. What are the differences between news groups and Listserv discussion groups? Which is preferred?

7. How do you accomplish the following Listserv discussion group activities?

   a. subscribe to a discussion group

   b. read the postings in the discussion group

   c. unsubscribe to a discussion group

   d. start a new discussion group

8. In setting up your own discussion group, you should join a news group that deals with setting up a discussion group. How would you find out the names of suitable Listserv news groups?

## Exercises

*Note: You may not have the same news and discussion groups available on your news server. It would be appropriate to substitute a similar group from your choices.*

1. Identify the number of news groups that are available to you at your campus. Write down the name of the *first* and *last* news groups. Does your campus censor the groups?

2. Using your own newsreader software, subscribe to the *rec.audio* news group. Read the first article in that group and print a copy. Prepare a reply and e-mail it to your *own* mailbox address.

3. Subscribe to the *rec.arts.tv* news group. Find an article in that group, then follow the thread to other articles replying to that message. Print the complete set of messages.

4. Subscribe to a news group of your choice, then read a message that interests you. Print out that message, then create an e-mail reply to the originator of that message. Print your reply and any reply you get from the originator.

5. Join the *comp-org-eff-talk* discussion group at *listserv@eff.org* for a few days and receive the daily postings; then request to be dropped from that group. Print at least one day's worth of postings from that group.

6. Join the CleanStuff humor mailing list by accessing the Mercury Communications Web site at *http://www.mercurycommunications.net/*. Select Cool Mail, and choose the CleanStuff mailing list. Fill in your own name and e-mail address, and then click Subscribe. The list should send you a confirming e-mail message. You will receive occasional humorous messages.

7. Join the Anchordesk mailing list to receive a daily electronic computer magazine with the latest news about the industry. To subscribe or unsubscribe, go to *http://www.anchordesk.com/whoiswe/subscribe.html*. You will receive a daily e-mail message with links to and descriptions of the articles that appear at the Anchordesk Web site found at *http://www.anchordesk.com*. Print at least one posting for this mailing list.

8. If your Web browser is functional, open *http://www.tile.net/tile/listserv/index.html/* and note the five ways this Web page organizes mailing lists found on the Internet. Switch to the "grouped by host country page," and select CA (Canada). Give a brief description of the following mailing lists from Canada.

   a. YESCAMP

   b. WESTNET

   c. SING-OUT

   d. LENSTEST

   e. CSOCWORK

## Working with Discussion Groups

Use the Internet search tools to locate news groups *and* mailing lists about each of the following subjects. Give the complete news group name along with the name and subscription address for each mailing list.

Golden retrievers (or dogs in general)
Java (programming, not coffee)
Microsoft Access (database)
Folk dancing
Acupuncture
Breast cancer
Mailing lists
Politics

### PROJECT TEAM OPTION

Explore genealogy discussion groups that would be pertinent to the background of each member of the team. For instance, if someone is of Scottish ancestry, locate discussion groups that are appropriate for that ancestry. Don't forget that some discussion groups may be located in the country in question.

# File Transfer Protocol (FTP) and Telnet

This unit describes two important tools for retrieving information from the Internet. FTP is used to retrieve files from host servers, while Telnet is used to make a remote connection to an Internet server. You will learn how to use the Windows 95 built-in FTP program as well as the popular WS_FTP program with a graphical user interface.

## Learning Objectives

At the completion of this unit, you should be able to

1. explain the uses of FTP to transfer files from a remote server,

2. discuss the various kinds of file transfers possible with FTP,

3. connect to an FTP server and select the proper directory,

4. transfer a single file from a remote server,

5. transfer a group of files from a remote server,

6. use Telnet to make a remote connection,

7. initiate a Telnet session,

8. quit a Telnet session.

## Key Terms

*The following terms are introduced in this unit. Be sure you know what each of them means.*

Anonymous FTP
ASCII file
Binary file
Download
File Transfer Protocol (FTP)
PKZIP
Self-extracting file
Subdirectory
Telnet
Upload
WinZip
WS_FTP client
Zip

## Transferring Files with FTP

Thousands of useful programs and data files are available to users over the Internet, most of them free of charge. To transfer files to your computer, you can use the file transfer protocol, or FTP for short. FTP represents the set of standards for accomplishing the file transfers as well as a particular program for doing the transfers. Your Web browser also supports FTP operations.

# File Transfers

We need to review some terminology before learning how to use FTP. With respect to FTP, the *host computer* is a remote computer that is accessible via the Internet. The *client computer* is usually considered to be your computer, but in some cases it may be your Internet provider's host computer that also is connected directly to the Internet. Ordinarily, we **download** or transfer files from the host computer to the client computer; but some FTP systems allow **upload** transfers in the other direction.

If the file is small enough, we transfer it in its normal state. Larger files are usually compressed before being stored on the host. The most common compression standard for PC-compatible files is called **zip**, found in such programs as **PKZIP** and **WinZip**. Files compressed this way usually have the *.zip* file extension. After transferring the file to your own hard drive, you use the program to expand the file. It is typical to have several normal files compressed into one *.zip* file so that only one file must be transferred. Some compressed files may have the *.exe* extension; these are **self-extracting files** and already contain the expansion program inside. To expand these files, just run the program, and it automatically extracts all the compressed files. After expanding a compressed file, you can copy it to a floppy disk and remove it from your hard drive to save space.

## TYPES OF TRANSFERS

For FTP transfers there are two kinds of files. **ASCII** (pronounced as-key) **files** contain text characters and can be displayed on your screen just by viewing the file itself, without a word processor or special viewer program. Files with names like *Readme.txt* are usually ASCII files and can be viewed with the Notepad accessory.

**Binary files** contain special character codes and generally represent executable programs or specially encoded files such as word processing documents. Most files that you can transfer with FTP are binary files. Some FTP programs require that you specify the type of file before it can be successfully transferred. WS_FTP will automatically determine the file type when you perform the transfer.

## SUBDIRECTORIES

Although each FTP host is organized differently, they all subdivide the hard drive space in a hierarchical fashion. A **subdirectory** represents a particular area on the host computer's disk storage system. When you use FTP to transfer files, you must know both the name of the file and the subdirectory within which it is stored. In Microsoft's Windows 95 operating system, subdirectories are called *folders*.

Subdirectories are stored in a tree or hierarchical fashion, with a root directory and subdirectories of the root directory. Subdirectories frequently have subdirectories of their own. Figure 7.1 shows a sample disk structure with subdirectories (folders) on a typical client computer that runs Windows 95. Your computer might be similar to this, but most client computers reflect the unique choices made by their users.

**TIP**

The Windows 95 file compression product called WinZip can handle long file names. Visit the WinZip Web site at *www.winzip.com* for more information and to download an evaluation copy. You can obtain the PKZIP and PKUNZIP DOS programs at many FTP sites, including *ftp://papa. indstate.edu.* Look in the */winsock-l/ Misc_Utils/ Compression* directory for the *pkz204g.exe* file. This is a self-extracting compressed file that contains the programs and a license agreement.

**FIGURE 7.1**
*Windows Explorer
view of
subdirectories
(folders)*

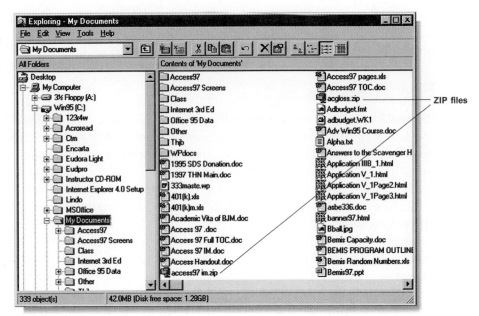

You can use FTP commands to navigate from one subdirectory to another subdirectory so that you can select the file to be transferred. We will cover subdirectory navigation later in the unit.

### BASIC FTP OPERATIONS

There are three main steps in performing an FTP operation:

- Make the FTP connection by logging in to the host computer.

- Navigate to the subdirectory where the desired file is stored.

- Transfer the file from the host computer to your client computer (or vice versa).

The first step begins with loading the FTP client program on your computer. We first describe how to use a command line FTP program in the next section. Use this client to download a Windows version of the FTP software discussed in this book. You will learn how to use a Windows-based FTP client in the following section.

---

NET TIP
**Web Addresses**

Current links to most Web sites in this book can be found on the *Understanding & Using the Internet* Home Page. Choose **Resources** at **computered.swep.com**. Remember that a Web address may change at any time. An address given in this book as an example may no longer be valid. If this is so, either access the Home Page for the current link or do a search to find a similar site (see Unit 5 for a discussion of search methods).

# Using Command-Line-Based FTP

Traditional FTP software packages that run under UNIX or DOS utilize commands that you type in at the ftp> prompt, very similar to MS-DOS commands. They are called command-line programs because you must type in each command. With a Windows client you can use the mouse to click buttons and menu bars. With a command-line FTP client, you see text-only results of each command.

Windows 95 comes with its own command-line FTP client that runs in an MS-DOS Prompt window. To open an MS-DOS Prompt window, click *Start*, choose *Programs*, and then select the *MS-DOS prompt*. (We will refer to this as the DOS prompt.)

## STARTING FTP

To start the command-line FTP program, connect to the Internet, and type ftp at the DOS prompt.

C>ftp

**TIP**

To save time, you can give the name of the server when you start FTP by typing the domain name after the initial FTP command, thus avoiding the open command:
C>ftp mama.indstate.edu

In a moment, you should see the ftp> prompt that signifies that you may key in an FTP command. You must open a connection with the host computer. Use the open command and specify the domain name of the server to which you wish to connect. For instance, to open an FTP connection with the server called *mama* at Indiana State University, use this FTP command:

ftp>open mama.indstate.edu

## LOGGING IN TO THE HOST

After making the connection, the FTP host will ask you to log in. You will see the User and Password prompts or something similar. If your FTP site requires preauthorized user names and passwords, enter the appropriate value after each prompt. When you have entered the correct values, the FTP host will let you select files to be transferred.

However, most FTP sessions will be made to a host where your username is *not* preauthorized to do file transfers. In that case, use the anonymous FTP login method. When asked for your user name, type in anonymous. If asked for the password, type in your full e-mail address. If the FTP host allows **anonymous FTP** sessions, you will be permitted access to the host files.

Many FTP hosts are exceptionally busy and may not be able to accept new logins when you connect. Try again in a few minutes or later in the day. The busiest times for FTP servers are in the daytime, and particularly from 11 a.m. to 2 p.m. local time.

## SELECTING FILES

Before you can *download* a file from the host to your computer, you must locate the proper directory and file. At the ftp> prompt you can use the cd directory-name command to change to the named subdirectory *beneath* the current one, or the cd .. command to change to the parent directory. For example, if you are in the docs subdirectory, the command cd pub-docs will change to the pub-docs subdirectory within the docs directory. The pwd command will print (display) the name of the working (current) directory.

Use the dir command to display the names of the files in a subdirectory. A sample output appears in Figure 7.2. The first letter in each line tells the kind of entry: a "d" means that entry is a directory, and a "-" means the entry is a file. In this case the first two entries are directories, the next four are files, and the remainder are directories. The last entry on each line is the name of the file or directory. Preceding it are entries for the date and time the file was stored in the FTP server, and just before that is the size of the file, in bytes. Other entries on the line give security information and are not necessary to transfer a file.

**FIGURE 7.2**
*Typical UNIX FTP
directory display*

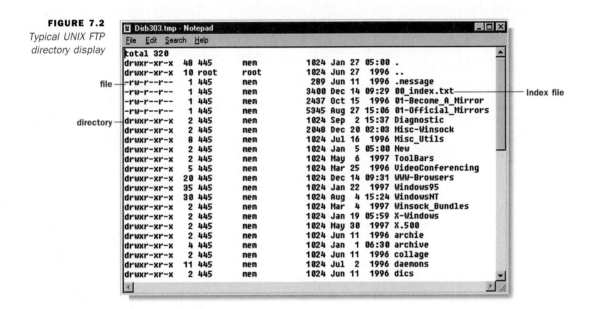

If you don't know the exact name of the file, look for a file that contains a listing of available files. It could have the name *readme*, *index.txt*, *list*, or other similar phrase. These are usually ASCII files and thus can be downloaded and viewed on your client machine. Remember that spelling is critically important when requesting a specific file, so double-check that you spell the file name correctly, *including* capitalization of letters. On some computers, notably UNIX machines, a file called *FILE22* is different from one called *file22*.

## GETTING HELP IN COMMAND-LINE FTP

To receive a list of commands, type help and press *Enter*. You can get help about any particular command by typing help <command>. Remember that capitalization in command names is important, particularly if you are working on a UNIX computer or in DOS. Capitalization is *not* important when using the Windows 95 FTP client commands.

## TRANSFERRING A FILE TO YOUR COMPUTER

Before you initiate the download of the file to your computer, determine the type of file and use the proper command to tell the host to send the file in ASCII or as a binary file. At the ftp> prompt type `binary` for a binary file or `ascii` for an ASCII (text) file. To see the current status of the FTP session, use the `status` command. It will tell you whether you are set up for ASCII or binary transfers. In most cases you will do binary transfers.

When you have changed to the subdirectory of the file you want to download, at the ftp> prompt type `get filename` and the host will begin to transfer that file to your computer. Other than seeing the disk drive activity light come on periodically as the file is copied to your computer, you may not be aware of what is happening in the transfer. Some host computers will display a progress report while the file is being transferred. Keep in mind that large files may take a long time to transfer over the Internet, and even longer if you are connected to the Internet with a dial-up connection. When finished, the host will give a message indicating that the transfer is complete.

The actual time it takes for the file to transfer depends on:

- The size of the file to be transferred.

- The speed of the network connection between you and the Internet.

- The number of other clients the FTP host is serving.

- The amount of other traffic flowing over the Internet.

## TRANSFERRING GROUPS OF FILES

It is also possible to transfer a group of files at one time by tagging each file in the group and sending the files in one group. Each FTP program will have its own way to tag files. With a Windows-based FTP package, click on the first file, then *Ctrl*-click each remaining file that you want to tag. With a text-based FTP program, use the `mget` command and specify multiple file names. They will be transferred in a batch and saved on the local disk drive without further action required.

## TRANSFERRING A FILE TO THE FTP HOST

The `put` or `send` command will *upload* a file from the local machine to the host computer. You must be authorized for that operation, and most users will not use this feature. However, if you use FTP for transferring files, this service can be useful. Before you transfer the file, you will need to change to the host subdirectory in which the file will be stored.

## COMPLETING THE FTP SESSION

When you are finished with the FTP session, use the `bye` or `quit` command. The FTP session will be closed and you will return to the command-line prompt.

## GUIDED ACTIVITY

# 7.1    Using Command Line FTP

In this activity, you will use a command-line FTP client to transfer a text file to your computer. If you do not have a command-line FTP client, you may skip this activity.

1. Log in to your network and establish the command-line prompt. In MS-DOS this will probably be F> or C>. The UNIX command-line prompt is >.

2. At the command prompt type `ftp` and press *Enter.* Your computer will load the FTP command-line client and display the ftp> prompt.

3. Next type `open mama.indstate.edu` to connect to this FTP server at Indiana State University. Press *Enter.*

4. When asked, type your user name as `anonymous`. Use your full e-mail address as the password. The password does not display for security reasons.

**Checkpoint 7A**    Why do we use anonymous FTP logins?

5. At the ftp> prompt type `dir` to see the files and directories at this level as shown in Figure 7.2. You will download the *README.1ST* file first to find out more about this FTP site.

6. At the ftp> prompt type `ascii` to switch to ASCII file transfer mode. At the next ftp> prompt type `get README.1ST`. Your capitalization should match exactly.

**Checkpoint 7B**    Why must capitalization match exactly?

7. Your computer will receive the short text file and save it under the same name in the default directory.

8. Now change to the internet_book subdirectory. Type `cd internet_book` and press *Enter.*

9. Type `dir` to see a list of available files.

10. Now we'll download a file to be used in a later unit. Type `get photo.gif` and press *Enter.* The file will be copied to the default folder, probably C:\Windows.

11. Use the `quit` command to quit from the FTP client and view the *README.1ST* text file. In many cases there are further instructions that tell you where to find files on the host.

12. To view the file from the DOS prompt, you can use the text editor. Type `edit README.1ST`. When finished, use the *File→Exit* command to return to DOS.

13. Type `Exit` and press *Enter* to close the MS-DOS window and return to Windows 95.

TIP

In case you don't have this program, you can use the Windows 95 FTP program to download the LE version from *ftp.ipswitch. com.* It is stored in the */Ipswitch/ Product_Down- loads/* directory on that FTP server. Log in as anony- mous, then use the `cd /Ipswitch/ Product_ Downloads/` com- mand to switch to that directory. The file is called *ws_ ftple.exe*, and is about 669 KB. Make sure you switch to binary mode before you download the file. Both Windows 3.1 and Windows 95 versions are stored in the same file. Run this program and follow installa- tion instructions.

# Using the Windows WS_FTP Client

In this section you will learn how to use the popular Windows-based WS_FTP client to transfer files. As with most Windows packages, this one is significantly easier to use than a command-line-based FTP program. You don't have to memo- rize commands with the Windows FTP. Also, you can click your way through sub- directory changes without having to spell out a subdirectory name. And, it is easy to mark several files to be downloaded at one time.

We will use the popular WS_FTP95 LE (limited edition) client that comes in both 16- and 32-bit versions. Although we selected the 32-bit version that runs un- der Windows 95 for this edition, the 16-bit version is nearly identical. The 32-bit version displays long file names. Your own Windows FTP client probably will be similar to this one.

### CONNECTING TO AN FTP SERVER

From the Start button select *Programs* and select the *WS_FTP program group;* choose *WS_FTP95 LE* from that group. Figure 7.3 shows the opening FTP screen with the Session Profile box open. In this box you can specify the FTP host name, give your user name and password, and select the type of system you are connecting to. In this case *mama.indstate.edu* is a UNIX system. The WS_FTP client also has an Auto- matic Detect setting where it tries to determine the host system type. Once you have specified the host settings, click *OK* and WS_FTP will try to connect with that host.

### USING THE MAIN WS_FTP WINDOW

In a few seconds you should see the main WS_FTP window shown in Figure 7.4. In the left part of the window is a directory of the Local (client) system, and at the

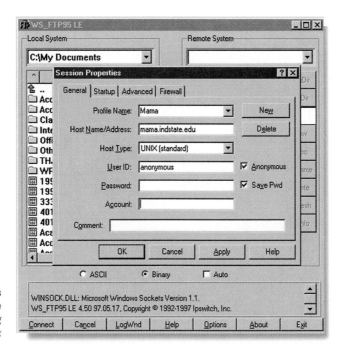

**FIGURE 7.3**
*WS_FTP Session Properties dialog box*

**FIGURE 7.4**
*The Main WS_FTP window*

Current local directory

Switch to a higher directory

File mask

Session log

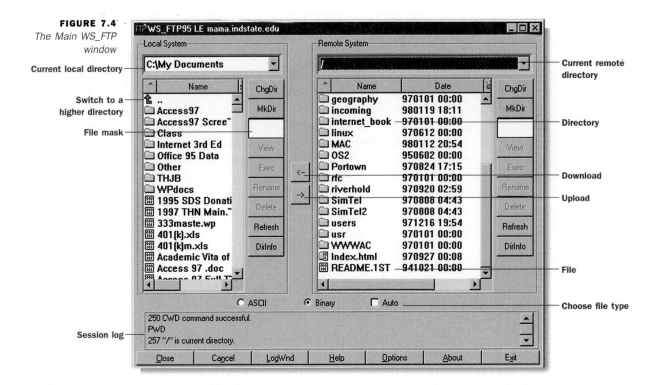

Current remote directory

Directory

Download

Upload

File

Choose file type

right side is the directory for the Remote (host) system. The white areas of the display are used to select different subdirectories and to choose particular files. The top box on each side shows the current directory for each system. This window was resized to display more remote system information.

The session message log appears in the lower part of the WS_FTP window. Double-click this area (or click the LogWnd button) to open a larger version of the log. You will see a log of your FTP commands and their results. To the right of each panel is a set of file manipulation buttons as shown in Table 7.1.

**TABLE 7.1**
*WS_FTP file manipulation buttons*

| BUTTON | MEANING |
|---|---|
| ChgDir | Change to a different directory (specify name directly). |
| MkDir | Create a new directory. |
| [File Mask] | This empty box lets you specify a file mask so that only files that match that pattern are displayed. Example: ws* will display files starting with "ws". |
| View | Display text file in Notepad window. You can choose the viewer in Options. |
| Exec | Execute selected file. |
| Rename | Rename selected file. |
| Delete | Delete selected file or subdirectory. (Be careful!) |
| Refresh | Ask system to redisplay subdirectory and file names. |
| DirInfo | Provide directory display in a Notepad window. |

## CHANGING DIRECTORIES

Before you transfer the file, select the proper directory in the remote directory panel by double-clicking its name. To move to a higher level directory, double-click on the .. entry at the top of the pane. As you change directories, the FTP client will automatically display the files found in that directory in the lower part of that panel. In the case of Figure 7.4, there are numerous subdirectories in the remote system panel, so we scrolled that window down to show the two files at the bottom. To see directory information about files on the local or remote system, click the *DirInfo* button in the proper panel. Figure 7.2 was obtained in this manner.

## TRANSFERRING A FILE

Select the file to be transferred by clicking its name. If you want to transfer several files in one operation, *Ctrl*-click each file name to be selected. Before you transfer the file, be sure that the proper directory on the local machine has been selected. The transfer type (ASCII or Binary) is selected in the lower part of the FTP window. WS_FTP automatically selects binary mode for all but *.txt* files, but you can change that in the Options menu.

When you are ready to transfer the file, click on the appropriate arrow button in the center of the window. Clicking the left arrow will download that file to your local system; clicking on the right arrow will upload a file from the local system to the remote system. Most FTP hosts will not permit uploads from a local machine to the FTP host for anonymous logins. Figure 7.5 shows the FTP window with one highlighted file. You will retrieve this file in Exercise 2 at the end of this unit.

When you are finished with the FTP host, click the *Close* button in the lower left corner to disconnect from the remote host. You can click *Exit* to leave WS_FTP.

**FIGURE 7.5**
*WS_FTP window
with highlighted file*

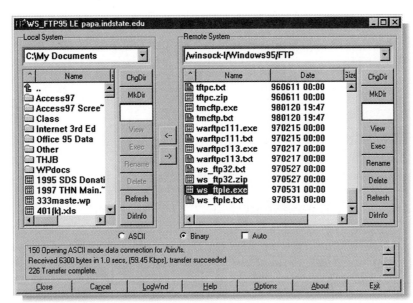

# 7.2    Using the Windows WS_FTP Client

In this activity you will use the Windows WS_FTP client to transfer a file to your computer.

1. If you are not already in Windows 95, start it now. Locate your FTP client and start it. We will use the WS_FTP client shown earlier in Figure 7.3.

2. Use the Connect command to open the Connect dialog box. Click *New,* then enter `Papa` in the Profile Name box. Enter `papa.indstate.edu` in the Host Name/Address: box. Select *UNIX* as the Host Type. The User ID is `anonymous` and Password is your full e-mail address. See Figure 7.6.

**FIGURE 7.6**
*Session Properties box for Papa FTP host*

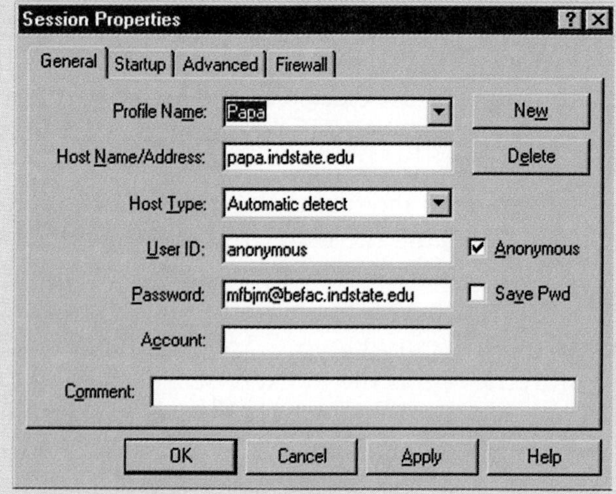

3. Click *OK* to connect to this FTP host. After a few moments, you will be connected. FTP will transfer directory information from papa to your computer and display it in the right side of the display.

4. In the Remote Directory window scroll down until you see *winsock-l.* Double-click on that entry to switch to that subdirectory.

**Checkpoint 7C**    Is there a difference between using a "1" (one) and an "l" (letter ell) for the last character in winsock-l?

5. Next scroll down the Remote Directory window until you locate the *Misc_Utils* directory. Double-click that entry to view the entries within that subdirectory. Double-click the *Compression* directory to display its files.

6. Click on the *00_index.txt file* to select it as shown in Figure 7.7.

7. To display this text file with WS_FTP, first click the *ASCII file type* button. Then click the *View* button in the *remote* side of the WS_FTP window. The contents of this file are shown in Figure 7.8.

**FIGURE 7.7**
*WS_FTP window for index file*

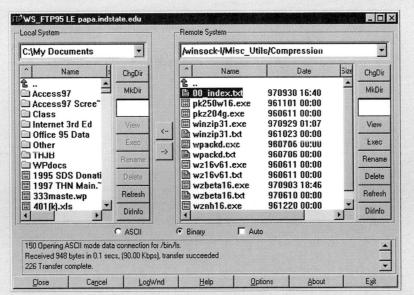

**FIGURE 7.8**
*Contents of 00_index.txt file*

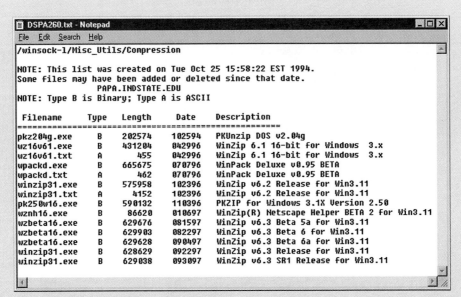

8.  If you want to download the *pkz204g.exe* compression file, repeat the process in this activity but select that file instead and click the *Binary file type* button. To copy it to your computer in the current Local Directory, click the *left arrow* button.

**Checkpoint 7D**  How would you copy this file to the *floppy* disk in the A drive?

9.  Click the *Close* button in the lower left corner to close the connection. Click again on *Disconnect* to confirm. If you are finished with FTP, click the *Exit* button to close the WS_FTP window.

## CHANGING WS_FTP OPTIONS

Click the *Options* button in the lower portion of the WS_FTP window to display the configuration menu. Although we will not illustrate any options in this unit, Table 7.2 shows an assortment of changes that you can make.

**TABLE 7.2**
*WS_FTP
configuration
options*

| MENU | ITEMS |
|---|---|
| Program Options | Change how window displays; set text viewer program. |
| Session Options | Set warning sounds on or off (sounds can be annoying). |
| Pro Options | Options available under WS_FTP Pro version. |

You can also customize the startup directories in WS_FTP for any connection. Figure 7.9 shows the Session Properties dialog box shown earlier in this unit. With the Startup tab displayed, note that you can choose the initial remote and local directories for a particular session. Here you can customize each session for where files pertinent to that session are stored.

**FIGURE 7.9**
*Session properties
dialog box*

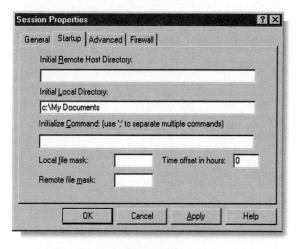

## WS_FTP PRO VERSION

Although WS_FTP95 LE is free for certain users, including academic and nonprofit institutions, the Pro version offers a few features that may be useful to frequent FTP users. Figure 7.10 shows the About WS_FTP screen available by clicking the *About* button in the lower part of the WS_FTP window, then choosing the *WS_FTP Pro tab*.

**Net Ethics**    *Username and Password Privacy*

Some FTP hosts require that you provide your username and/or e-mail address to log in. Have you ever wondered what is done with that information after you log off? And for those FTP hosts that permit anonymous FTP operations, is it ethical to provide a *false* e-mail address as your password?

**FIGURE 7.10**
*WS_FTP Pro
features*

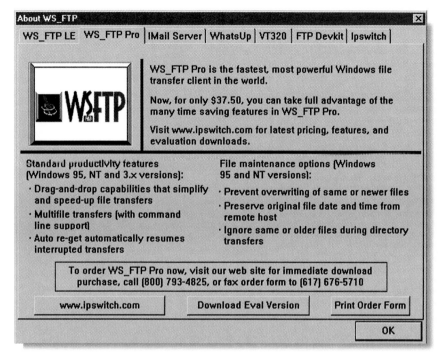

## Other FTP Methods

We have demonstrated two stand-alone FTP methods in this unit. FTP also may be accomplished in menu-driven Web browsers such as Internet Explorer and Netscape Navigator. Merely specify the FTP site's URL by prefixing it with *ftp://*. These programs show you a menu of information choices, and you can download a file merely by clicking on the hyperlink to that file. In this case the specific location and technical details are already stored in the menu. More FTP transfers are now being done through Internet Explorer and Netscape than through stand-alone FTP programs.

When publishing a home page to a Web server, you also need to use FTP. Many Web editors such as Netscape Gold and Netscape Composer provide for a built-in FTP that is accessed when you click the *Publish* button. See the next unit on creating your own home pages for information about publishing Web documents via FTP.

## Remote Logins—Telnet

You can use **Telnet** to log in over the Internet to a remote host computer. The terminal session is virtually identical to one you would have if you were present at the host computer's site, connected over its own LAN. Once you are connected, you can use all the resources made available on the host computer. Telnet is the software product that is used to perform the remote connection.

For example, you can connect to the Library of Congress Information System (LOCIS) and search the collection from nearly anywhere in the world. We'll show you a LOCIS example later in the unit. You can use Telnet to connect to the weather system at the University of Michigan. If you have an account on another computer system, you may be able to run a Telnet session to it from your regular host computer without logging off your regular host. Figure 7.11 shows the initial LOCIS display within a Telnet window.

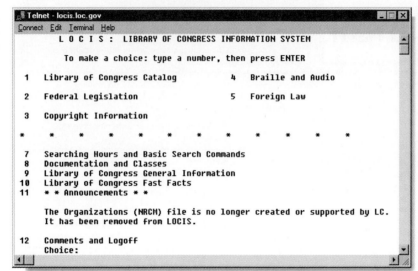

Popular Web browsers like Internet Explorer and Netscape Navigator permit Telnet sessions directly from the browser by prefixing the remote site's URL with *telnet://*. With these applications you don't have to remember the specific Telnet commands. However, you may need to inform your browser of the name and location of the Telnet program on your computer.

## Telnet Session with a Windows Telnet Program

A Windows-based Telnet program is easy to use. You set up your own username and password the first time you use the program. This information will be saved and transferred whenever you initiate a Telnet session. You can create a directory of Telnet sites and pick the site from a list rather than providing the detailed address each time you want to connect to that site. Windows 95 contains a Telnet program, called Telnet.exe, that usually is installed when TCP/IP is placed on your computer. This is the normal Telnet client program that emulates the DEC VT100 terminal. It is located in the C:\Windows folder on your computer.

## GUIDED ACTIVITY

## 7.3 Connecting to the Library of Congress via Telnet

In this activity, you will connect to the Library of Congress Information System (LOCIS) via Telnet and then search for information about a book.

1. Start Windows 95. Select *Run* from the Start menu and specify *Telnet* as the name of the program to run. Click *OK* to start Telnet.

2.  Use the *Connect→Remote* system menu bar command to specify the location of the remote host. Figure 7.12 shows the Telnet Connect dialog box, with the LOCIS host name entered. Click *Connect* to open the Telnet session.

**FIGURE 7.12**
*Telnet Connect dialog box*

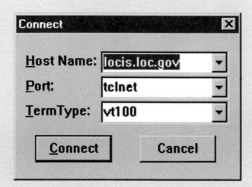

3.  In order to see your own commands with the LOCIS host, you need to turn on local echo. Use the *Terminal→Preferences* command and put a check next to Local echo.

**CAUTION**   If you get a double-echo of each typed character, go into the *Terminal→Preference* menu and remove the check next to Local echo. Each Telnet host is configured differently.

4.  The opening LOCIS menu was previously shown in Figure 7.11. Type 1 and press *Enter* to access the Library of Congress Catalog.

5.  Figure 7.13 shows the various catalogs available in LOCIS. We want the third one, BOOKS cataloged since 1975. Type 3 and press *Enter*. The Telnet box will scroll as you proceed with the Telnet session. You can review previous material by using the vertical scroll bar at the right side of the box.

**FIGURE 7.13**
*LOCIS catalogs available*

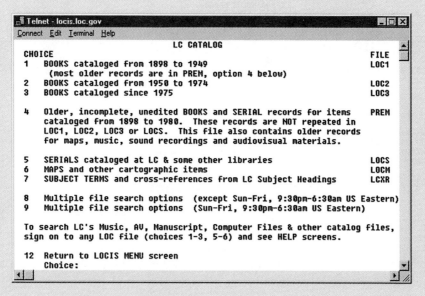

6. Figure 7.14 shows the next LOCIS search menu within the Telnet client window. We're going to look for books written by John Grisham, so type `browse grisham, john` and press *Enter*.

```
Telnet - locis.loc.gov                                    [_][□][X]
Connect  Edit  Terminal  Help
To choose from list, see examples at bottom.              FILE: LOC3
Terms alphabetically close to:GRISHAM, JOHN

B01 Grisham, Charles M//(AUTH=2)
B02 Grisham, Edith P//(AUTH=1)
B03 Grisham, J. David//(AUTH=1)
B04 Grisham, Jim//(AUTH=1)
B05 Grisham, Joe W//(AUTH=1)
B06+Grisham, John--//(AUTH=13; SUBJ=1)
B07 Grisham, Matthew B//(AUTH=1)
B08 Grisham, Noel//(AUTH=1)
B09 Grisham, Roy A//(AUTH=1)
B10 Grisham, Violet//(AUTH=1)
B11 Grishanina, M. A//(AUTH=1)
B12 Grishanov, Eduard//(AUTH=2)

---EXAMPLES: s b6       (SELECTs line b6; creates a SET for each term type)
             f b6-b8/b10 (FINDs b6-b8 and b10; combines sets, displays result
             r b6       (RETRIEVEs term on b6; searches text in some files)
             r subj=b6  (RETRIEVEs term type specified; e.g., SUBJ, TITL)

  Next page of BROWSE list, press ENTER key.  More info, type HELP BROWSE.
  READY:
```

7. The next screen will list different records from different authors. The John Grisham that we want should be set to 6. Type `f b6` and press *Enter*. LOCIS should return the set of Grisham books shown in Figure 7.15. Notice the information displayed in the citation for each title including the first book that has not yet been received by the Library. Press *Enter* to see the next screen of Grisham books

```
Telnet - locis.loc.gov                                    [_][□][X]
Connect  Edit  Terminal  Help
  For more information on the BROWSE command, type:  HELP BROWSE

  BRWS0003  Ready for new command:

ITEMS 1-4 OF 14              SET 3: BRIEF DISPLAY           FILE: LOC3
                               (DESCENDING ORDER)
1. 97-47484: Grisham, John.  The street lawyer /  1st ed.  New York :
   Doubleday, 1998.  p. cm.
   CIP - NOT YET IN LC
2. 96-54702: Grisham, John.  The partner /  1st ed.  New York : Doubleday,
   c1997.  366 p. ; 25 cm.
   LC CALL NUMBER: PS3557.R5355 P35 1997
3. 96-35026: Pringle, Mary Beth, 1943-  John Grisham : a critical companion /
   Westport, Conn. : Greenwood Press, 1997.  xi, 139 p. ; 25 cm.
   LC CALL NUMBER: PS3557.R5355 Z82 1997
4. 96-13872: Grisham, John.  The runaway jury /  1st ed.  New York : Doubleday
   1996.  401 p. ; 25 cm.
   LC CALL NUMBER: PS3557.R5355 R8 1996

NEXT PAGE:        press transmit or enter key
SKIP AHEAD/BACK:  type any item# in set          Example--> 25
FULL DISPLAY:     type DISPLAY ITEM plus an item# Example--> display item 2
READY:
```

8. Finally you need to log out from LOCIS. At the Ready prompt type `bye` and press *Enter*. At the next menu type `12` to log off, then type `12` once again to confirm your log off. Telnet will inform you that the connection was lost as you disconnected. You can close the Telnet window with *Connect→Exit* or by clicking the *Close* button.

## Other Telnet Applications

As you will see in later units, it is possible to Telnet into an Internet host and run programs on that host. The Telnet session causes the output from that session to be sent to your own computer. For example, some schools allow you to Telnet into the student information system and retrieve information about e-mail addresses, class schedules, grades, financial aid, and so forth. For example, Figure 7.16 shows a Telnet session with Purdue University's SSINFO system.

**FIGURE 7.16**
*Purdue SSINFO System*

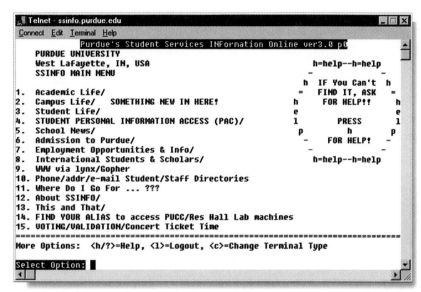

Another application for Telnet occurs when you want to log in to your own computer while away from your office or residence. If you have set it up as a Telnet host on the network, you can find another computer, and then use Telnet to get into your computer and have access to its resources. For instance, you might create a private e-mail system that avoids going through normal e-mail channels. When users want to send or read mail, they would Telnet into that host and then use its own internal mail system.

File Transfer Protocol (FTP) is the method used to upload and download files over the Internet. In FTP files are divided into two categories: text (or ASCII) and binary. You must select the correct type before you transfer the file. Zip files are compressed and transfer more quickly than uncompressed files. Zip files often contain multiple files that are transferred with one command. Programs like PKZIP and WinZip can be used to compress and uncompress these files. Some EXE programs are compressed and contain the decompression software within the file itself.

Windows 95 comes with a built-in command line FTP program that permits you to exchange files with FTP hosts. Anonymous FTP allows you to retrieve files without having an authorized username; you must provide your e-mail address as the password.

WS_FTP is an easy-to-use FTP program with a graphical interface for Windows users. You can change directories by double-clicking the desired directory name. There are command buttons for viewing the contents of text files and renaming a file. You can see the contents of the file directory in a Notepad window. Your Web browser is also capable of doing FTP downloads; specify the URL by prefixing it with ftp://.

Telnet is used for remote logins to a host computer. Windows 95 comes with a built-in Telnet program, and others are available to download. With Telnet you see a text screen as though you were running a terminal session with the remote computer.

## Command Review

**Command-Line FTP:**

| | |
|---|---|
| ascii | Set file transfer type to ASCII (text). |
| binary | Set file transfer type to binary. |
| bye | Close FTP connection and exit program. |
| cd *directory* | Change to the specified subdirectory. |
| cd .. | Change to the parent directory. |
| dir | Display file names and related information from the current directory. |
| ftp | Begin the command line FTP program. |
| get *filename* | Transfer specified file from host to your local computer. |
| help | Get list of FTP commands. |
| mget *file1, file2* | Transfer specified list of files from host to your local computer. |
| open *hostname* | Connect to the specified FTP host. |
| put *filename* | Transfer specified file from your local computer to the host. |
| send *filename* | Transfer specified file from your local computer to the host. |
| pwd | Show the name of the current directory. |
| status | Give current FTP status including transfer type. |

**Windows WS_FTP buttons:**

| | |
|---|---|
| ChgDir | Change to specified directory or folder. |
| Close | Close connection with FTP host (not Close window). |
| Connect | Specify host name and connection parameters, including username. |
| Copy | Copied selected file(s) in specified direction between Remote and Local computers. |

| | |
|---|---|
| DirInfo | Give information about specified directory. |
| Exit | Close WS_FTP window. |
| Rename | Rename selected file. |
| Transfer arrow | Click ASCII or Binary button to set transfer type, then click arrow. |
| View | Display text file in Notepad window. |

## Vocabulary Exercise

*Write a short definition for each term in the following list.*

| | | |
|---|---|---|
| Anonymous FTP | File Transfer Protocol (FTP) | Upload |
| ASCII file | Self-extracting file | WinZip |
| Binary file | Subdirectory | WS_FTP client |
| Download | Telnet | Zip |

## Review Questions

1. What is the purpose for FTP on the Internet?

2. Why do we use zip when transferring files? How do we get the files back to their original state?

3. Describe the use of ASCII and binary transfer types in FTP. When is each used?

4. What is anonymous FTP? What other information should you provide when using anonymous FTP?

5. Why is it preferable to use FTP with a Web browser rather than with an FTP client like WS_FTP?

6. Suppose you want to transfer a file over the Internet to your computer. What factors affect the time it takes to complete the transfer?

7. Describe the purpose of each of these FTP commands:

   a. open          e. status

   b. cd            f. get

   c. cdup          g. mget

   d. pwd           h. put

8. Contrast use of a Windows FTP client with a command-line client. Which is preferred, and why?

9. Explain *why* one would want to perform Telnet sessions with remote hosts.

10. How would you obtain a Windows Telnet program?

## Exercises

1. Write the precise DOS FTP commands necessary to connect to the imaginary FTP server at *ftp.noplace.com*. The file to be transferred is called *wsg-12.exe*, and it is located in the */pub/wsapps/gophers* subdirectory. The file type is binary. Assume that you are performing an anonymous FTP login. Do *not* attempt this FTP transfer.

2. Use your own FTP client software to retrieve the file called *ws_ftple.zip* from the FTP server called *ftp.ipswitch.com*. Hint: the file is located in the */Ipswitch/ Product_Downloads/* subdirectory.

3. Expand the *ws_ftple.zip* file you downloaded in Exercise 2 and count the number of files contained inside. Examine the *Common.txt* file stored in the *.zip* file and write down the last sentence from that file.

4. Use your own Windows FTP client software to retrieve the file called *photo.gif* from the FTP server whose address is *mama.indstate.edu*. The file is found in the */internet_book/* subdirectory. Be sure to match case.

5. Use your Web browser to access the Microsoft FTP server at *ftp://ftp.microsoft.com/*. Print the contents of the DISCLAIM.TXT file, then switch to the */Products/Windows/Windows95/CDRomExtras/FunStuff/* subdirectory. Download the file called *clouds.exe* and expand it in a temporary folder on your hard drive or network account. This is a 123 MB file. What is contained in this compressed file?

6. Continue the Telnet activity begun in this unit by using your own Telnet client to connect to the Library of Congress Information System (LOCIS). The address is *locis.loc.gov*. Once there, choose the first entry, *Library of Congress Catalog*. Select *BOOKS cataloged since 1975* and you should see a screen similar to Figure 7.13. Continue as in Guided Activity 7.3 and use the *browse* command to locate the catalog information for the 2nd edition of this textbook, *Understanding & Using the Internet*. Write down the LOCIS number for that book.

7. Point your Web browser to the WinZip home page at *http://www.winzip.com*. Follow instructions to download the evaluation version of the WinZip compression software. Install this in your computer if possible. What is the purpose of this program?

## Download a Browser

If you do not already have a current browser version on your computer, visit the Web site of Netscape or Microsoft to download a copy. The Netscape home page is found at *http://home.netscape.com*, while Microsoft is located at *http://www.microsoft.com*. Follow the links to the download sections. Both products are free to all users. Remember that the FTP sites are busiest right after a new browser version is released.

**CAUTION**

Be careful what options you select for downloading—these files can be very large and can take several hours to download from the FTP server via modem. Avoid downloading during the middle of the day when the Internet is busiest.

### *PROJECT TEAM OPTION*

Download *both* products and prepare an instruction sheet for the download process for each company. If you have limited time or space on your local computer, cancel the download of the second product after you have begun the download.

# Creating Web Documents in HTML

This unit presents an introduction to creating Web documents—or home pages—using HTML. The material in this unit is based on Windows Notepad and the Netscape Composer home page editor. You also may use other Web editors such as the one packaged with Internet Explorer. The unit is *not* necessary for those who are interested only in surfing the Internet.

## Learning Objectives

At the completion of this unit, you should be able to

1. explain the steps in creating a home page,

2. list the five basic elements of a home page,

3. describe how Web documents are formatted with HTML tags,

4. use Notepad to create a simple home page,

5. create a hyperlink to another Internet resource,

6. use a Web editor like Netscape Composer to create a home page,

7. add an image to a Web page,

8. apply formatting to a home page with Composer,

9. create a table in a home page.

## Key Terms

*The following terms are introduced in this unit. Be sure you know what each of them means.*

Anchor
Common Gateway Interface (CGI)
Frame
HyperText Markup Language (HTML)
Image
Image map
Link
Microsoft Front Page
Netscape Composer
Notepad
Ordered list
Script
Table
Tag
Text file
Unordered list
Webmaster

## Basics of Web Documents

You learned in earlier units that pages on the Web are actually documents written in the HyperText

Markup Language, or HTML. These documents contain normal text phrases but have special format codes, called tags, to activate and deactivate hypertext features. As discussed in previous units, Web browsers such as Netscape are able to display HTML formatted documents. Although not every browser reacts identically to a particular format tag, most are similar.

Netscape Navigator has a source viewer that enables you to see the hypertext commands that produce the final formatted page. Use the *View→Document Source* command to view the HTML source document in a read-only window; you cannot make any changes to the HTML source document in this window. With Internet Explorer use the *View→Source* command; it will open your document in a Notepad window where you can display or edit the HTML commands. One of the simplest ways to create new HTML documents is to save favorite pages on your disk drive. You then open the source documents in a word processor and examine the tags used, copying them into your own document.

It is *not* necessary to know how to create HTML documents in order to retrieve information from the Web. For those who are interested in writing their own HTML documents, we present a brief overview of HTML in this section. Numerous documents located on the Web are available to help you create your own HTML pages. An excellent primer on HTML is called *A Beginner's Guide to HTML* and is found at *http://www.ncsa.uiuc.edu/General/Internet/WWW/HTMLPrimer.html*.

In order to create a home page or Web document, you must follow these steps. Each is important—don't leap right to the HTML editor.

- Decide on the content of your Web site.

- Design each document on paper first.

- Use an editor to create the home page.

- Test the home page as a file.

- Upload (publish) the home page to the Web server.

- Maintain the home page making changes as necessary.

## Basic Structure of a Home Page

A home page or Web document is a text file. A text file contains only regular text characters, also called *ASCII characters*. It is not formatted and can be viewed and modified with any text editor such as Notepad. The formatting is done by a Web browser such as Netscape Navigator.

A home page usually contains five or more kinds of elements. Each is previewed next. A complete discussion of commonly used HTML tags follows this overview.

---

NET TIP

**Web Addresses**

Current links to most Web sites in this book can be found on the *Understanding & Using the Internet* Home Page. Choose **Resources** at **computered.swep.com**. Remember that a Web address may change at any time. An address given in this book as an example may no longer be valid. If this is so, either access the Home Page for the current link or do a search to find a similar site (see Unit 5 for a discussion of search methods).

## HEAD SECTION

The head section appears at the top of a home page and provides the title for the document, reference information such as the creator, creation/modification date, and name of the editor used to create the page. The head section begins with **<HEAD>** and ends with **</HEAD>**. Capitalization does not matter with HTML codes—use uppercase or lowercase or mix them. A typical head section appears below with the HTML tags shown in bold.

```
<HEAD>

<META NAME = "Author" CONTENT="Bruce Mclaren">

<META NAME="GENERATOR" CONTENT="Mozilla/4.03 [en] (Win95; I)
[Netscape]">

<TITLE> Understanding & Using the Internet </TITLE>

I) [Netscape]">

</HEAD>
```

## BODY SECTION

The body section contains most of the remainder of your Web page. It has the words that users see when they access your page and contains other settings that affect the entire document such as background color, wallpaper, and so forth. Anything that is not interpreted as an HTML tag in your document is considered body text and displayed as is.

HTML has one frustrating characteristic—it does not preserve your own horizontal spacing between words, sentences, and paragraphs. In fact, Web browsers will happily insert one space, even if you put in 30 spaces, six tab characters, or press *Enter*. The special tag to indicate the beginning of the paragraph is **<P>**. If you want to preserve your own spacing, surround your text with **<PRE>** and **</PRE>** preformatted tags as shown later in the unit.

## HEADLINES

Headlines serve the same purpose in a home page as they do in a newspaper or magazine. They subdivide sections of your page, grab your eye, and set things apart. HTML documents can have up to six levels of headlines. We'll discuss **<H1>** through **<H6>** headline tags later in this unit.

## IMAGES

Most Web documents contain images. They could be large image maps, such as those appearing on the first page of the ISU home page, or tiny icons that say "New" or "Under Construction." Horizontal lines are images. Images make your page more attractive and convey meaning that would be difficult with words alone. Unfortunately, too many Web page designers clutter their document with images that take a long time to download. We'll discuss the appropriate roles of images and image maps later in the unit.

## LINKS TO OTHER DOCUMENTS

Most home pages point to other resources on the Internet. We talked about links in Unit 4—they can be underlined words or image maps with embedded buttons. The basic concept of hypertext implies that you can jump to other pages in a hierarchical fashion. We'll show you how to create links later in the unit.

# HTML Tags

The format codes known as HTML tags are surrounded with < > bracket characters, and they often come in pairs. That is, there is a tag to turn on a feature and a paired tag to turn off that feature. For example, an HTML document should begin with an **<HTML>** tag and end with **</HTML>**. Likewise,

```
<TITLE>Krannert School of Management</TITLE>
```

means that "Krannert School of Management" will be placed in the title bar of your Web browser. Case does not matter in HTML documents, so **<title>** is the same as **<TITLE>**.

If you make an error, your Web browser will ignore lines containing those tags. A common error made by new users is to create a tag with mismatched brackets, such as **<H2)**. Some commercial HTML editor products will let you apply HTML formatting codes just as easily as you format text in your own word processor. These packages will even let you try out new HTML documents without having to take your page live on the Internet. We'll demonstrate Netscape Composer, the HTML editor module found in Netscape Communicator, later in this unit.

## BASIC HTML CODES

Several appearance codes are used in most HTML documents. **<B>** turns on bold face; **</B>** ends the bold style. **<I>** turns on italic; **</I>** turns off italic. **<H1>** through **<H6>** activate headline fonts, with H1 being the largest and H6 the smallest; the headline ends with a matching **</Hn>** tag. **<CENTER>** will center the text that follows, up to the **</CENTER>** tag.

In HTML documents, paragraph formatting is done automatically. If the user switches to a wider window, your Web browser will automatically adjust where lines break. A hard return or blank space inserted into the document will be ignored. To end a paragraph, use the **</P>** tag. The Web browser will start a new paragraph after that tag.

The **<HR>** tag produces a horizontal ruler (line) that extends across the entire width of the browser window. Use this to separate items on the page.

## OTHER HTML TAGS

Tags are available for creating lists of items, inserting graphic images, and inserting preformatted text. The examples below demonstrate use of these tags.

**DISPLAYING A NUMBERED OR BULLETED LIST**  To display an ordered list or itemized list with numbers, use the following HTML tags:

```
<OL><LI> Accounting
```

```
<LI> Finance

<LI> MIS</OL>
```

These tags will produce the following output in a Web page:

1. Accounting

2. Finance

3. MIS

If you substitute **<UL>** for **<OL>** above, your Web browser will display the same items as an unordered list with bullets instead of numbers.

**DISPLAYING AN IN-LINE IMAGE** To display an in-line image, use the **<IMG>** tag with appropriate information inside the brackets. For instance,

```
<IMG SRC="logo.gif" ALT="ISU Libraries">
```

will display the graphic image file called *logo.gif* found on the current server. For those browsers without graphics capability, you can (optionally) display alternate text such as ISU Libraries. Add ALIGN=TOP or ALIGN=MIDDLE to the **<IMG>** tag to align the image with adjacent text.

**USING EXTERNAL IMAGES AND SOUNDS** To display external images or sounds, use the normal anchor method but specify the file's URL as part of the **<A>** tag. For instance,

```
<A HREF="Welcome.wav">Welcome to our Page</A>
```

will play a wave (sound) file called *welcome.wav* located on the current server. If the file is found on another server, provide the full path to that file. The file extension is the key to what type of file it is. Use the *Edit→Preferences→Navigator→ Applications* menu in Netscape to learn the file extensions for various types of external files. Movies or animations frequently come with the *.avi, qt,* or *.mov* file extension. Netscape uses helper applications for all but *.html, .txt, .gif,* and *.jpeg* files.

**DISPLAYING PREFORMATTED TEXT** Because Netscape ordinarily wraps each line of text at the current right margin, depending on the width of the window, you may want to insert preformatted text with the line breaks already inserted. Use the **<PRE>** tag before the text, and **</PRE>** after that text. For example, this text will be displayed as it appears with spacing and line breaks at the indicated places:

```
<PRE>Four score and seven years ago

Our fathers brought forth on this continent a new nation,

conceived in liberty,

and dedicated to the proposition that all men are created equal. </PRE>
```

### *CREATING A LINK TO ANOTHER WEB DOCUMENT*

To create an anchor with a link to another HTML document, use the **<A>** tag and include the type and address of the linked document within the tag. For example, the following tag would retrieve a document called *home.html* found on the *www.indstate.edu* Web server:

```
<A HREF="http://www.indstate.edu/home.html">Main menu</A>
```

The *Main menu* phrase would be highlighted in the Web page, signifying that the user could click anywhere on that line to activate the link to the home page.

Here's another example that shows how a linked item would appear in HTML:

```
<FONT SIZE=4><A HREF = "Busweek.html">Krannert Rated Top 20 in
Business Week!</A></FONT SIZE=4><P>
```

In this case, *Krannert Rated Top 20 in Business Week!* will appear on a separate line and will be highlighted as a link. This relative link is to another HTML page called *Busweek.html* on the *same server* as this page. The tag **<FONT SIZE=4>** activates that font size for this line, then the matching **</FONT SIZE=4>** deactivates that font size. Although not demonstrated here, the **<BASEFONT=n>** tag sets the size of the base font that is in effect unless a separate font size command is issued.

## Web Page Design Considerations

Before you fire up your HTML editor, think carefully about what you want to convey with your Web document. Creating a good Web document is probably tougher than creating a good term paper. You have more elements to work with and need to have a sense of artistic style to make everything work together.

Here are some tips for good page design:

- Keep document size to a minimum to allow quicker downloads. It is better to subdivide larger documents into smaller ones that can be called from the first home page.

- For larger home pages, use good hierarchical design in which the user can jump directly to the desired material, then return. Use a table of contents approach at the top of your document.

- Use fewer (or smaller) graphic images in your Web document. We suggest limiting graphic size to 20 KB or less if possible, particularly if you include multiple documents. Under typical busy Internet conditions, a 20 KB image may transfer at less than 2,500 bits per second with a modem; that means it will take more than a minute to receive the image, assuming 8 bits per byte. Users get anxious when pages load slowly.

- Consider alternate text-only pages for dial-up users that can be selected at the top of the page. Keep the basic text elements, but replace the graphic images with simple headings. Substitute simple link lines for image maps. Many commercial sites offer this feature.

**Net Ethics**     *Borrowing from a Web Site*

Is it ethical to "borrow" material from someone else's Web site to put into your own home page? In other words, are you free to copy graphic images, good designs, applets, and text phrases that you find on the Internet?

- Look for design guidelines from your college or organization. In many cases there will be a set of recommendations for Web documents—probably posted on the organization's home page.

- Also check your organization for a library of graphic images, icons, and other graphic elements that you can use in your own home page.

- Remember that your page will be viewed by people with many different kinds of browsers. Avoid using "special" features that work only in one browser because others may not be able to view those features. The worst case is that your page will not open in that browser.

- Take advantage of other pages that you find at your organization, using their best parts. Copy them, and then change the words and images to fit your situation. You'll save a great deal of time and learn about HTML as well.

- Review other pages critically, comparing them to your work. Ask other developers to review your page and make suggestions for improvements.

- Always put the last revision date and your name in the bottom of the Web page. That way you and your viewers can tell the version of the page on the screen. Add a *mailto:* command at the end of your page so that viewers can provide feedback. The link destination *mailto:mfbjm@befac.indstate.edu* would open a browser mail window with the recipient's e-mail address already in the message.

- Proofread your work before you put it out on the Internet!

- Check some on-line references such as "Composing Good HTML" at *http://www.cs.cmu.edu/~tilt/cgh/* and "A Basic HTML Style Guide" at *http://guinan.gsfc.nasa.gov/Style.html/*. You also might want to check out the "Bad Style Page" at *http://www.earth.com/bad-style/*.

- Many books about creating Web sites are available at your bookstore; they may come with CD-ROMs containing sample pages and HTML shareware software for Windows, Macintosh, and UNIX users.

## HTML Editors

Each of the programs in this section can be used to enter the contents of your home page, including the HTML formatting tags. They range from simple programs like Notepad, to friendly programs like Netscape Composer, to more sophisticated commercial programs like Microsoft's Front Page. For the work in this unit, we suggest you use Notepad or a beginner-level HTML editor program like Netscape Composer.

### WINDOWS NOTEPAD

Notepad is free because it has been built in to Windows and Windows 95. It is simple to use but requires the most typing. It is unaware of any HTML formatting tags so you must type those in yourself. The next Guided Activity shows you how to use Notepad to create a simple HTML document.

## WORD PROCESSOR ADD-IN

Free HTML editor add-ins are available for Microsoft Word (version 6.0a or later) and WordPerfect (version 6.1 or later.) That is, you can download and install these templates, and then create new HTML documents within your word processor. If you have MS Word 97 or later, the Web publishing tools add-in already comes with the CD-ROM but must be installed.

With a word processor add-in, use the *File→New* command, select the Web Pages or HTML template from the list, and begin typing your document. When you need to specify some HTML format, highlight the text and choose the HTML style from the word processor's menu bar or toolbar. You save the document in HTML format with an *.htm* extension. Word 97 has a built-in Web browser for previewing your home page. These products are convenient but don't offer a full range of HTML features.

## NETSCAPE COMMUNICATOR/COMPOSER

The Netscape Communicator Standard edition includes an easy-to-use Web editor called Composer. We'll have several Guided Activities that demonstrate how to create a home page with Composer. Netscape Composer is easy to use and produces Web documents quickly. Use the *File→New* command to open a new document, and then add elements by selecting them from the menu bar or toolbar. Save the document, and then click the *Netscape* button to preview your finished document in the Navigator browser module. The previous version of Composer was called Netscape Gold.

## MICROSOFT FRONT PAGE

Microsoft Front Page is a sophisticated Web site publishing product introduced in 1996. Front Page is designed to work best with Microsoft's Internet Explorer browser, but it will work with Netscape and other browsers as well. It has more features than any of the HTML editors mentioned previously and sells for approximately $100. Like Netscape Composer, it uses a WYSIWYG editor so that you can immediately see what the page will look like when someone views it in a Web browser. You can add sophisticated features including graphics—without programming. For more information about Front Page, see the Web site at *http://www. microsoft.com/frontpage/*.

## OTHER HTML EDITORS

Several other HTML editors are worth mentioning. Mostly designed for the serious HTML developer, they bring advanced capabilities and are somewhat more difficult to use. Each has built-in menus for HTML tags and styles. Some products are available in a free, lower-powered starter version that can be upgraded to the full package on the Internet. Some are shareware that come with a 30-day free evaluation period but then must be registered.

Several of these require that you use your own Web browser to see what the page actually will look like. Some of the better known products include:

- HTML Writer

**TIP**

An HTML add-in is useful when a word processor document already exists. Open it in your word processor, and then save it as an HTML document. Some of the formatting may be lost, but much is converted to HTML. You can "clean up" the remaining problems with an HTML editor.

**TIP**

You also can use Communicator to edit existing HTML files that you display in Navigator. From the browser window, use *File→Edit Page* to open the page in Composer. Then follow the same process as creating a new Web document.

- HTML Assistant
- HTMLed
- Hot Dog Professional
- Quarterdeck WebAuthor

# Creating an HTML Document Using Notepad

A quick way to enter HTML tags is to use a text editor like Windows Notepad. If you choose to use a word processor to enter the HTML tags, be sure to save the file as a text file and *not* in the native word processor format. Type in your Web document, including HTML tags. Make any changes, and then save the formatted document as a text (or ASCII) file. Finally, open the HTML file in your browser and view the results.

## Using Notepad for a Simple Document

Notepad is in the Accessories group on the *Start→Programs* menu. It will open up with a blank document as shown in Figure 8.1. If you already know how to use Notepad, you can skip to the next section.

**FIGURE 8.1**
*Windows Notepad window*

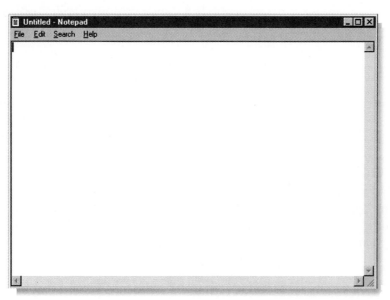

Notepad works like a mini word processor—it has word wrap, allows you to set margins and choose portrait or landscape mode, and works with the Windows Clipboard. You do not need to make any configuration changes to use Notepad for creating HTML documents.

Creating an HTML document in Notepad can be tedious because you have to type in each of the HTML tags. We recommend that you start with something small, such as the home page in the next Guided Activity. Create the document, *saving it frequently* with *File→Save* as you would with any paper you are preparing.

Use the *.htm* file extension (*not .txt*) when you save it. Remember *where* you save it because you will have to tell Netscape or your Web browser where to look for the saved file. Leave Notepad open for now while you load Netscape or your Web browser.

## Trying Your Home Page in Netscape

Use the *File→Open Page* (*Ctrl+O*) command in Netscape to retrieve and execute your HTML page. The Open Page dialog box is shown in Figure 8.2. You can open the file in Navigator for browsing or in Composer for editing. If you click the *Choose File* button, Netscape will show you the *.htm* and *.html* files in the Open dialog box; you must navigate to the folder containing the HTML document you created with Notepad. Select the file, and then click *Open.*

**FIGURE 8.2**

*Netscape Open Page dialog box*

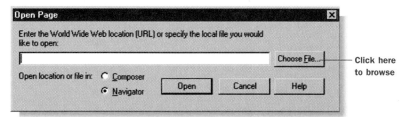

Click here to browse

Netscape will open the HTML document and format it according to your instructions. If you included image files, they should be stored in the same folder as the HTML document in order for Netscape to find them. Later on, you will upload those files to the Web server.

To make changes, return to the Notepad window and open by clicking on the *Notepad* button in the Taskbar. Make changes to your HTML document and then save it again. Switch back to Netscape and click the *Reload* button to see how the changes worked. Creating an HTML document is an iterative process (meaning you "run it over and over until it's right"), much like writing a computer program. Expect lots of trial and error!

## GUIDED ACTIVITY

## 8.1    Creating a Simple HTML Document

In this activity, you will use Windows Notepad to create a simple HTML document, save it as a disk file, and then load that document in Netscape. You may do this work away from the computer lab because it does not require a live Internet connection.

1.  If you haven't already started Windows 95, do so now.

2.  Click the *Start* button, select *Programs,* and then start Notepad from the Accessories program group.

**TIP**

**If you cannot find Notepad, any text editor should work in creating this simple HTML file, including the DOS EDIT program.**

3. Within Notepad, enter the following lines *exactly as listed*, pressing *Enter* at the end of each line.

   ```
   <HTML>
   <TITLE>My First HTML Page</TITLE>
   <H1>My Own Home Page</H1>
   <P><UL><LI>My Name<LI>My Address<LI>My Major <LI>My Telephone</P>
   </HTML>
   ```

4. Use the *File→Save* command in Notepad to save your document as *Example1. htm*.

5. Start Netscape or your own Web browser.

6. Issue the *File→Open Page (Ctrl+O)* command in Netscape (or the appropriate *File→Open* command in your browser); then specify the path and name of the file you saved in step 4. Make sure the Navigator button is selected, then click *Open*.

**Checkpoint 8A**  What is the meaning of the path of the file in step 6?

7. Netscape should display the page shown in Figure 8.3.

**FIGURE 8.3**
*Example1 home page in Netscape*

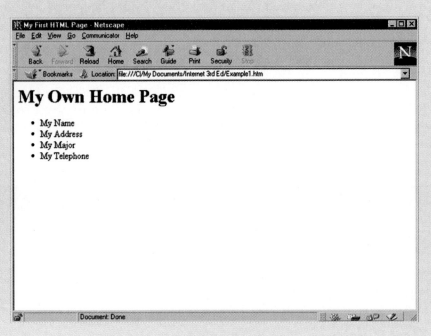

8. We will make some changes to this home page in the exercises at the end of the unit. Leave Notepad and Netscape open—we'll use them in the next activity.

## Adding Images and Graphic Elements

As mentioned previously, the HTML tag for inserting an in-line image is **<IMG>**. The basic format is **<IMG SRC="file">**. It has several options that may be specified within the tag. In the following table, "filename" refers to a valid URL address for a graphic image file, usually a *.gif* or *.jpg* file.

**TABLE 8.1**
*IMG Options*

| DISCUSSION | OPTION |
| --- | --- |
| Name of the file | SRC="filename" |
| Alternate text string if image is not available | ALT="text string" |
| Alignment for text on same line as image | ALIGN=TOP\|BOTTOM\|MIDDLE\|LEFT\|RIGHT |
| Alternate width of the image in pixels | WIDTH=nn—defaults to existing width |
| Alternate height of the image in pixels | HEIGHT=nn—defaults to existing height |
| Border size in pixels | BORDER=nn |
| Low resolution substitute file while hi res image is loading | LOWSRC="filename" |
| Image map declaration | ISMAP |

## GUIDED ACTIVITY

## 8.2   Adding an Image to a Home Page

In this activity, you will add an image to the home page you created in the previous activity. Your instructor will tell you where to locate the *Photo.gif* file; it is available on the textbook's home page at *http://computered.swep.com/* under Resources. You may use an image file of your own in this activity.

1. Start Windows 95 and open the Notepad editor. Use the *File→Open* command to open the *Example1.htm* file you created in the last activity.

2. In Notepad, scroll down to just above **</HTML>** and type the following line exactly as it appears.

   `<IMG SRC="photo.gif">This text appears to the right of the photo.</P>`

3. Use the *File→Save As* command to save the file under the name *Example2.htm*.

4. Open Netscape or switch to it if it is already open. Issue the *File→Open File in Browser* command and specify *Example2.htm*. You should see the home page as it appears in Figure 8.4.

 *If the photo displays as a question mark inside a small box, change the tag from step 2 to reflect the complete path where the* Photo.gif *file may be found, then resave the .htm file and click the* Reload *button in Netscape to fetch the revised HTML document.*

**FIGURE 8.4**

*Example2 home page in Netscape*

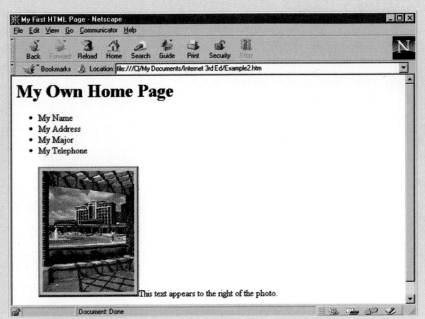

5. Now switch back to Notepad and add the following line just above the **</HTML>** tag, changing the size and placement of the image.

```
<IMG SRC="photo.gif" HEIGHT=100 WIDTH=75 ALIGN=RIGHT>This text is
at the left.
```

6. Save the file as *Example2.htm*, then switch to Netscape to see how it looks. See Figure 8.5.

**FIGURE 8.5**

*Example2 home page after step 6*

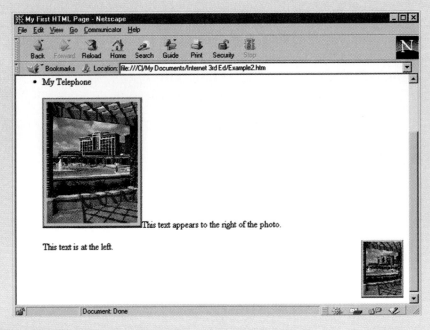

 **Checkpoint 8B**    What does the ALIGN=RIGHT parameter in the **<IMG>** tag of step 5 do?

7. Leave both Notepad and Netscape open for the next activity.

# Inserting Links

Links are called anchors in HTML and represent other Internet documents, usually HTTP files. As mentioned in Unit 4, Netscape is able to link to Gopher, Telnet, FTP, and Web documents. The **<A>** tag represents an anchor in HTML and requires a closing **</A>** tag at the end of the entry. There are several kinds of anchors in HTML, depending on the location of the other document.

### LINK TO ANOTHER WEB PAGE

Here you are creating a hyperlink to another Web page somewhere on the Internet. While it could be within the current document, this form assumes you are linking to the beginning of a different document.

Example: Here we create a link to the beginning of the HTML document called *access97.html* that resides on the server at *www.indstate.edu*. The text that comes next will appear as underlined words on the screen and can be clicked by the user.

```
<A HREF="www.indstate.edu/mclaren/access97.html">Access 7 Home Page</A>
```

### LINK TO A NAMED ANCHOR IN THE SAME DOCUMENT

Here we create a link to another named point within the same document. This link produces a faster jump than loading the entire document again. It does require that you first *define* the named point with an HTML anchor command such as **<A NAME="value"></A>** where *value* is the unique label that you use in the anchor link. Naming this point is equivalent to creating a bookmark in a word processor. In Netscape Composer, these named anchors are known as targets.

The anchor command to *jump* to a named point follows the notation, **<A HREF="#value">...</A>**. The # indicates this is a named anchor point within the current document.

Example: Suppose you have set up a document with section subtitles, each with a named anchor tag inserted. You want to set up different links to two points within the document, Summary and Details.

```
<A HREF="#Summary">Jump to Summary</A>

<A HREF="#Details">Jump to Details</A>

<A NAME="Summary"></A>

(... rest of summary text)

<A NAME="Details"></A>

(... rest of details text)
```

You will end up with Jump to Summary Jump to Details in your document.

**NOTE** **You must usually match capitalization for named anchors within your document. Thus Summary is not the same as summary.**

### SENDING E-MAIL FROM A WEB DOCUMENT

As mentioned earlier, Netscape and many other Web browsers provide an easy to use e-mail form. Create a regular anchor link, but specify "**mailto:***e-mail-address*" as the URL location in the anchor tag. Place any e-mail address in the "mailto" expression, and give some appropriate address. For example, the following expression will create an e-mail link to the author:

```
<A HREF="mailto:mfbjm@befac.indstate.edu">Mail to author</P>
```

The following activity will give you practice with links.

---

## GUIDED ACTIVITY

### 8.3  Using Links in a Home Page

In this activity, you will create a link to other Web documents and set up an e-mail link within your home page.

1.  Start Windows and load Notepad. We will create a new document from scratch, so if you still have the previous home page in Notepad, use the *File→New* command to clear it out.

2.  Type the following identifying lines as is. Press *Enter* at the end of each line.

```
<HTML>

<TITLE>Example Three</TITLE>

<H1>Example Three with Links</H1>
```

3.  Now we will create the link to several well-known Web sites. Type each line as shown.

```
<A HREF="http://home.netscape.com">Netscape Home Page</A></P>

<A HREF="http://www.microsoft.com">Microsoft Home Page</A></P>

</HTML>
```

4.  Now use *File→Save As* to save the file as *Example3.htm*.

5.  Either start Netscape or switch to it, and use the *File→Open File in Browser* command. Specify *Example3.htm* as the filename, and click *OK*. (See the Netscape window shown in Figure 8.6.) Move the cursor to one of the under-lined phrases and notice the pointer changes to a hand with pointing index finger. The address of each link is shown in the status bar when you move the mouse pointer over it.

6.  Switch back to Notepad, and add the following line just before **</HTML>**. Fill in your *own* e-mail address where indicated, without leaving any spaces.

**FIGURE 8.6**
*Example3 home
page with links*

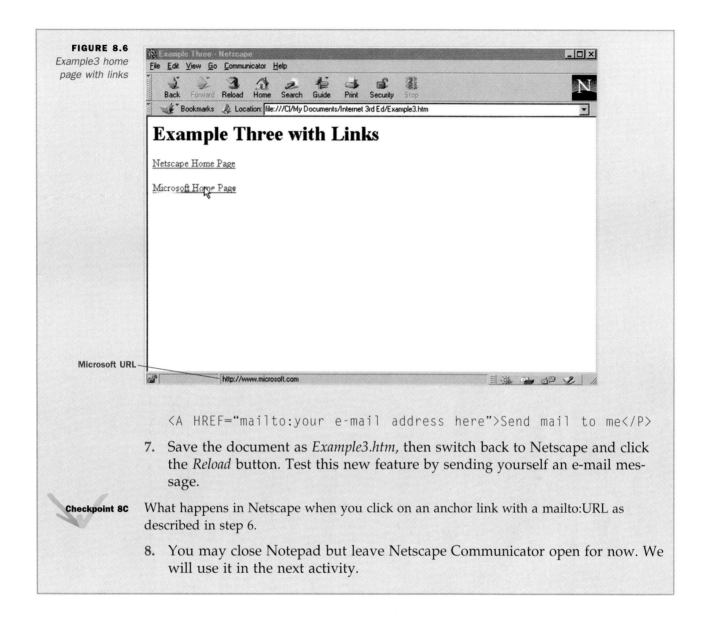

```
<A HREF="mailto:your e-mail address here">Send mail to me</P>
```

7. Save the document as *Example3.htm*, then switch back to Netscape and click the *Reload* button. Test this new feature by sending yourself an e-mail message.

**Checkpoint 8C** What happens in Netscape when you click on an anchor link with a mailto:URL as described in step 6.

8. You may close Notepad but leave Netscape Communicator open for now. We will use it in the next activity.

## Creating a Home Page with Netscape Composer

It is significantly less trouble to build a home page using a Web editor like Netscape Composer. When you open a new document in Netscape Communicator, an editor window opens in Netscape Composer. Type in your document, as with a word processor. Highlight the text to be formatted, and then select one of the HTML formatting styles by using the menu bar or toolbar. You will immediately see the results of most of your work in the editor window. Save the document, and then open another browser window for your file to see the final results. Finally, publish or upload the file to your Web server to make it available to others on the Internet. You will create a simple home page with Netscape Composer in the next activity.

# 8.4

## Creating a Simple Home Page with Netscape Composer

In this activity, you will create the same page as in Guided Activity 8.1, and then add a few extras. If you do not have access to Netscape Communicator or Internet Explorer, skip this activity. You do not need to be connected to the Internet to do this activity.

1. Begin Windows and start Netscape Communicator.

2. Use the *File→New* command and then select *Blank Page* (or press *Ctrl+Shift+N*). Netscape will create a second window for Composer as shown in Figure 8.7. The original browser window will remain open.

**FIGURE 8.7**

*Empty Netscape Composer editor window*

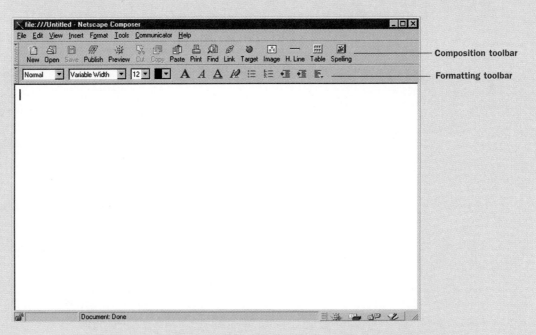

3. To name the document, use the *Format→Page Properties and Colors* command. Type My Own Gold Home Page in the Title box. In the Description box, type This is a sample home page created with Netscape Composer. Click *OK* to save the properties. See Figure 8.8. Netscape will display the new title in the title bar.

4. Click the down arrow next to the first button in the Formatting toolbar and select the Heading 1 style, meaning you will make this a large headline. Next type My Own Gold Home Page.

5. Press *Enter* to go to a new line. Composer should have gone back to the Normal font.

**FIGURE 8.8**
*Page Properties dialog box*

**Page Properties**    ☒

General | Colors and Background | META Tags |

Location:    file:///Untitled

T̲itle:    [My Own Gold Home Page]

A̲uthor:    [Bruce Mclaren]

D̲escription:    [                                    ]

┌─ Other attributes ─────────────────────────────┐
│         Use commas to separate multiple words or phrases.│
│  K̲eywords:    [                              ]  │
│                                                  │
│  C̲lassification:    [                          ] │
└──────────────────────────────────────────────────┘

[ OK ]    [ Cancel ]    [ A̲pply ]    [ Help ]

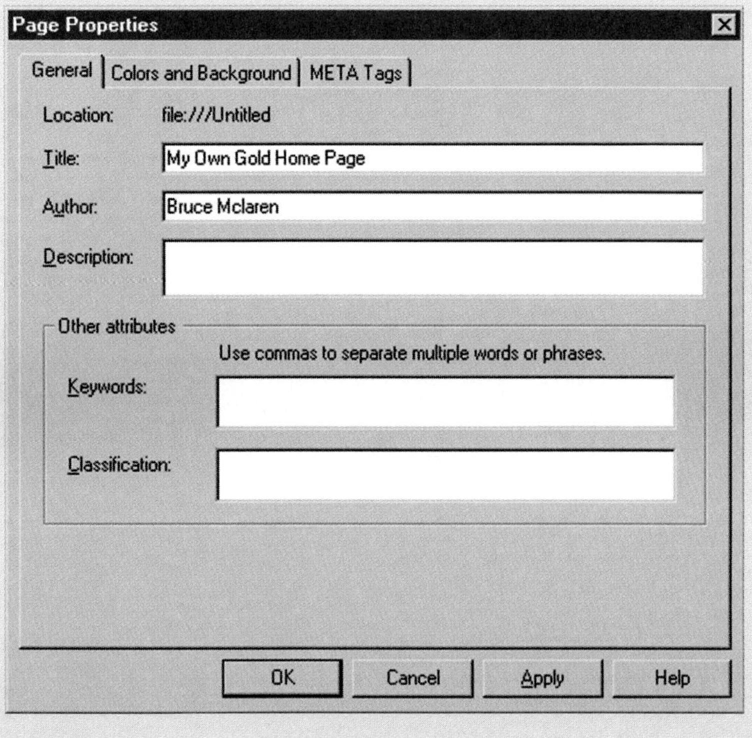

6. Next type in the following lines, ending each with *Enter*.

   My Name

   My Address

   My Major

   My Telephone

   My E-mail Address

7. Highlight these lines by dragging with the mouse, then click the *Bullet List* button in the Formatting toolbar, fifth from the right. Composer will move them closer together and place a bullet in front of each.

 **TIP**    You can save time by selecting the bullet list button before typing in the lines.

8. Click outside the list to remove the highlight. Press *Enter* once to go to a new line. If Netscape places a bullet on that line, click the bullet list button in the toolbar to remove the bullet.

9. Finally, we need to add the photograph used in a previous activity. Click the *Insert Image* button in the Composition toolbar, fourth from the right (or use the *Insert→Image* command). Next you will see the Image Properties dialog box, shown in Figure 8.9. Make sure the Image tab is displayed.

10. The name of the image file is *Photo.gif*. Make sure you specify the correct path to this file. For now leave the other properties unchanged. Click *OK* and Composer will place the image into your page.

**FIGURE 8.9**
*Image Properties
dialog box*

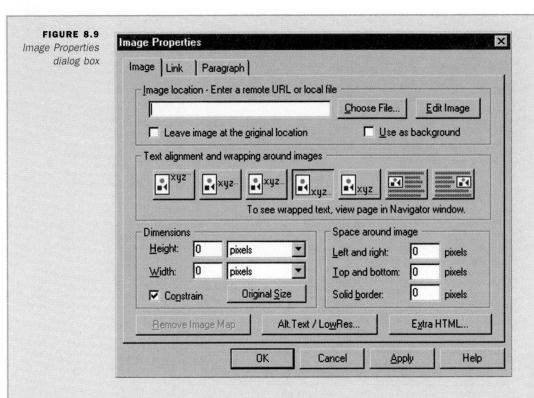

11.  Now we need to change the background color to gold. Issue the
     *Format→Page Colors and Properties* command again, but this time choose the
     *Colors and Background* tab, shown in Figure 8.10. In the lower center, click the
     *Background* button. From the Other menu, select gold, second element in the
     first row, and click *OK* two times to register your preference. Your page will
     now appear with a gold background.

**FIGURE 8.10**
*Colors and
Background
properties*

Change
background color

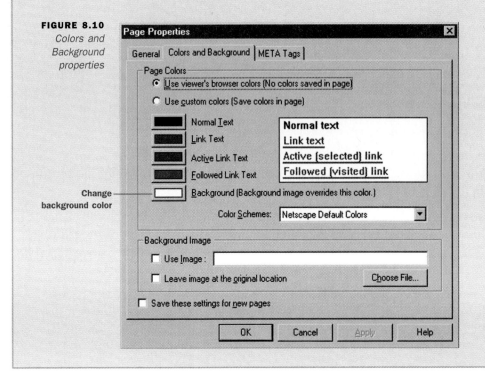

**TIP** You can create a true gold color by working with the Custom Colors portion of the Page Colors and Background Properties window. Click *Background*, click *Other*, and then pick the appropriate color from the color pattern.

12. To see the final result of your page, you must first save the document. Click the *Save* button in the Composition toolbar, and specify `Example4` as the filename.

13. Click the *Preview* button in the Composition toolbar. A new Netscape Navigator window will open with your page displayed, as shown in Figure 8.11.

**FIGURE 8.11**
*Netscape Example4 home page*

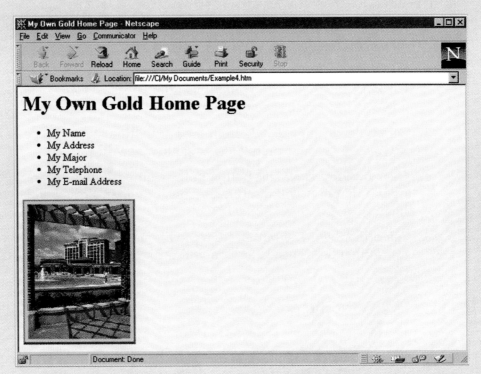

14. Switch back to Composer and close that application. Leave Netscape Communicator open for now.

 **TIP**

If you have a significant amount of text to enter that is already in a document, copy that text to the Clipboard and paste it into Composer.

# Creating a Complex Document with Netscape Composer

Netscape Composer supports most of the HTML 3.0 formatting extensions, including tables but not forms. This section will explore creating a more complex Web document using Netscape Composer. We will introduce Web formatting and hyperlinks in the next section.

## USING WEB FORMATTING WITH NETSCAPE COMPOSER

The usual text formatting options are available with Composer, including font name, font size, font color, bold, italic, underline, and text alignment. Composer supports numbered lists and unnumbered (bulleted) lists. The next activity gives you an opportunity to practice these skills.

## 8.5  Using Text Formatting and Hyperlinks

In this activity, you will build a formatted Web page that describes community volunteer programs. The page also features internal targets and links along with hyperlinks to external Web sites.

1. Switch to Netscape Communicator, and use the *Communicator→Page Composer* command to create a blank HTML document in the editor.

2. Use the *Format→Page Colors and Properties* command to set up the page title. Click the *General* tab and enter this title: `Community Volunteer Web Site`. Click *OK* to save the title.

3. Select the Heading 2 style from the Formatting toolbar, type `Community Volunteers`, and press *Enter* to go to a new line.

4. Click the *Horizontal Line* button in the Composition toolbar, third from the right. Composer will insert a horizontal divider. Press *Enter* to go to a new line.

5. Select the *Bullet List* button from the Formatting toolbar and type the following section headings. Later you will turn each one into a hyperlink.

   `United Way`

   `Heart Association`

   `Links to National Organizations`

6. Key in `United Way`. Then highlight that phrase, select *Heading 3* from the style list, and choose blue from the font color button in the Formatting toolbar. Press *Enter*.

7. Press the numbered list button, then type the following list of names, pressing *Enter* after each one: `John Richmond, Ellen Kimberly, Fred Garnett, Patty Dinten, Cate Lynn`.

8. Repeat steps 6 and 7 with `Heart Association` as the section heading. This time select red for the font color. The Heart Association volunteers are: `Amber Elkins, Bryce Adam, Peter Tennis, Wendy Labrecque`. Refer to Figure 8.12 to see how the page should look so far.

9. Now you can go back and fill in the targets and links. Move the cursor to the United Way section header above the list of volunteers. Click the *Target* button in the Composition toolbar to display the Target Properties dialog box shown in Figure 8.13. Key in `UnitedWay` and click *OK*.

 **TIP**    It is better to *not* use spaces in the middle of a target name because it ultimately becomes part of the URL.

**FIGURE 8.12**
*Community Volunteer home page after step 8*

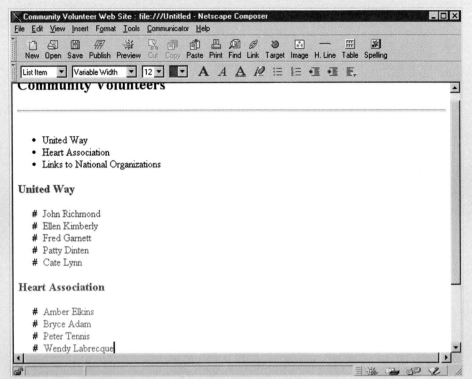

**FIGURE 8.13**
*Target Properties*

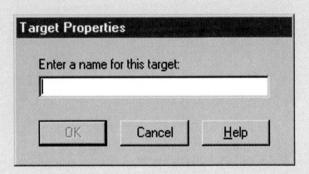

10. Repeat step 9 for the Heart Association section heading, this time choosing `HeartAssociation` as the target.

11. Now move the cursor up to the bullet list near the top of the page. Highlight the *United Way* label, then click the *Link* button in the Composition toolbar. You will see the Link properties as shown in Figure 8.14.

12. Select the *UnitedWay* target and click *OK* to assign this target to the United Way label. Composer will underline the label and display it as a hyperlink.

13. Repeat step 12 for the Heart Association label and select the *HeartAssociation* target.

14. Finally, highlight the *Links to National Organizations* label and click the *Link* button. In the Link section in the center of the box, type `http://www.unitedway.org` and click *OK*. Composer will create a hyperlink to the National United Way Web site.

FIGURE 8.14
*Link tab of
Character
Properties*

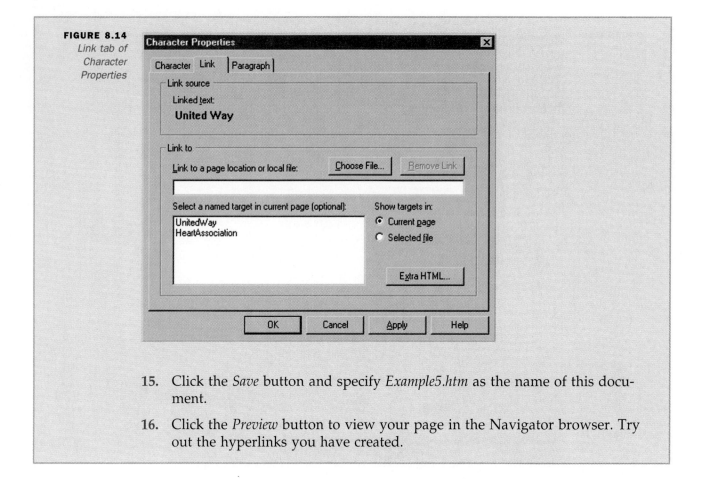

15. Click the *Save* button and specify *Example5.htm* as the name of this document.

16. Click the *Preview* button to view your page in the Navigator browser. Try out the hyperlinks you have created.

## USING TABLES WITH NETSCAPE COMPOSER

Web **tables** resemble word processor tables—they present tabular data in rectangular rows and columns. You can choose special formatting or let it default to the usual cell borders and colors. There are three steps to creating a table with Netscape Composer:

1. Set up the table in Netscape—specify the number of rows and columns.

2. Fill the table with data.

3. Optionally set up formatting for borders, characters, and so forth. You can mark individual items by highlighting them, and then choose a format from the menu bar or toolbar.

The *Insert Table* button is second from the right in the first Netscape Composer toolbar. Click it to display the New Table Properties dialog box shown in Figure 8.15. The first two choices represent the number of rows and columns for your table. Other choices for borders, cell spacing, color, and caption can be made in this dialog box.

**FIGURE 8.15**
*New Table Properties dialog box*

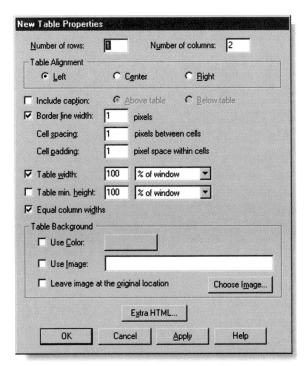

## GUIDED ACTIVITY

## 8.6 Creating a Web Page with a Table

In this activity, you will build a Web page with a formatted table.

1. Open Netscape Communicator, and use the *Communicator→Page Composer* command to create a blank HTML document in the editor.

2. Use the *Format→Page Colors and Properties* command to set the title of the document to `Example 6`.

3. Add this title in Heading 1 style: `Media Web Sites`

4. Click the *Insert Table* button in the top toolbar, second from the right. Choose three rows and two columns for the table. Select 75 percent for the table width and use all other default settings. After you click *OK* to confirm your choices, Composer will create a 3×2 table.

5. In the table, fill in the following values. When you finish filling in the first cell, press the *Tab* key to move to the next cell. Use *Ctrl+Tab* to move to the previous cell, or click in it with the mouse.

| New York Times | *http://www.nytimes.com* |
|---|---|
| CNN | *http://www.cnn.com* |
| Time magazine | *http://www.pathfinder.com/time* |

6. Highlight each cell in the first column, one at a time, and click the bold **A** button in the top toolbar. Repeat the process in the second column, this time choose the italic *A* button in the top toolbar. Your screen should resemble the table on the previous page.

7. Save the document as *Example6.htm*. Now you will convert the entries in the second column into links.

8. Highlight the *http://www.nytimes.com* entry, then click the *Link* button in the Composition toolbar. The Link tab of the Character Properties dialog box will appear. In the Link to box, enter the same address, *http://www.nytimes.com* and click *OK*.

9. This time highlight the *http://www.cnn.com* line in row 2 and use the *Edit→Copy* command to put this address into the Clipboard.

10. Click the *Link* button, then use *Edit→Paste* to place the CNN URL into the Link to box. Click *OK*.

11. Repeat steps 8 and 9 with the third row in the table.

12. Finally, save your Web document under the same *Example6* name.

13. To test your simple table, establish an Internet connection, and then click the *Preview* button to load your Web page in Netscape Navigator. Figure 8.16 shows the finished home page.

**FIGURE 8.16**
*Example6 home page in Netscape*

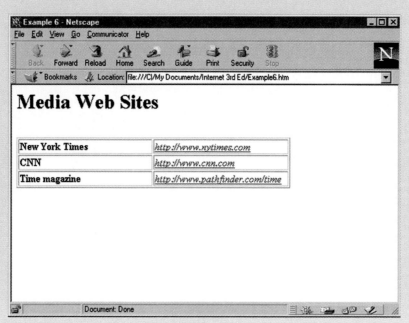

14. Experiment with the links you just created.

15. When finished, you may close the Netscape Composer editor. Leave Navigator open for the next activity.

## PUBLISHING YOUR HOME PAGE

So far you have only previewed your Web document in Netscape Navigator by opening its file from your hard drive. The final step in creating a home page is to use FTP to upload your HTML file to a Web server. FTP is covered in Unit 7, and WS_FTP works very well with Composer or Notepad HTML files.

Before you can upload your Web documents, you must have an account on the Web server with the appropriate user name and password. See your instructor or system administrator for this information. If you are using WS_FTP for uploading your Web file, create a new session with the name of the host and your account authentication information, then click *Connect*. After you are connected to the remote Web server, navigate to the desired directory in the right panel, then click the transfer button to upload your file.

Composer has a built-in upload facility in the Publish button of the Composition toolbar. After you save your HTML document, click the *Publish* button to start the upload process. Figure 8.17 shows the Publish dialog box for the *Example4.htm* file you created earlier. Notice that the filename has been inserted for you at the top, along with the name of the graphic file that is a part of the page. Fill in the URL for your FTP or HTTP server location, along with your user name and password for that location.

**FIGURE 8.17**
*Composer Publish dialog box*

Filename —

Fill in your information —

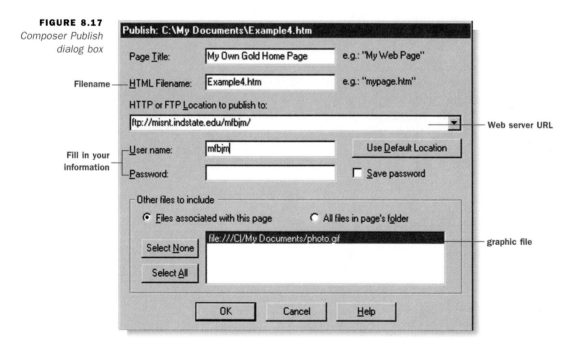

Click *OK* to begin the transfer. After a few moments, Composer will display a message that your files were uploaded successfully. Click *OK* to clear that message, and then open that Internet URL (not the filename on your computer's hard drive) in your browser to make sure all was done properly.

## USING NETSCAPE WIZARDS TO BUILD HOME PAGES

Netscape offers some useful Wizards for building complex Web pages at its online Web site. When starting a new page in Netscape Composer, use the

**FIGURE 8.18**
*Netscape Page Wizard*

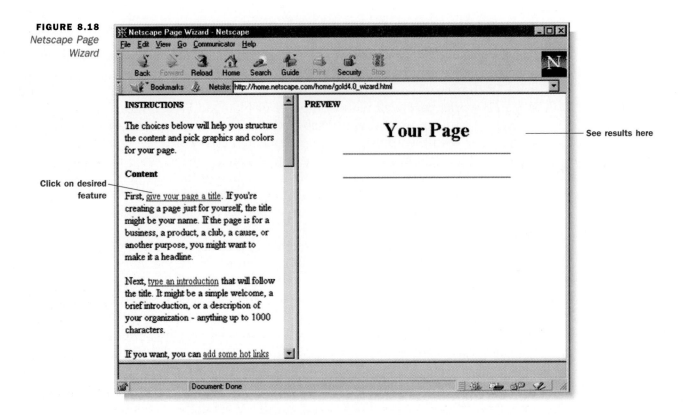

*File→New→Page From Wizard* command. You must, of course, be connected to the Internet to use this service. Figure 8.18 shows a part of the Netscape Page Wizard.

Following the instructions page in the left pane, you can click on features that you would like to place in your home page. Netscape will construct the HTML commands to make it happen. You can add the following items, and more:

- title

- introduction

- hot links to other Web sites

- add an e-mail link to the page creator—you

- set a color combination

- choose bullet style

- choose horizontal ruler style

Finally, click the *Build* button and Netscape will create the page for you. We will not demonstrate this feature here, but you can try it on your own.

## *Advanced HTML Features*

This section describes some miscellaneous features associated with newer HTML technology. It covers HTML standards, image maps, frames, 3D, and scripts such as Java programming. It concludes with a discussion about usage logs and access counts. The details of implementing these features are beyond the scope of this book. They are included here to give you an idea about the capabilities of advanced technologies.

# HTML Standards

The HTML standard is maintained by the W3 Consortium, led by MIT, CERN, and a France-based group. Based on SGML, Standard Generalized Markup Language, HTML 2.0 (Level Two) provided basic Web features such as headlines, anchor links, in-line image support, and various character styles. Virtually all GUI Web browsers handle HTML 2.0 tags in a satisfactory fashion. Even Lynx and other text browsers will display Web pages that are formatted with HTML 2.0 commands.

HTML 2.0 has been updated to HTML 3.0. Most Web current GUI browsers will handle HTML 3.0 tags with few problems. HTML 3.0 introduced such new features as tables, mathematical equations, style sheets, horizontal tabs, and form support. The proposed HTML 4.0 standard is under discussion.

The "official" HTML standard has been extended by Netscape and Microsoft in their battle for desktop browser supremacy. Standards have long been "winked at" in the browser business. You may have seen a small graphic logo in some pages that says "Best when viewed with Netscape 2.0" or "Designed for Internet Explorer." These logos indicate that the Web designer used HTML commands that are specific to that browser, and they may not work in another browser. When the best-selling packages adopt their own standards, the official standard is strongly influenced. Expect to see the new standards reflect these extensions.

# Image Maps

An **image map** is a graphic image that contains a clickable interior region. The **image** is mapped to links to other Web resources. The ISU home page discussed earlier and seen at *http://web.indstate.edu/* contains 14 buttons that are part of a single graphic image. By setting up an image as a map, the Web designer can make it easy for the user to select a jump to another part of the Web document or to another document altogether. The Southwest Airlines home page at *http://www. iflyswa.com/* shown in Figure 8.19 is another example of an image map: click on various objects in the map to access that section of the Web site. For instance, click on the slot marked "Resumes" to get information about employment with the firm.

The first step in inserting an image map is to create a usable graphic image that is easy for the user to understand. That is, make sure it is clear what the choices are and that the user would know to click in that area to make the choice. User testing is very helpful here—find someone who is not already experienced with image maps and see if they can understand the choices.

Then insert the graphic, and mark it as an image map. (In Netscape Composer, the Image Properties window has a check box for image map.) Then you must create a map between the pixel coordinates in the image with actual URL links. This must be accomplished by an external program that runs on the server. Specific information about the external mapping program are beyond the limits of this introductory textbook. The FrontPage HTML editor handles image maps well.

Netscape Composer allows you to mark the entire image as a link to a single URL. Right-click the image, and then use the Link tab of the Image Properties dialog box to set up the location. You will do this as an exercise.

**FIGURE 8.19**

*Southwest Airlines
image map*

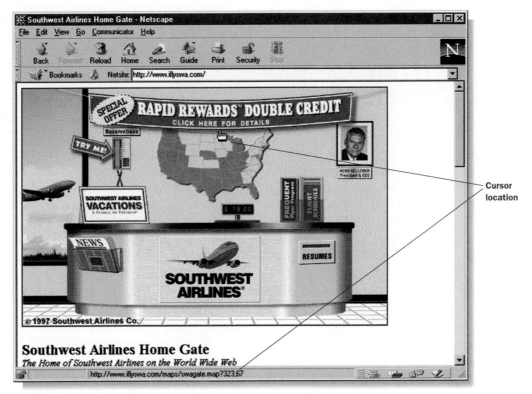

## Frames

A **frame** is a subdivision of the normal browser window into two or more separately scrollable regions. Frames allow the user more control over what is seen. For instance, the Web designer could place a menu in one small frame at the left side of the screen, and then put a larger area that displays the content of that menu choice in the right part of the window. Figure 8.20 shows an example of a Web page with three frames.

There are several limitations with frames. The window size of each window is smaller, making it more difficult to display information. Some developers tend to place lots of graphic information in a frame, thus taking longer to download the contents of that frame. Some Web browsers do not display frames or do not handle frames well. For instance, clicking the *Back* button may take you back in the frame *or* take you back to the previous screen, before the frame windows opened.

To get around these limitations, fewer designers use frames for commercial Web sites. Rather, they program a navigation menu or bar that is copied to *each* home page in the Web site. A good example is the Microsoft home page that places a thin graphic bar at the top of most pages, as shown in Figure 8.21. Others create a similar effect by running a vertical navigation block down the left side of the screen.

## Java and Other Web Programming Tools

Many Web designers take advantage of server-based programming tools called scripts. A **script** is a macro or program that performs some interactive task within a Web document when needed.

**FIGURE 8.20**
*Web Page with frames*

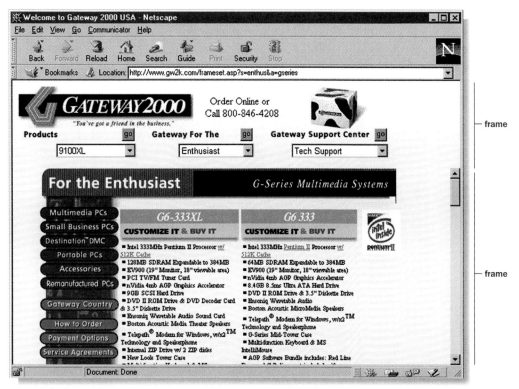

**FIGURE 8.21**
*Microsoft home page navigation bar*

Scripts are based upon Common Gateway Interface or CGI. CGI represents the pathway between the script and the user. The browser places data into a form, and then passes the data to a script or other program. For example, you could use a script to search text or retrieve a certain piece of information from a database that is based upon the reader's specific request. This could be the closing price of a common stock or the marketing catalog page for a particular product. Scripts are used to submit searches to a search engine, based upon the user's keyword input.

Scripts are written in various languages, including Java, C, Visual Basic, PERL, and even the DOS SHELL program. Nearly all Web server software comes with a scripting language. The newest and hottest programming environment was developed by Sun Microsystems and is called Java. Based upon C++, Java goes beyond the traditional script operations. With Java you can insert action into your Web page. Java is also beyond the scope of this book, but you can read about Java in many on-line locations, including the Netscape home page at *http://home.netscape. com/* and the Sun Microsystems home page at *http://www.sun.com/*.

Microsoft introduced ActiveX applications to compete with Java. Based on Visual Basic, the ActiveX language is used in active server pages whose file extension is *.asp,* another Web standard. Although some *.asp* Web documents will display in Netscape, many only work properly with Microsoft's Internet Explorer.

## Usage Logs and Access Counters

Virtually all Web servers keep a log of files that are requested by Internet visitors. Typically, these logs include the date and time of the request, the file requested, the address of the requester, some status code about the transfer operation, and the number of bytes transferred. Because in-line images are stored as separate files, a request for a Web page with several images will generate multiple log entries. Needless to say, an active Web site will generate an enormous number of log entries.

Most Web page developers are curious to know how many people visit their site (Web page developers who design and maintain sites for businesses and institutions are typically called **webmasters**.) Some commercial sites may need to know the number of Web site visitors in order to make decisions about the effectiveness of advertising on the Internet. You may have seen a site with an odometer-like image showing the total number of visitors since a certain date.

You can use CGI scripts to search the log entries and develop a count of the number of visitors. Visit *http://www.ics.uci.edu/WebSoft/wwwstat/* for information about the WWWStat PERL script. Gwstat is another program designed to run on UNIX platforms. Gwstat takes output from the WWWStat program and converts it to a graphical format.

# SUMMARY

This unit presents an overview of creating home pages. You learned about the overall process to follow, including planning the page, creating the HTML document, uploading it to the Web server, and checking the page. The unit contains tips for designing and creating good Web documents.

Home pages are text files that contain HTML tags that appear in angle brackets. You can create these files directly in a text editor, inserting your own HTML commands, or use a suitable word processor or HTML editor to insert the codes. Save the home page as a text file on your own computer's hard drive. Use FTP or the built-in publishing function to upload your home page to a Web server. Then view the home page with your Web browser.

You can add different font sizes, colors, special effects like bold and underline, bulleted lists, numbered lists, and images to a home page.

---

## Command Review

**Netscape Composer**

| | |
|---|---|
| Communicator→Page Composer | Start Composer |
| Edit→Copy | Copy selected object to clipboard |
| Edit→Paste | Copy clipboard at current location |
| File→Browse Page (or Preview button) | Preview page in browser |
| File→New→Blank Page (Ctrl+Shift+N) | Create new blank page in Composer |
| File→New→Page From Wizard | Use online Wizard to make page |
| File→Open Page (Ctrl+O or Open button) | Open .htm file in Composer |

| | |
|---|---|
| File→Print (or Print button) | Print document |
| File→Publish (or Publish button) | Upload document to server |
| File→Save (or Save button) | Save document as HTML file |
| Format→Page Colors and Properties | Change page colors and properties |
| Insert→Horizontal Line (or H. Line button) | Insert horizontal line |
| Insert→Image (or Image button) | Insert graphic image file |
| Insert→Link (or Link button) | Insert hyperlink |
| Insert→Table (or Table button) | Insert table |
| Insert→Target (or Target button) | Insert target as bookmark |
| Edit→Preferences | Change preferences in Composer |
| Tab (Ctrl+Tab) | Move to next (previous) table cell |

**Windows Notepad**

| | |
|---|---|
| File→New | Create new text file |
| File→Save | Save document under current name |
| File→Save As | Save document under new name |

**HTML Tags**

| | |
|---|---|
| <A> and </A> | Give specifications for anchor link |
| <B> and </B> | Bold on and off |
| <CENTER> and </CENTER> | Center line on and off |
| <FONT SIZE> | Adjust font size |
| <H1> through <H6> | Choose headline style 1 through 6 |
| <HEAD> and </HEAD> | Begin and end head section |
| <HR> | Insert horizontal rule (line) |
| <HTML> and </HTML> | Begin and end HTML document (optional) |
| <I> and </I> | Italic on and off |
| <IMG> | Specifications for in-line image |
| <LI> | Indicates this item is part of a list |
| <OL> | Set up ordered (numbered) list |
| <P> and </P> | Begin and end paragraph |
| <PRE> and </PRE> | Surround preformatted text area in document |
| <TITLE> and </TITLE> | Surround title of Web document |
| <UL> | Set up unordered (bulleted) list |

## Vocabulary Exercise

*Write a short definition for each term in the following list:*

| | | |
|---|---|---|
| Anchor | Image map | Script |
| Common Gateway Inter- | Link | Table |
| face (CGI) | Microsoft Front Page | Tag |
| Frame | Netscape Composer | Text file |
| HyperText Markup | Notepad | Unordered list |
| Language (HTML) | Ordered list | Webmaster |
| Image | | |

## Review Questions

1.  What is HTML? Do all Web users need to know HTML?

2.  How do you set colors for text and background in a home page? Give the specific HTML commands to use blue text on a white background.

3.  Explain how to create and test a Web page if you do not have access to a Web server.

4.  Define the purpose of each of the following HTML tags.

    a.  <B>

    b.  </I>

    c.  <H2>

    d.  <P>

    e.  <TITLE>

5.  Define the purpose of each of the following HTML tags.

    a.  <HR>

    b.  <OL>

    c.  <UL>

    d.  </HEAD>

    e.  <CENTER>

6.  Explain in detail how to create a hypertext link to a Web document called *home.html* at the site called *http://www.indstate.edu/pub/*. The text of the link should be called "Link to home page."

7.  How would you examine the actual HTML codes in a particular home page you are viewing?

8.  Discuss the advantages of using an HTML editor like Netscape Composer instead of Notepad or another plain text editor.

9. Define the following HTML features. Explain why they would be useful for your Web page.

   a. Table

   b. Frames

   c. Image map

   d. Java

10. Describe how you would build your personal home page and what kinds of information you would store there.

## Exercises

1. Retrieve the home page for this textbook at the following location: *http://www.indstate.edu/internet_book/*. Print the contents of the file with Netscape or your Web browser. Save it as a disk file on your computer using the name *inbook.htm*.

2. Repeat Exercise 1, but this time open the file in Notepad or your own text editor and print the contents.

3. Modify the *Example2.htm* file from Guided Activity 8.2 so that *your personal information* appears in the home page. Instead of displaying My Name, insert your own name. Save the results in a Notepad text file called *mypage.htm* then try out the revised home page in your Web browser. Print a copy of the modified page with your Web browser.

4. Create a home page for the Internet course that you are currently enrolled in. Include information about that course that someone from another campus would find useful. Save the home page as *course.htm* and print a copy of the HTML code in your document.

5. Go to the home page at *http://misnt.indstate.edu/mfbjm/home.html*. Print a copy of the HTML codes in the first screen page only, and then annotate the print out with the meaning of each HTML tag on that page. It would help you to print out the document with your Web browser as well.

6. Suppose you have been hired by a retail computer store in your home town to prepare a home page for them. Lay out on paper what you would include in that Web site, including specific Web pages, graphic images, headlines, text, and links. It might help to interview someone at a similar store, or visit one on the Web. You will implement this Web site in the next exercise.

7. Beginning with the design you created for the previous exercise, implement the Web site using Composer. Print a copy of each page from your browser, and the HTML codes from a text editor like Notepad.

8. If your Web browser supports tables, create a home page that contains the following table that is entitled **MIS Courses for MIS Minors**. Duplicate the formatting shown here (bold, centered first column, italicized middle column) including the outside borders.

| COURSE NUMBER | COURSE TITLE | PREREQUISITES |
|:---:|---|---|
| **MIS 276** | *Introduction to MIS* | Consent of Instructor |
| **MIS 376** | *Advanced Micro Applications* | MIS 276, ACCT 201 |
| **MIS 310** | *Intro to Programming* | MIS 276 |
| **MIS 300** | *Business Systems Analysis* | MIS 276, Jr. Standing |

9. Create a Web document that contains an image that also serves as a hyperlink to the South-Western home page at *http://computered.swep.com*. If possible, use the collage *.gif* file from that table as the image.

10. Use the Netscape Page Wizard to create a home page for your favorite club or organization. Print a copy of the finished page.

## Creating a Home Page Web Site

Use Composer or another HTML editor to create a home page about creating a home page. The home page is called *website.htm* and should contain title information and links to other helpful home pages. The home page should have several graphics and give basic steps. Your page should employ targets as bookmarks to organize the material with a table of contents. The page should talk about all phases of developing a home page, from design tips through creating the page to uploading the page to the Web server. Make sure that you put your name and the date your page was last modified at the bottom. Include an e-mail link to your e-mail account so that viewers can send you comments about your page. Print a copy of your page.

### PROJECT TEAM OPTION

Expand your home page into a Web site with several related home pages in the site. Each page should describe a major part of the process and should have a link to return to the main page.

# UNIT 9

# Electronic Commerce and the Future of the Internet

This unit describes additional applications found on the Internet—including business use of the Internet, commonly called electronic commerce. It also discusses additional personal technologies as well as the issue of Internet security. The security issue is especially important when dealing with sensitive financial data used in business applications. The unit concludes with some of the concerns our society has about the Internet.

## Learning Objectives

At the completion of this unit, you should be able to

1. discuss how businesses might use the Internet,

2. discuss personal uses of the Internet,

3. explain the use of intranets,

4. describe various emerging technologies related to the Internet,

5. discuss the Internet's societal implications.

## Electronic Commerce on the Internet

Although most of the action on the Internet has been in the personal use area, many companies have found that the Internet provides unique opportunities for conducting business. According to a report by Netscape Communications Corporation, commercial addresses compose more than 50 percent of network registrations now and are growing as a percentage of total network use.

A thorough guide to the advantages of doing business on the Internet is found at

## Key Terms

The following terms are introduced in this unit. Be sure you know what each of them means.

Channels
Chat
CoolTalk
CU-SeeMe
DealerNet
Digital cash
Doom
Electronic shopping cart
Encrypt
Extranet
Finger
Firewall
Hacker
Handle
Internet Relay Chat (IRC)
Intranet
PGP (Pretty Good Privacy)
RealAudio
SportsZone
Sub-cent charges
Videoconferencing
Zines

*http://www.usa.uu.net/html/internet_business_guide.html/*. This site is provided by UUNET, a pioneer ISP for commercial applications. Another useful resource is IBM's electronic commerce Web site at *http://www.ibm.com/e-business/*. It contains case studies and pointers on setting up your business on the Web.

The Access Business Online site at *http://www.bizwiz.com/* contains hundreds of links to all sorts of on-line business activities for registered members. It contains news catalogued by industry type, links to news sources such as CNN and *USA Today*, and other useful information. It also contains advertising. Visit this site and follow the sample links.

Many organizations now provide multiple contact methods. For instance, advertisements appear in national magazines that contain information such as the following:

> Another Company, Inc.
> Voice: (800) 555-1234
> Fax: (123) 456-7890
> E-mail: info@company.com
> Web site: *http://www.anothercompany.com/*

As research for this book the author sent an e-mail message to several Internet service providers. Using advertised e-mail addresses (similar to *info@company.com*), reply messages with answers to frequently asked questions were received almost immediately. The cost of servicing an e-mail request for more information is about $2 to $4 per request; handling a toll-free phone call costs from $10 to $15 per call. Thus, an organization is able to lower costs by handling requests on-line. Of course, the cost of creating and maintaining the link to the Internet is not included.

## Typical Business Uses

Not surprisingly, many business applications use the same personal tools that we have already explored. The big three applications—e-mail, WWW, and FTP—are frequently encountered. The World Wide Web is *the* place to be on the Internet today. Because Web browsers like Netscape offer HTTP, FTP, Gopher, and Telnet (among others), these protocols are particularly useful for business opportunity.

Electronic commerce applications (also called e-commerce) can be organized into four categories—roughly corresponding to the four marketing phases known as pre-sale, taking the order, delivering the goods, and post-sale. Typical e-commerce techniques supporting each phase are discussed next.

---

NET TIP

**Web Addresses**

Current links to most Web sites in this book can be found on the *Understanding & Using the Internet* Home Page. Choose **Resources** at **computered.swep.com**. Remember that a Web address may change at any time. An address given in this book as an example may no longer be valid. If this is so, either access the Home Page for the current link or do a search to find a similar site (see Unit 5 for a discussion of search methods).

## PRE-SALE

Pre-sale techniques provide information to potential customers who are comparing products and vendors. Businesses often use the Internet for additional advertising targeted at users who frequently use the Internet. Those users tend to be the kinds of customers the businesses most want to reach. Some companies use the Internet as a repository for information that customers may access directly, rather than going through a human operator and requesting that it be mailed. For instance, one firm has had an intensive advertising campaign for its new software product. A trial copy of this software is readily available for downloading from the Internet.

Some companies use e-mail to send sales flyers that target specific customers, often matching buying preferences through database analysis. The rationale is that a customer who purchases a certain product might be more likely to purchase similar or complementary products. Unlike mass mailings of catalogs that are often discarded, targeted e-mail is more likely to be read. Moreover, the cost of processing an e-mail request is a fraction of the cost of providing a live operator. Most of today's e-mail clients will display an embedded Web URL as a clickable hyperlink, making it easy to bring the customer to a home page that colorfully describes the product or service.

Another pre-sale method involves placing banner advertisements in Web pages of complementary products. Users visiting that page see an ad containing a link to other sites with products of interest. Those kinds of ads tend to be more effective in attracting qualified buyers than those that appear before the general audience. A similar phenomenon occurs with search engine sites—the ads tend to be selected to match the subject interest of the keywords used for the search. Thus, if you search for the word "basketball" in Yahoo, an ad appears for CBS SportsLine. Search Lycos for the word "Maui," and you'll see a Travel Network ad. Many Web sites come with hit counters to measure the activity at that site, making it easier to assess the effectiveness of a particular medium or advertising campaign.

Most Web browsers can display forms on which users may fill in information. The forms may be returned to the company via e-mail. For instance, Eudora Light is available from the Eudora home page at *http://www.eudora.com/*. You can receive a free copy of this software by filling out an information form. Other companies like Toshiba and Texas Instruments use forms to survey potential customers prior to sending them literature about products.

Netscape Communicator and Internet Explorer 4.0 feature **channels**, to which requested personalized information is sent automatically and continually to the user's browser. Similar to the television channel metaphor, Web channels provide a way of organizing this personalized information. Thus, a user can select a particular channel and access the information that has been downloaded to that channel. Companies are finding this to be an excellent way to provide information to customers and employees. Figure 9.1 shows the Internet Explorer active channel guide.

Car dealers in several states have combined to offer a Web home page at *http://www.dealernet.com/* as shown in Figure 9.2. This page provides information about many makes and models of cars. Called *DealerNet*, this "virtual showroom" features hundreds of car dealers representing dozens of nameplates. The home page also offers e-mail access to the member dealers. DealerNet includes information about used cars, boats, and recreational vehicles as well.

**FIGURE 9.1**
*Internet Explorer
Channel Guide*

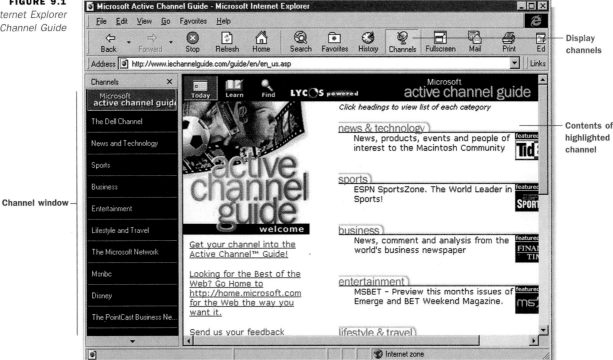

**FIGURE 9.2**
*DealerNet home
page*

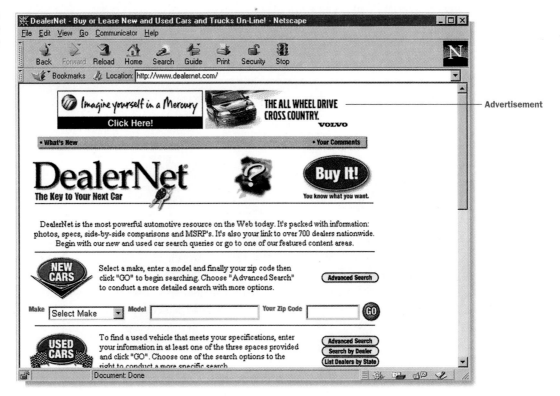

**TABLE 9.1**

*URL locations for automobile manufacturers*

| MANUFACTURER | URL |
|---|---|
| Chrysler | *http://www.chrysler.com/* (divisions also available) |
| Ford | *http://www.ford.com/* |
| General Motors | *http://www.gm.com/* (divisions also available) |
| Honda | *http://www.honda.com/* |
| Lexus | *http://www.lexus.com/* |
| Mitsubishi | *http://www.mitsucars.com/* |
| Nissan | *http://www.nissanmotors.com/* |
| Toyota | *http://www.toyota.com/* |

Most car manufacturers have individual home pages for their vehicles. Table 9.1 contains URL locations for popular makes. Manufacturers' home pages include specifications, photographs, and links to dealers that carry those models. Some of these pages even contain an on-line inventory list of specific vehicles showcased by an individual dealer. You can configure a Dodge or Chrysler car and get the sticker price for that vehicle. Residents of some states can even get real price quotes from participating dealers.

General Electric has a large home page on the Web at *http://www.ge.com/*, shown in Figure 9.3. The Web site contains separate pages for various GE divisions with detailed product information. You can find phone and fax numbers for GE offices worldwide. Financial information from GE also is available on-line and

**FIGURE 9.3**

*GE home page*

is formatted with HTML and hypertext to make it easier for investors to locate information. From the GE home page a potential customer can be directed to an appropriate specialist in any of GE's major businesses. You can even get on-line help for fixing your GE appliance. This page also can help you search the job opportunities at GE or even locate a GE employee.

High-quality product literature is often available through the Internet. For instance, with some home pages you can order a brochure to be sent to your home by filling out a Web form. In other places you can view the literature on-line. For instance, GE maintains product literature in PDF (Portable Document Format) that can be viewed on-line and printed locally. You must have a copy of the free Adobe Acrobat Reader installed on your computer before you can view PDF documents. The PDF installation manual for a refrigerator as displayed by Acrobat is shown in Figure 9.4.

**FIGURE 9.4**
*PDF manual displayed by Acrobat*

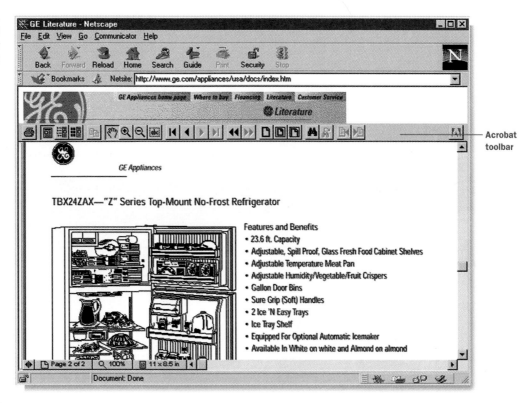

Acrobat toolbar

**TIP**

**You can download Adobe Acrobat Reader from the Adobe Web site at *http://www.adobe. com/prodindex/ acrobat/readstep. html.***

Some companies place electronic catalogs on the Web, making it easy to browse and search for products. Figure 9.5 shows the opening OfficeMax OnLine Web site. You can select a special, browse any of the product categories, or search directly for a particular product. The Cross writing instruments catalog is shown in Figure 9.6.

The *Amazon.com* book seller exists only on the Internet—as of this writing there are no Amazon retail locations. The Web site offers sophisticated search capabilities, one of which allows you to locate other books by a selected author. The Web site is personalized for your tastes, suggesting other books similar to those you have purchased there already. It also can bring up books *similar* to the one you have just found. Prices are shown in the catalog, along with expected stock avail-

**FIGURE 9.5**
*OfficeMax Web site*

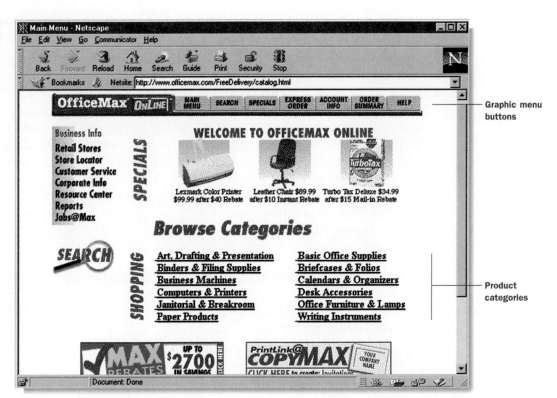

Graphic menu
buttons

Product
categories

**FIGURE 9.6**
*Cross writing
instruments catalog
page*

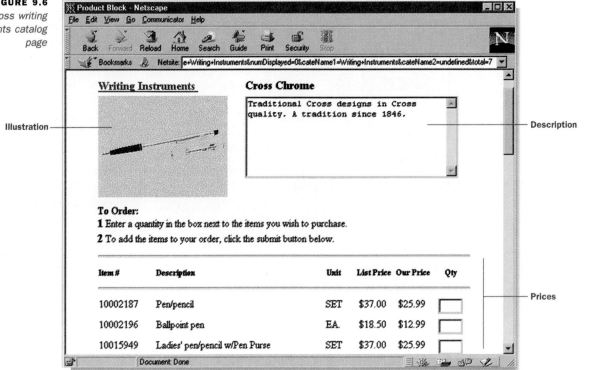

Illustration

Description

Prices

**FIGURE 9.7**
*Amazon.com Web site*

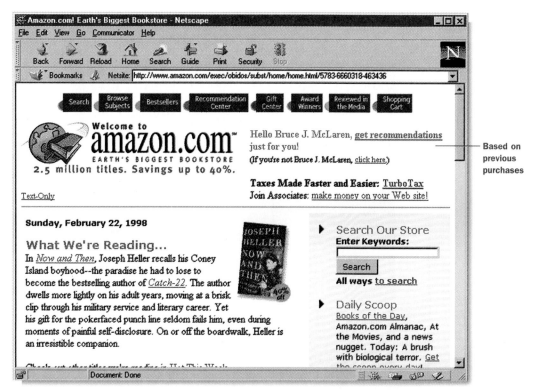

ability. This Web site also has a chat feature that allows readers to post reviews of books and correspond with authors. Figure 9.7 shows the *Amazon.com* Web site.

## TAKING THE ORDER

The Internet offers a low-cost method of taking orders and accepting payment. Both Gateway and Dell have massive on-line Web sites for people to configure and purchase customized personal computers. Dell is cited frequently as the model for on-line sales via the Internet. By the end of 1997 it was generating $4 million in sales *per day* from its Web site and received 10 million visits in the fourth quarter alone. The opening Dell Web site is shown in Figure 9.8. From this page you can build a custom computer, check on an order, access hundreds of pages of technical support information, and find out more about Dell, including career information.

SHOPPING CART

Many sites use an **electronic shopping cart** to keep track of the items you have selected for purchase. Figure 9.9 shows the Web form for a Dell notebook computer. Each drop-down box in this form lets the buyer configure that item. Notice that the standard computer comes with 32 MB of RAM; in this case, an extra 32 MB of RAM costs an additional $200. There is no option for the Variable CD-ROM that comes with this computer. When finished with the options, the buyer should update the price and then add it to the shopping cart or print out the quote. The buyer can stop the process at any time. Most visitors at this point are just looking, not buying.

You can pay for the goods with a credit card, purchase order, prearranged line of credit, or make other arrangements. The section on Internet security will present options for maintaining private information on the Internet.

**FIGURE 9.8**
*Dell on-line
computer store*

Custom
configuration

Add Dell as a
channel

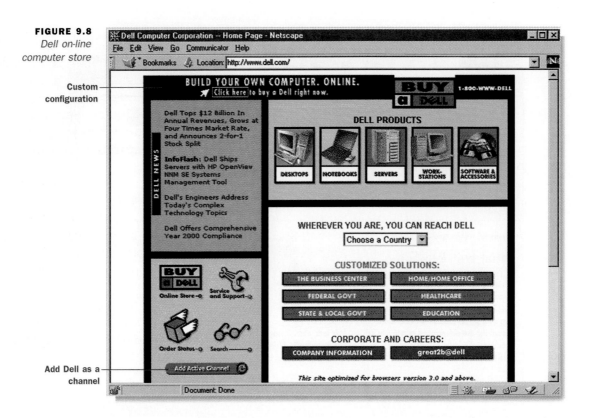

**FIGURE 9.9**
*Dell order Web form*

Optional RAM

No option

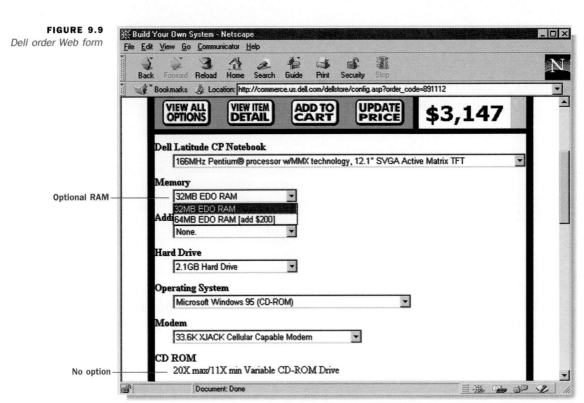

### DELIVERING THE GOODS

Some goods can be delivered electronically over the Web. Software may be a good candidate for immediate delivery, but larger programs can take a long time to download. In some circumstances you can receive a registration code that will "unlock" a trial version that you already have installed. For example, you can download a trial version of WinZip from *http://www.winzip.com*; when you purchase the product and install the registration code for your copy, more features become available.

Many services constitute *information* and are excellent candidates for delivery over the Internet. For instance, newspapers like the *Washington Post* (*http://www.washingtonpost.com*), the *Los Angeles Times* (*http://www.latimes.com*) and *USA Today* (*http://www.usatoday.com*) have on-line editions that carry the latest news. The same thing is true for magazines and television news sources. Companies that sell financial information such as Wall Street firms also have developed extensive Web sites. Information is provided for paying customers.

Of course, the Internet is ideal for checking on the status of an order through the company database. The best-known examples of this come from the express package delivery companies. Both FedEx and UPS maintain on-line sites for checking delivery status of a shipment.

## GUIDED ACTIVITY

## 9.1   Connecting to the FedEx Home Page to Track a Package

In this activity, you will connect to the FedEx home page and attempt to track a package containing the manuscript for this textbook by its airbill number.

1.  Establish your Internet connection as usual, and open your Web browser.

2.  In the Location or Address box enter *http://www.fedex.com/us/tracking/* and click *OK*.

**CHECKPOINT 9A**   Is there an easier way to return to this particular Web site in the future?

3.  In the Airbill Tracking Number box type 800468588402 and then enter 021698 in the Ship Date box. Click the *Request Tracking Info* button to activate the tracking process.

 **NOTE**   **This airbill will be unavailable because airbills remain in the database only up to 120 days. Your instructor may provide you with an alternate airbill number.**

4.  The results of this search will be the following message: "An invalid ship date was entered. The ship date must be in the range from 120 days in the past to the present." If you had tracked this package within the 120-day range, your display would be similar to that shown in Figure 9.10.

5.  Leave your browser open for now.

FIGURE 9.10
*FedEx airbill
tracking results*

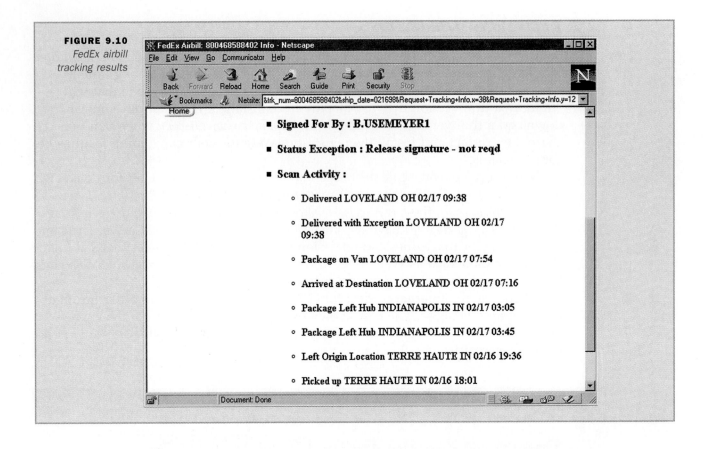

FIGURE 9.11
*UPS tracking
results*

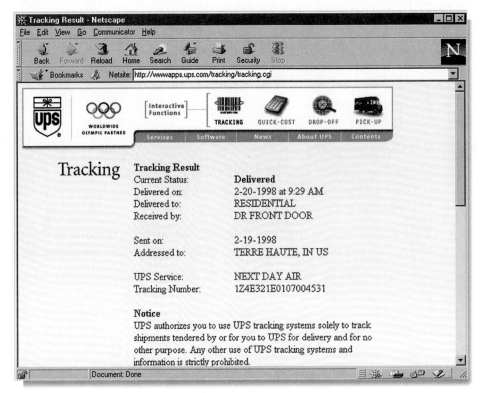

FedEx also provides a shipping service on the Internet with which you can create an airbill on-line, to avoid having to hand write it. You must have a FedEx account number to register for this service. After entering the shipping information in an on-line form, the information is automatically entered into the FedEx computer system. You then print a barcoded shipping label with your laser printer and drop your package off for shipment. You can also use the FedEx home page to search for drop-off locations or to schedule a pickup at your site.

The UPS tracking service is very similar. Found at *http://www.ups.com/tracking/ tracking.html*, this service is only authorized for packages delivered to you or shipped by you. The results of a UPS tracking search are shown in Figure 9.11 on page 208. You can also locate UPS drop-off locations at the main home page.

## POST-SALE

Most e-commerce methods in this category relate to customer service and technical support. E-mail links provide a way for the customer to contact the vendor about specific problems. A mailing list represents a way to provide follow-up information to customers, including operating suggestions, product improvements, and information about related products or services. (Of course, this implies that the customer provide an e-mail address.)

Some companies participate in technical support forums in which customers may leave messages, pick up FAQ files, and comment on questions left by other customers. Forums have long been available on CompuServe, but companies have begun using news groups directly on the Internet. I have found that other users often provide an accurate response faster than the authorized support person on that forum.

A Web site can provide much of the same information as e-mail, but it does require that the user open that site and navigate to the desired page. Of course, many firms send e-mail containing their Web site URL as a hyperlink. The Web site can offer answers to *frequently asked questions,* or *FAQs.* Users can display or print instruction sheets and technical notes for products. For instance, suppose you have lost the jumper settings sheet for your Maxtor hard drive. Connect to the Maxtor home page at *http://www.maxtor.com,* select Service and Support, and scroll down to the menu shown in Figure 9.12. You will complete this process in the next activity.

For thorny technical support problems, send an e-mail message describing your problem and then wait for a customized response to be e-mailed back. You can attach copies of critical files to the initial message, giving the technical support person as much background information as you think helpful. Although this method avoids your playing telephone tag, it sometimes requires that additional messages be sent back and forth if you were not specific enough at the outset about certain aspects of your problem.

Some services may continue to be provided after the initial sale. For newspapers such as the *New York Times,* the on-line edition is updated 24 hours a day. Readers can tune in at any time and find current information. Of course, most of these newspapers carry advertising in both the on-line version and the print version.

**FIGURE 9.12**
*Maxtor Service &
Support page*

Jumper settings ——

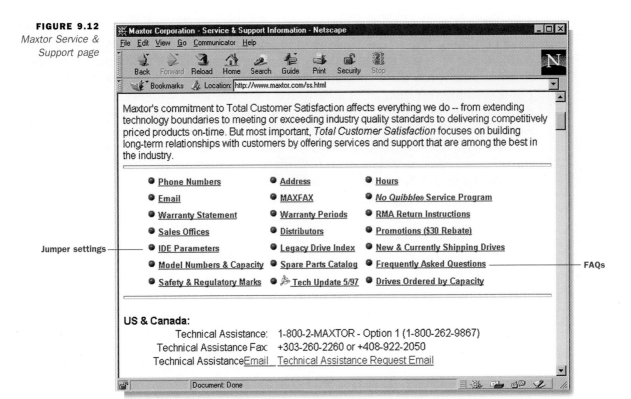

—— FAQs

## GUIDED ACTIVITY

## 9.2 Connecting to the Maxtor Tech Support Home Page

In this activity, you will retrieve the master and slave jumper settings for a hard drive from the Maxtor home page.

1. Start your computer and connect to your Internet service provider.

2. Open your browser and connect to the Maxtor home page at *http://www. maxtor.com.*

3. Navigate to the Service & Support page and scroll down to the menu as shown in Figure 9.12.

4. Select the IDE Parameters link. The drives are listed in descending order by drive capacity within each product series.

5. Locate the 71260A drive in the second product series whose capacity is 1.2 GB. Click its link to display the parameters for this drive.

CHECKPOINT 9B   What is a quick way to find a line containing "71260A"?

6. Scroll down to the jumper section to display the master and slave jumper settings, shown in Figure 9.13. Note the use of jumper 20 to designate whether this drive is the master or the slave. You could print the page or simply make a note of this information.

**FIGURE 9.13**

*Jumper settings*

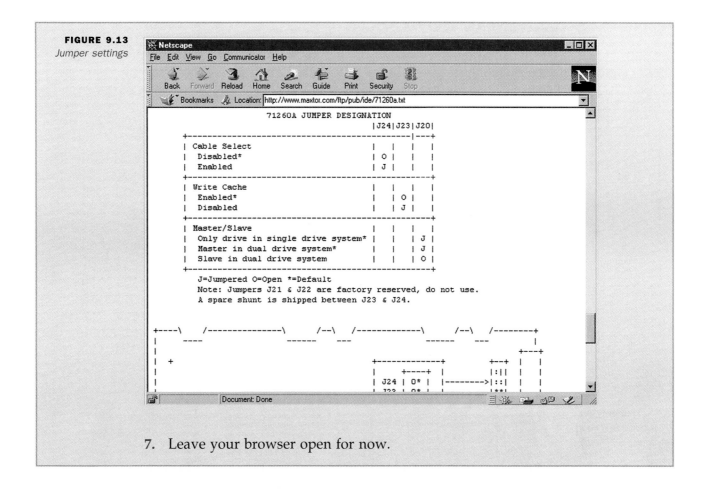

7. Leave your browser open for now.

## Security on the Internet

A long-standing business concern has been the protection of consumers' credit card numbers and other private information. Although e-mail messages generally reach their destinations without being read by anyone other than the recipient, the possibility remains that someone could capture packets and examine them for sensitive information.

### USE A PHONE CALL

There are several methods to prevent spying on private information. The first method is the simplest, yet requires an extra step. Customers can view information about products and services on the Internet but must make a phone call to place the order. Although this is simple, it requires human intervention to handle the phone call, and it may deter some people from placing an order. Other customers may be reassured that their confidential information remains reasonably secure.

## SEND ENCRYPTED DATA

A better solution is to **encrypt** the data in a transaction. That is, before the information is put out on the Internet, it is encoded in a way that prevents someone else from knowing its contents. Then, the encrypted information is sent across the open Internet. At the destination end, the information is *decrypted,* or converted back to the original form. The recipient must have a special software key to decrypt the message.

Netscape Navigator and Internet Explorer have built-in security which is activated if you are talking to a secure server. The security icon at the lower-left of the Netscape screen shows whether the current transaction is secure. If the lock is open, the transaction is sent as plain text; if it changes to closed lock, it is sent as an encrypted transaction. Internet Explorer shows its security icon in the center of the status bar; it uses a closed lock for secure documents and *no* icon for regular Web pages.

The *https:* prefix denotes a Web document that is encrypted by the secure sockets layer (SSL) method. Encryption is *not* a guarantee that sensitive information will not be stolen, but it prevents the majority of information snooping. Not all businesses offer secure transactions, but most protect customer information in this way. Figure 9.14 shows a portion of a secure document from Time Warner's Pathfinder Network; notice the lock symbol in the Internet Explorer status bar.

**FIGURE 9.14**
*Secure document from the Pathfinder Network*

https: prefix

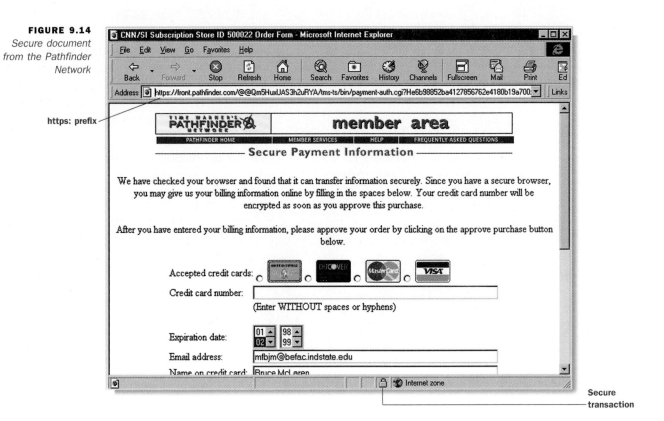

Secure transaction

## PGP—PRETTY GOOD PRIVACY

There is a *personal* method for encrypting information over the Internet that allows you to encode such things as e-mail messages. **PGP** or **Pretty Good Privacy** was developed as an easy-to-use encryption program. It is based on the concept of a key value that you exchange with your correspondent before creating the message. The message is sent in coded form. Someone without the key would just see gibberish. With the key your recipient can decode the encrypted message.

First, create the message as plain text in a text editor such as Notepad. Then use PGP to do a mathematical transformation of the bits in a message. Attach the encrypted message file to an e-mail message. When the message arrives at the other end, the recipient uses the key to reverse the mathematical transformation and produce the original message. PGP for various operating systems and e-mail systems can be downloaded from *http://home.earthlink.net/~cybermule/wherepgp.htm.*

## FIREWALLS

Some companies want to isolate themselves from hackers—those users who wish to do damage or steal information. By building a firewall between the company's computers and the Internet, some protection is afforded. A firewall is a secured gateway that prevents some kinds of access to unauthorized net visitors. Some firewalls are set up to permit access but keep detailed records about the whereabouts of visitors.

For those interested in computer security topics, there are several good news groups. See the FAQ archives at *alt.security* and *comp.security.misc* for more information about computer security, firewalls, and PGP.

## DIGITAL CASH

Digital cash is a fairly new concept in which the user makes a normal cash or credit card deposit with a firm that maintains on-line accounts for customers. Then the user can spend digital cash from this account at many different on-line vendors. Because no confidential information is transmitted over the Internet, much of the risk is eliminated. It does, however, require the cooperation of a wide variety of on-line vendors.

## HARDWARE ACCESS CARDS

Another idea that has been proposed is to make hardware access cards that contain a microchip with a certain code or algorithm. To make a purchase you would insert the card into a reader slot in your computer similar to the PCMCIA (PC Card) slot popular in many notebook computers. The card would transmit a certain code that is received by the system, thus authenticating the user. Only someone with physical possession of the card would be able to make the transaction.

A related idea is to create a cash card that contains a preset amount of funds, similar to the "smart cards" in use today. An embedded microprocessor subtracts the amount of the sale from the card. When the balance on the card is depleted, you take it to a financial center and have it refilled.

# Intranets

An intranet is a Web site that is designed to serve *internal* users only. It is isolated from the Internet via a firewall or other mechanism, discussed in the following sections. The intranet serves the information needs of an organization and can augment—even replace—the traditional paper publishing operations of the organization. It enables users to communicate and share information pertinent to that organization.

Most colleges have elaborate Web sites with all sorts of information that its constituents would need. Students, faculty, staff, and administrators can access bulletin boards, read minutes of meetings, work on group-shared documents, seek answers to questions, and perform other tasks. Although most schools make this information available to outside users, companies generally are more private about their material.

As the information stored in intranets explodes, organizations employ search engines to find specific information. They are similar to the general search engines you might use on the Internet but are tuned to find information stored within the confines of the intranet. Most commercial Web server software comes with a built-in search engine, but some organizations choose to purchase a third-party product for better performance.

Many organizations have multiple locations and use a TCP/IP communications network to connect points in their intranet. For companies with remote users, there must be an alternate method of connecting to the intranet. For example, the sales force may need to access the orders database and check on the status of an order or enter an order. An extranet is an intranet that is accessible from the Internet outside of the company. Users must enter a valid username and password before gaining access to information on the extranet. The extranet may be appropriate for sensitive information.

Companies like Microsoft have published Internet access tools for retrieving information from external databases such as Microsoft Access. Thus, a user can prepare a database query as part of a Web page and then access that information directly from the database.

Because intranets are based upon open standards, they are easier to administer. Some companies are building their information systems around intranets, and it is changing the way new applications are viewed.

# Personal Applications on the Internet

Previous units described the major Internet tools, including e-mail, news groups, FTP, Telnet, and Web browsers such as Netscape Communicator and Internet Explorer. Although most users will be satisfied with the major tools, there are more tools that are designed for personal applications.

## Finger

A tool called finger helps you identify other users. Different versions of the finger command are available. The UNIX version gives the name of the person whose user name is entered, along with some personal information. Other versions let you determine who is now logged on to a particular server. Check with your instructor to see if finger is operational at your campus.

## Chat

A popular feature of the Internet, chat is a way for two people to talk or chat back and forth over the Internet. The screen is divided into two parts, with one for your comments and the other your partner's. When you send chat messages, you can see each other's comments.

A similar service is IRC, or Internet Relay Chat. Here you can converse with groups of people in real time about various topics. The Internet is divided into topic areas, each with its own dedicated chat channel. Someone will open a channel and then permit other users on that forum to participate. Each user is given a handle, or nickname, that identifies them to the group. When you send a message to the group, it is repeated on everyone's screen in the forum.

## Personal Finance

Families have found that computers can help them do financial planning and carry out transactions. Programs like Quicken have made it easy to budget, keep track of expenditures, prepare tax forms, and plan for financial events such as paying for a college education and retirement. CheckFree is a way to write checks electronically, sending them for clearance through the Federal Reserve system. CheckFree connects directly with Quicken. So far, these programs have used dedicated dial-up connections rather than the Internet, probably for security reasons. We discussed Internet security earlier in this unit.

The Wells Fargo Bank pioneered a banking presence on the Internet. Its address is *http://www.wellsfargo.com*. The Security First Internet Bank at *http://www.sfnb.com/* is the first financial institution chartered exclusively for the Internet. The Online Banking and Financial Resources Directory home page at *http://www.orcc.com/banking.htm* is a directory of financial institutions that have home pages. You can get links to these home pages, organized by continent and type of institution.

You can use the Internet to check stock prices (*http://www.secapl.com/cgi-bin/qs/*) using the CheckFree Investment Services Quote Server. Open this Web page, enter the Wall Street ticker symbol for your stock or bond, and then click *Get Quotes*. For example, to check Hewlett Packard, enter HWP as the ticker symbol. If you don't know a ticker symbol, click the *Ticker Search* link. The system will bring back information about your security on a 15-minute delay basis. This company has a variety of subscription-basis stock-quote programs available.

You can subscribe to specialized business information services that provide electronic clippings of new stories about companies you are following. Some services provide detailed security prices and stock history data. You can create an electronic portfolio and download closing price data to your computer at the end of a trading day.

## GUIDED ACTIVITY

## 9.3    Checking Stock Prices

In this activity, you will check stock prices on the Internet.

1.  Connect to the Internet and open your Web browser.

2.  Connect to the quote server at *http://www.secapl.com/cgi-bin/qs/*.

3. Enter the ticker symbol AHP and click the *Get Quotes* button.

4. Click the *AHP* link in the first column of the table to open the details screen for this company.

**CHECKPOINT 9C** How would you get the detailed information into a word processing document?

5. Next, click the *Ticker Search* button. When prompted, type `Guidant` and click the *Search* button.

6. In a few moments, the quote server should supply GDT as the ticker symbol. Click the symbol to bring up the detailed quote server screen.

7. You can leave your browser open for now.

## Recreational Applications

Many games are available on the Internet, either to be downloaded to your computer and played off-line or to be played against other Internet users while on-line. Perhaps the best known of these games is MUD, which stands for Multi User Dungeon. Based on the Dungeons and Dragons adventure game, MUD connects users in a network and allows them to interact while logged on to the Internet. For more information about MUD games, join the news group called *rec.games.mud.announce* and read the FAQs (frequently asked questions).

Another popular game on our campus is called **Doom**. Some students have become literally addicted to interactive games on the Internet. We recommend moderation when playing any computer game. Set an ending time, and quit when you get to that time.

ESPN has created a sophisticated sports home page called **SportsZone**. The Web address is *http://espn.sportszone.com/*. You can follow games in progress and will find pages about each of your favorite pro sports teams. Full box scores of recent games are included. There is no basic subscription fee as of this writing, but some features are restricted to paying customers. The opening Web page appears in Figure 9.15. Similar sites include CNN/SI at *http://www.cnnsi.com/* and CBS SportsLine at *http://www.sportsline.com/*.

For those interested in flight simulators, there are news groups and mailing lists. The Flight-Sim mailing list contains numerous references for realistic shareware scenery files available via FTP. Roughly every three weeks a flight mission called Round Robin is published. Round Robin provides specific flight instructions for a geographic area, including airport departure data, navigational way points, and destination airport data including runway and instrument landing settings. You can discuss the mission with other flight enthusiasts and exchange ideas about various flight simulation software.

## The Arts

Although the screen resolution is not high, some organizations have placed samples of their artistic products on the Internet. For example, you can visit the Louvre Web page in Paris at *http://mistral.culture.fr/louvre/*. The site appears in four different languages for the convenience of visitors. Duplicates of that site exist elsewhere—North American users can access the SunSite Web Museum in North

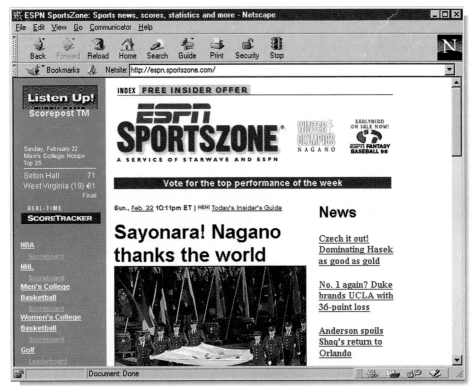

Carolina (*http://sunsite.unc.edu/wm/*) to shorten data transfer times significantly. You can view famous paintings and read about many exhibits. It also provides links to other Web pages with similar content. Of course, the Yahoo home page (*http://www.yahoo.com/*) has many Internet links to Entertainment and other related subjects.

# Emerging Technologies

Although the promise of direct universal connectivity has not yet been fulfilled, many of us can reach the Internet at a reasonable cost via telephone and modem. However, many of these new Internet technologies will depend on employing a larger bandwidth to the user so that a larger volume of information can be sent.

## CU-SeeMe

One way to engage in videoconferencing over the Internet is to use CU-SeeMe. A small video camera mounted above the monitor provides a slow-scan video signal that is compressed and sent over the Internet to the destination. Users will see their own image in the corner of the screen and the other person will appear in the remainder of the screen. Rapid motions are blurred because a new video frame is sent only 3 to 12 times per second, as compared to 30 times per second, with regular television signals. Your frame rate depends on the speed of your connection to the Internet. CU-SeeMe also contains an audio signal for voice communications, and in addition, can forward written messages.

To participate in CU-SeeMe you must have a high-speed Internet connection. Although it can work with a minimum modem connection of 28.8 Kbps, a direct connection is preferred. To originate video, you need a video camera and a video capture board. The board converts the NTSC output signal from the camera into a digital format that can be processed by the CPU (central processing unit) in your computer. If your computer has a fast CPU (such as a Pentium), it will be able to compress and uncompress the signal faster, resulting in less-jerky motion.

Through the use of CU-SeeMe reflectors, more than two people can participate in a video conference. A reflector is an Internet host, typically a UNIX machine, that can retransmit video signal packets to several users simultaneously so that they all see roughly the same image on their screens. The first full movie was transmitted over the Internet via CU-SeeMe in June 1995.

## Internet Radio

An article in *Time* magazine commented on sending radio programs in real time over the Internet. RealNetworks developed a method of Internet Radio called **RealAudio** that lets you listen to a program as it was broadcasted, or listen to recorded sound clips. It uses sophisticated digital compression algorithms. There are well-organized Web pages for ABC News and NPR broadcasts such as *All Things Considered* and *Morning Edition*.

You must have a copy of the RealAudio player in order to decode the transmission. Look for it at *http://www.realaudio.com* on the Web. Some Web browsers already come with an audio player. You can have either a direct Internet connection or a dial-up PPP account to use this service. The National Public Radio Web page containing links to various RealAudio broadcasts is found at *http://www.npr.org/*.

AudioNet makes use of the RealAudio player when it broadcasts live sports events. Figure 9.16 shows the AudioNet Purdue University basketball Web site.

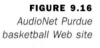

**FIGURE 9.16**
*AudioNet Purdue basketball Web site*

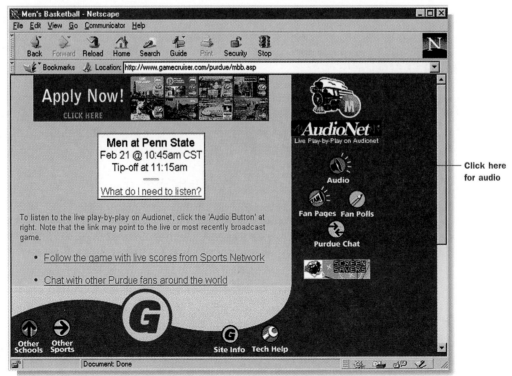

FIGURE 9.17
*RealAudio Player*
*dialog box*

Play/pause

Stop

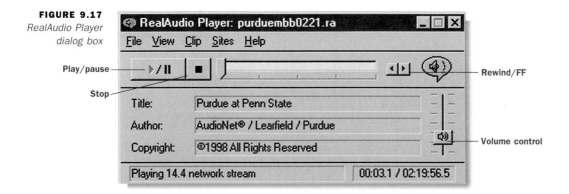

Rewind/FF

Volume control

Click on the Audio button to receive the actual live radio account of the game via RealAudio. Figure 9.17 shows the RealAudio player for this game. The Internet broadcast only lags the actual play-by-play by about 10–15 seconds, even with delays in the Internet.

## Internet Phones and CoolTalk

This group of applications goes beyond the chat utilities mentioned at the beginning of this unit. Here you can actually place and receive voice "phone calls" over the Internet. Netscape Navigator bundles a telephone tool called CoolTalk. To use CoolTalk you should have a microphone to capture your voice and a sound card and speaker to play the voice from the other end. Currently, there is no additional cost to use CoolTalk.

CoolTalk users can share a whiteboard while on-line and viewing and editing a graphic image. CoolTalk also can handle audio conferences with more than two people participating. Internet users who have Direct connections will hear much better audio quality, but CoolTalk does work with dial-up users. CoolTalk also includes a text chat utility. A Web phone book lets you find addresses of other CoolTalk users. CoolTalk even includes an answering machine to record messages if you are unable to take the call.

## High Bandwidth Connections

Although discussed in earlier units, it is worth mentioning again that graphics-intensive Web screens transfer very slowly using a typical 28.8 to 33.6 Kbps modem connection. Video conferencing adds greatly to the bandwidth requirements of your Internet connection. Although the best connection to the Internet is a direct connection at 10 Mbs, few of us have that luxury. Thus, a new set of high-speed connections are about to flourish.

You can use an ISDN line to communicate up to 128 Kbps or lease a line to connect at higher speeds. Although the Telecommunications Act of 1996 authorizes TV cable companies to provide telephone and high-speed data transmission services, at this writing few cable companies have begun to compete in this area. Cable modems are capable of 1.5 Mbps. The DSL (Digital Subscriber Line) technology may permit the phone company to increase the capacity of your home telephone line up to 1.5 Mbps or higher. Expect to see DSL installations in late 1998 or early 1999. The cost for such high-speed connections is likely to be much higher than the $20 per month fee for 28.8 ISP connections.

# Societal Implications of the Internet

It may be too early to tell what will happen to society as a generation of "surfers" grows up in the Internet environment. Some say that surfing the Internet is a significant waste of time and will lead to mindless clicking. Author William Gibson, who coined the term "cyberspace," described the Web in the *New York Times* as "a procrastinator's dream," giving us opportunity to wander aimlessly. Others say that those with Internet access—mostly people who live in affluent suburbs—will have another substantial advantage over the have-nots.

Some psychologists say that surfing the Internet may be addictive. The interactive features, particularly chat rooms, have led to psychological dependence. Some people have been known to call in sick to work so they can stay home and surf the Internet. Others have developed destructive long-distance romances with individuals they met on the Internet. A research study about Internet dependence was presented at a meeting of the American Psychological Association.

## Colleges and Universities

The Internet is having great influence in the college and university arenas. Higher education was probably the first big user of the Internet and still leads its use. Students are asked to do more research using resources found on the Internet. Libraries have found their role to be substantially different in this electronic era.

Faculty place syllabi and other course materials in Web pages instead of printing and duplicating them. Listserv groups and other discussion groups permit virtual discussions to take place around the clock.

Distance education is beginning to take hold in many parts of the country. Early forms involved closed-circuit television—sometimes two-way but often just one-way. Some schools sent videotapes to remote sites. The Internet provides the following new ways to offer courses off-campus:

- Web pages are used for making course assignments.

- E-mail provides a convenient means of communicating between students and instructors.

- Discussions can be done via mailing lists or news groups, permitting those with conflicting time schedules to participate.

- Assignments can be submitted with FTP or through a Web page.

Most college admissions offices have set up shop on the Internet. Prospective students can search for schools that meet their criteria and even conduct virtual visits via Web pages. Although colorful Web sites have not replaced the traditional college guide books, some students conduct all their admissions work electronically through the Web and e-mail. Many colleges now have electronic applications on-line, making it easier than ever to apply to a school.

## Medical Information Searches

Much medical and health information is available on the Internet, providing a valuable resource for patients and others who wish to educate themselves. Use the standard search tools such as Yahoo and Lycos to search for a particular disease or treatment by name. Or refer to the search tools' subject browsers and access health topics. Some of the information, such as the Medline archive, is available only to subscribers. Refer to the Knowledge Finder at *http://www.ariessys.com/* for information about such on-line archives.

Many newspapers and news services maintain on-line health columns and libraries of past stories. Refer to MSNBC at *http://www.msnbc.com/* and CNN at *http://cnn.com* for health stories. The CNN Health main page is shown in Figure 9.18.

**FIGURE 9.18**
*CNN Health main page*

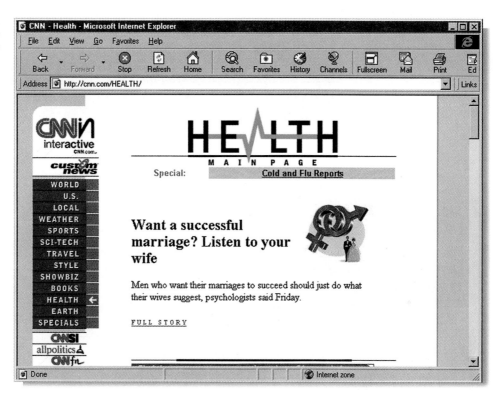

CAUTION    **Medical information found on the Internet is not necessarily current or applicable. *Always* corroborate such information with your own physician or health professional.**

# Telecommuting

The Internet has made telecommuting more interesting. Home workers can retrieve assignments easily from Web pages and FTP sites. Some prepare Web pages at home and post them electronically. Most importantly, communication via e-mail is inexpensive and makes telecommuting more effective than phone calls and faxes alone. Workers feel more "connected" when they can communicate easily with co-workers at other locations.

# New Industries

A whole new industry has grown up around the Web. Companies are hiring HTML programmers to build their Web sites. Advertising companies need computer-literate graphic designers to create attractive home pages. Nearly every town has an Internet service provider, or someone thinking about opening such an organization.

Another new phenomena is the hundreds of magazines that appear only on the Internet. Called zines (short for Web magazines), these magazines have all sorts of unusual agendas. A Washington scandal was first broken by a zine called the Drudge Report, found at *http://www.drudgereport.com/*. This site, shown in Figure 9.19, averaged 125,000 hits per day in February 1998!

**FIGURE 9.19**
*Drudge Report Web site*

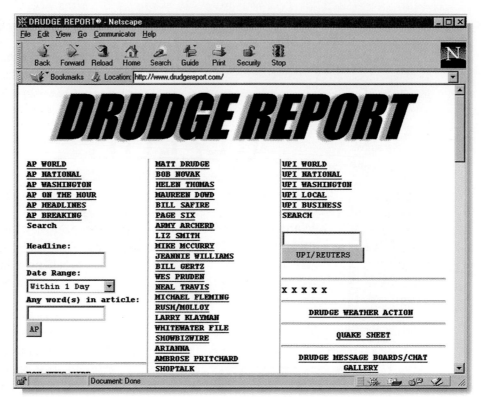

Zines can take advantage of the unique medium of the Internet. With hypertext the reader can jump around in an issue, or go back to previous issues with one click. Most zines lack the slick production quality of Drudge; they may look more like the public broadcast channels on your local cable TV network. The best-known zine is probably *Slate*, located at *http://www.slate.com*. It had more than 200,000 hits per day in early 1998 and the publisher expects to begin charging users $19.95 per year to access the page.

On-line dating services are flourishing on the Internet. Based on the personal pages section of your newspaper, Internet-based dating services are interactive and can feature more information if you would like to give it. The Internet also boasts

## Net Ethics        *Is Cybergossip Harmless?*

Are on-line gossip columns like the Drudge Report and others harmless entertainment? When they report rumors, are they subject to libel suits? Must they follow the same rules as ordinary publications?

numerous on-line job placement bulletin boards. People looking for jobs can post their resumes and even include an electronic pointer to their own personal home page. Hiring companies can leave job descriptions and even receive applications electronically.

# Will It Crash?

Most experts believe that the rapid growth of the Internet must be accompanied by expansion of the telecommunications infrastructure. Otherwise, the Internet will become saturated more frequently, leading to very slow response time, lost data, or even total breakdowns.

How do we pay for the increased capacity? Some argue that the government needs to get more involved. Others are pleased that the government has reduced its presence in the backbone portion of the Internet, letting competition lead the way. The latter group believe that the free-access nature of the Internet may give way to a system whereby a very small charge is made for use of the Internet.

# Paying For Use

Paying for use of the Internet may yet become a reality. Every time you transfer something through the Internet, a small fee—sometimes called sub-cent charge—may be levied and charged against your account. Most schemes would have you prepay an amount into the account and then use it up like a debit card. Others would bill you on a monthly basis. In either case, downloading a large program like Netscape Navigator would only cost a small amount. But those who use the Internet most would pay more for that privilege.

On August 7, 1996, America Online (AOL) had a nineteen-hour system-wide outage. More than six million customers went without e-mail and Web access for a day. It was notable enough to make the national TV news broadcasts that evening. Although AOL blamed the outage on human error when new routing software was installed, it nonetheless demonstrates how important e-mail and Internet access has become.

# Content Decency Issues

Parents have expressed concern about the Internet material available to their children. Other than direct parental supervision, there are several software solutions to this problem. You can purchase a filtering or blocking program that restricts access to certain sites or to Web documents that contain key phrases. See the Web site at *http://www.netnanny.com/* for one such program. The Learning Company publishes another program called CyberPatrol, found at *http://www.cyberpatrol.com/*. You can run a demonstration before purchasing the software.

Internet Explorer 4.0 contains a built-in screening service called Content Advisor, shown in Figure 9.20. With this dialog box, a parent or responsible adult can set levels of acceptable content for language, nudity, sex, and violence. The site ratings are supplied by the Recreational Software Advisory Council. CompuServe announced that it will include content ratings for all of its internal content. The ratings are based on PICS—Platform for Internet Content Selection—standards.

Some free speech advocates have argued that the First Amendment allows anyone to say anything on the Internet. Many argue that children should not be exposed to adult material. These packages help those who want to establish limits.

**FIGURE 9.20**
*Internet Explorer
Content Advisor*

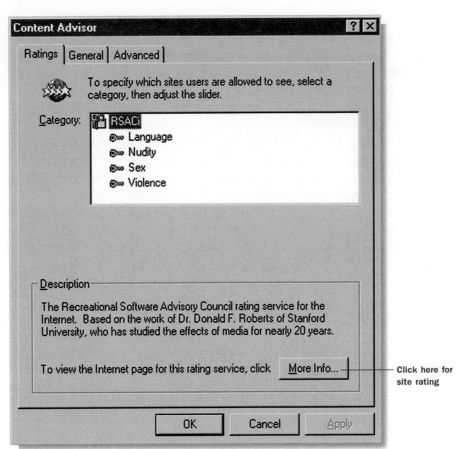

Click here for
site rating

# SUMMARY

This unit presents a summary of marketing phases and suggests ways in which the Internet can be used to facilitate electronic commerce. The Internet is ideal for pre-sale advertising, including mass e-mail, banner ads, and electronic catalogs. Many Web sites come with hit counters to measure the activity at that site, making it easier to assess the effectiveness of a particular medium or advertising campaign.

Many Web sites can take orders electronically, adding items to an electronic shopping cart. You can pay with a credit card or electronic money. In either case, most e-commerce Web sites offer encryption to protect sensitive information such as credit card numbers. Secure Web documents use the *https:* protocol and appear in your browser with a closed padlock icon in the security part of the status bar. Some Web sites are equipped to handle payments with electronic money, including smart cards, electronic tokens, and EFTS.

Some products lend themselves to electronic delivery, including software, financial information, and other knowledge-based products. Many organizations use the Internet to offer customer service and post-sale technical support. Both FedEx and UPS provide on-line tracking features for products shipped with those companies.

The Internet offers many personal uses, including virtual museums, chat rooms, personal banking, and recreation applications. You can purchase add-on filter programs to prevent children from accessing certain Web sites containing objectionable material.

## Vocabulary Exercise

*Write a short definition for each term in the following list:*

| | | |
|---|---|---|
| Channels | Encrypt | PGP (Pretty Good |
| Chat | Extranet | Privacy) |
| CoolTalk | Finger | RealAudio |
| CU-SeeMe | Firewall | SportsZone |
| DealerNet | Hacker | Sub-cent charges |
| Digital cash | Handle | Videoconferencing |
| Doom | Internet Relay Chat (IRC) | Zines |
| Electronic shopping cart | Intranet | |

## Review Questions

1. Discuss the four marketing phases as they pertain to e-commerce.

2. Discuss at least three reasons for a company to develop a Web page.

3. The Louvre has a Web site near its home in Paris. Why would it be better for people in the United States to access the copy in North Carolina?

4. What is ESPN's SportsZone? List the things you can find on this Web page.

5. What is CU-SeeMe? Why is this an important Internet development?

6. Discuss the use of digital compression algorithms for such things as videoconferences and RealAudio. What other parts of the Internet use compression technology?

7. How do you purchase a custom computer from a Web site like Dell Computers?

8. What security problems exist in doing business over the Internet? Discuss the solutions that have been developed.

9. What is an intranet, and why is it important? How does an intranet differ from the Internet? How can someone outside the company still access the intranet?

10. Discuss how colleges and universities use the Internet.

## Exercises

1. Access the Louvre Web Museum page at the North America site: *http:// sunsite.unc.edu/wm/*. Make a list of the five most impressive parts of this exhibit. Print a copy of something memorable from this Web site.

2. Connect to the J. Crew Web site at *http://www.jcrew.com/* and locate an article of clothing that suits you. List its item number, available sizes and colors, and its price. Find out what it would cost to ship the item to you.

3. Connect to DealerNet and print specifications about the car you would most like to have *and* can afford. Find the dealer closest to you.

4. Connect to the Southwest Airlines home page at *http://www.iflyswa.com* and determine the flight times and costs for a flight between Albuquerque and San Diego. Assume your travel is a month after the current date. What is the cost of the same flight taken in two days?

5. Connect to the *Amazon.com* home page and search for this textbook. What is the cost, and what other books are available by the same author?

6. Contact your school or company's computer center to see if there is a video-conferencing facility on your campus. Ask for a demonstration of this technology, if available.

7. Connect to the RealNetworks home page at *http://www.realaudio.com/* and obtain a copy of the RealAudio player. Download the contents of an NPR news broadcast and listen to a segment.

8. Connect to the Gamecruiser AudioNet College Sports Network at *http://www.gamecruiser.com* and listen to the college game of your choice. Prepare a list of the schools whose games are covered by this service.

9. Access ESPN's SportsZone and print the box score for the most important game played on that day.

10. Access the CheckFree Investment Services quote server and check the prices of Hewlett-Packard (HWP), Boeing (BA), Eli Lilly (LLY), Intel (INTC), and Conseco (CNC). Print the resulting display.

## Company Web Site

Select a local company or organization, and prepare a report about how a business home page could help them. Your design should focus on *what* the home page should do; don't actually implement the home page. Visit the company to discuss how using the Internet can help it conduct its business.

### PROJECT TEAM OPTION

Locate the home pages of other organizations similar to the company you have chosen. Develop a list of the features that are common to most of those sites. Prepare a report for the management of your company that describes those common features. Examples from those sites would be helpful for your report.

## Sports Sites

Compare the contents of the ESPN SportsZone, CBS SportsLine, and CNN/SI sports Web sites. Prepare a table that shows the common features and another table that shows the features that are unique to each service. Which parts of the service are available only at extra cost to subscribers?

### PROJECT TEAM OPTION

Print the stories from each of the sports services for the same game or sporting event. Which service's coverage is preferred for that game or event?

# APPENDIX

## *Answers to Checkpoints and Selected Review Questions*

2A, (p. 22): In Windows 95, Click Start, select Control Panel, and open the Modem icon. All the modems installed in the computer will be listed in the Modem Properties dialog box. You could also look at the back of the computer to see if a modem card has been installed. Of course, just because it is physically in the computer, the modem is not functional until it has been installed in the operating system.

2B, (p. 25): The *adapter* refers to a physical part of the system, such as the dial-up adapter (modem) or a network card. The *protocol* describes the procedures that the physical device follows in order to transfer data. You can right-click the Network Neighborhood icon on the desktop and select Properties to view all the adapters and protocols installed in your computer.

2C, (p. 27): Click Start, select Programs, then Accessories, and then scroll down to Dial-Up Networking. Many people will drag the particular dial-up networking icon to the Start button so that it appears in the first menu of the Start button.

2D, (p. 30): Line conditions always determine the fastest speed at which two modems can safely connect. If you get a relatively slow speed, hang up and try again to get a faster speed.

2E, (p. 32): If you move the mouse to the Connected To icon in the task bar, a pop-up menu will tell how many bytes have been received and transmitted so far in the session.

3A, (p. 44): Use Shift+Tab to move backwards to a previous header block; use Tab to move forward to another header block.

3B, (p. 49): Move the cursor to the edge or corner of the window until it turns into a two-headed arrow. Drag the side of the window out to enlarge the space. The message window will automatically expand to fit the new space you create.

3C, (p. 55): You can create your *own* e-mail address as an address book nickname. Then, when you put your nickname in the Cc: box, Eudora will expand it to the full e-mail address.

3D, (p. 55): Send yourself an e-mail message. Open the message, and read the end of it to see how Eudora has inserted your signature.

4A, (p. 75): Http: refers to hypertext transfer protocol, the default protocol for Web pages.

4B, (p. 86): The sequence of sites in the bookmarks or favorites list will vary for each user. To print the bookmarks list in Netscape (not asked in this question), open the bookmark.htm file in your browser. Then use the File→Print command.

4C, (p. 90): To print the contents of the legal message, simply click the Print button or use the browser's File→Print command.

4D, (p. 91): When you first click the link to a multimedia file, your browser may ask whether you intend to save the file on your disk or open the file. If you choose to save the file to disk, it will be saved for future use. Otherwise, it is saved in a temporary place and released after you close the audio player.

5A, (p. 101): You can open a Web site by (1) typing its URL into the Location box, (2) using the File→Open command in your browser, or (3) choosing it from a bookmarks or favorites list. Netscape "remembers" previously visited sites and will complete your URL entry as you type it into the Location box.

5B, (p. 104): Click on one of the underlined compass directions (e.g., South) to move (pan) the map in that direction.

5C, (p. 107): You could click the Back button until the home page reappears, or right-click the Web page and select Back from the quick menu. Use the Go→menu in Netscape and click on *www.yahoo.com*. You could also retype the home page URL in the Location box or select it from the bookmarks list.

5D, (p. 108): The search criteria "Windows NT" will look for this as a single phrase, rejecting any sites that do not have the keywords together. Some search engines default to this condition even if the quotes are omitted, while others would return sites that contain either word, or both, not necessarily together.

5E, (p. 109): If you are using dial-up networking with Windows 95, there will be an icon in the tray area of the toolbar (or a Connected To box in the toolbar) that indicates the name of the connection, the connection speed, the duration of the call, and how many bytes have been transferred in each direction. If you have a direct connection to the Internet, it should always be "live" so no further tests are necessary. To be certain your direct connection is working, you could open the MS-DOS Prompt window and type *ping www.indstate.edu* (or any other URL) and press Enter. Your computer will attempt to transmit information to that computer.

6A, (p. 126): The Newsrc file contains the names of each subscribed group and the posting numbers of articles you have already read. When you start the newsreader client, it goes out and fetches the new articles in your subscribed news groups. New articles are constantly being received by the news server. In the preparation of the manuscript for this book, it was frustrating to not be able to see the same set of articles at two different times because some had expired and were removed from the server. Although not recommended for new or inexperienced users, it is possible to manually edit the Newsrc file. You can subscribe to news groups by removing the exclamation point from the end of a group, and unsubscribe from a group by adding an exclamation point to the end of the group. You can also change the "see articles" reference numbers in the Newsrc file.

6B, (p. 128): Other ways of responding include sending an e-mail message to the individual who submitted the posting or creating an article that will be posted to the news group itself for everyone to see. Use the e-mail method if the reply is specific to the sender and the article posting if the reply is of wider interest to the news group.

6C, (p. 133): You should turn off the Signature feature because the mail server may interpret your signature as an extra command and will send you an error message for each (unrecognizable) line in your signature.

7A, (p. 146): Anonymous FTP lets you transfer files without having an account on the FTP server.

7B, (p. 146): Some computers, notably UNIX machines, treat lowercase and uppercase letters differently.

7C, (p. 150): The computer interprets the number "one" and the letter "ell" as different characters. You must use the correct one, in this case the letter.

7D, (p. 151): Scroll down to the bottom of the root folder in the left window, then select the A drive icon.

8A, (p. 172): The path indicates the drive letter and folder that contains the file. The default path in Notepad for Windows 95 is probably Desktop or Windows.

8B, (p. 174): ALIGN=RIGHT means that the image will be aligned with the right edge of the browser window.

8C, (p. 177): When you click on an anchor link with a mailto:URL, Netscape and most other browsers will open an e-mail message window with the URL address in the TO: box. You can fill in the message, and then send it to the recipient.

9A, (p. 207): The simplest way to access this page in the future is to add it to your bookmarks or favorites list. Once it is in the bookmarks list, you can open the book window in Netscape and then drag the bookmark to the desktop of your computer. Clicking that shortcut will open Netscape and fetch that page.

9B, (p. 210): Use the *Edit→Find* command to search the current home page for the desired target string.

9C, (p. 216): Block the desired text and then copy it to the Clipboard. Open the word processing document and paste the text in from the Clipboard.

# Answers to Odd-Numbered Review Questions

### Unit 1

1.  a. **Server** is the part of the network that provides shared resources such as hard disk space, specialty printers, tape drives, communications gateway, and so forth. The server frequently provides software and data for users of the network.

b. **Workstation** or **client** is the personal computer attached to the network for each user. The workstation or client typically has its own CPU, hard disk and other local storage, video, and keyboard and can act as a stand-alone computer.

c. **Cabling** connects the components of a network. Most local area networks use telephone-type or coax wiring while wide area networks use high speed cabling that may go through a satellite or microwave channel.

d. **Packets** represent information that travels over a network. The packet contains data and identifying information that allows it to be routed error-free to its destination. The packet is routed from node to node in the network until it reaches its destination.

3. To connect a personal computer to the Internet you must have a connection to a network attached to the Internet. This connection could be through a local area network or via a modem. You need the proper software drivers that allow the connection to take place. A more thorough discussion of connecting to the Internet appears in Unit 2.

5. a. For a student, **e-mail** can be used to correspond with faculty and other students. You can send e-mail messages to family members, other students, or co-workers. Some instructors request that students submit homework assignments via e-mail. In many businesses, virtually all routine communication is done through e-mail.

b. **Discussion groups** let a group of people talk about items of common interest. You might find a discussion group about your hobby and begin an electronic dialogue with other members of that group. Some schools have local discussion groups for items of interest on that campus, such as a discussion about campus politics, student parking, and other important topics.

c. **FTP** is used to transfer files over the network. A student could download via FTP the files containing the Internet tools described in this book. You could use FTP to transfer a file from your instructor's computer to your own computer. FTP can also be used to upload files such as homework assignments from your computer to another machine.

d. **Telnet** is the mechanism for doing a remote login to another computer system. You could use Telnet to connect to your library's electronic catalog system or to the Library of Congress catalog.

e. **World Wide Web** is the part of the Internet used for multimedia documents containing text, pictures, animation, video, and sounds. WWW documents contain hypertext links to information stored elsewhere on the Internet. The WWW is the fastest growing part of the Internet.

7. Netscape Navigator and Microsoft Internet Explorer are the two most popular Web browsers used today.

## Unit 2

1. The TCP/IP protocol is the name for a suite of telecommunications protocols that enable us to communicate over the Internet without errors. TCP is used

for routing information without errors; IP handles the data packets that form each message on the Internet. Because the Internet is based on TCP/IP, any computer fully connected to the Internet must have TCP/IP.

3. Use the Ping program that is built into Windows 95, and specify the URL address. Ping will convert the URL address into the IP address and tell you how long it takes to receive information from that address. The www.nasa.gov address converts to 128.183.243.36. Ping requires that you strip off the http:// prefix.

5. SLIP and PPP are types of TCP/IP connections established between the user and the Internet over the telephone, using a modem. SLIP was developed first and works well when lone conditions are good. PPP works better for noisier phone lines and for high-speed dial-up connections.

7. The V.32bis modem standard provides for 14,400 bits per second (bps) for dial-in connections. The V.34 standard provides up to 28,800 bps connections. Both work over normal telephone lines and test the line before each connection is made to determine the fastest speed that the line can support without data transmission errors.

9. First install your modem. Then make sure that dial-up networking is installed on your computer. Use the Make a Connection icon to create a new PPP connection. Configure the connection for your ISP's parameters: telephone number, IP address, DNS addresses, and domain name.

11. Authentication is the process of verifying that the user is authorized to use the service. Typically this means that the user must provide a valid user name and password.

## Unit 3

1. E-mail involves keying a message with an editor similar to a word processor and then sending it electronically to its destination. The e-mail message arrives almost instantaneously without postage or other fees. The recipient can read the message and print a copy if desired. The recipient is able to prepare and send a reply within moments. Regular mail takes a long time to reach its destination and must be created for each recipient. E-mail can be mailed to multiple recipients by listing their e-mail address in the message header area.

3. a. The **To:** box is where you place the recipient's e-mail address. You may list several recipients' addresses here, separated by commas.

   b. The **Subject:** box is for a brief description of the contents of the message. Some people decide whether or not to read an e-mail message by the contents of this box.

   c. The **Cc:** box is for the e-mail address where a "carbon copy" of the message is to be sent.

   d. The **Bcc:** box is where you place the e-mail address for the person who is to receive a blind carbon copy of this message. The To: recipient will not see the e-mail address of someone in the Bcc: box.

e. The **Attachments:** box is where you specify the names of files that are attached to the e-mail message. The recipient receives the message and is given the opportunity to extract the attached file.

5.  a. **Edu** refers to educational institutions. Some community colleges and other institutions do not use the Edu domain suffix.

    b. **Net** refers to a network provider, or an organization whose business is providing network access.

    c. **Mil** refers to a military organization.

    d. **Gov** represents a government organization.

    e. **Com** refers to a commercial or business organization.

7.  a. **Flame mail** refers to hateful or emotionally charged mail messages. Flame mail sometimes occurs because the original sender did not use common network etiquette (netiquette) or because the original sender made flamboyant comments. Flame mail is to be avoided whenever possible.

    b. **Message priority** is the ability to make an e-mail message appear at higher (or lower) importance. Many e-mail systems provide this feature and display the message header in a different color or with a different prefix.

    c. **Mailbox folders** or mailboxes let you organize your messages by subject. Most e-mail systems provide this feature with a way to transfer messages between folders.

    d. **Message signature** is an electronic file that is added to the end of an e-mail message. The signature contains text, not a graphic representation of your written signature, that identifies you. The signature typically contains your name, address, telephone numbers, affiliation, and e-mail address.

    e. **Message filter** is a way to filter out messages according to the sender's e-mail address or subject box. You can set up filters to remove messages meeting those criteria or to bring them up to read first.

9.  An emoticon is a small icon constructed from ordinary text characters that can lend subtle meaning to a message. For example, a :-) is equivalent to a grin or smiley and can indicate that you are teasing.

11. To send a message to a group, list the entire set of e-mail addresses, separated by commas, in the To: box in the message header. Or you can create a Eudora nickname for that group if you expect to send multiple messages to the same group. Some e-mail systems let you create a group or distribution list, another term for the nickname.

## Unit 4

1.  The World Wide Web represents that portion of the Internet that supports multimedia and hypertext documents. WWW documents following the HTTP protocol are called home pages or Web documents.

3. Web documents can contain such multimedia components as text in different fonts and colors, sounds, pictures or graphic images, animation, and video or moving images.

5. a. The **home page** is the opening document at a particular WWW site. It generally contains references to other pages.

   b. **URL** stands for Universal Resource Locator. The URL provides the protocol type (ftp:, http:, telnet:, gopher:, file:) for a particular document and the Internet address or domain name of that document.

   c. **HTTP** stands for HyperText Transfer Protocol and is the basic protocol used for WWW pages. The language used in HTTP is HTML or HyperText Markup Language.

   d. **Link** refers to the URL reference of another HTML document. Thus, a home page might have links to other kinds of information. In HTML documents the links are usually underlined and appear in a different color. You can fetch that information by clicking on the link.

   e. **.GIF file** stands for Graphic Image File and is the most common file type used in HTTP documents. A .GIF file is a picture, logo, or other single graphic image. .GIF files are larger than the newer .JPEG file format.

7. The URL provides the protocol type (ftp:, http:, telnet:, gopher:, file:) for a particular document. **ftp:** is used for transferring files to your computer. **http:** is the usual HTML document found on the WWW. **telnet:** establishes a remote terminal session with another host on the Internet. **gopher:** sets up a Gopher session with the WWW browser. **file:** refers to reading a HTML file from your own disk drive, useful when you are developing a new home page.

## Unit 5

1. You can open the Web site of a search engine by typing its URL into the Location box, using the File→Open command in your browser, or choosing it from a bookmarks or favorites list. Netscape "remembers" previously visited sites and will complete your URL entry as you type it into the Location box. Netscape Communicator and Internet Explorer both have Search buttons in the toolbar—click that button to display lists of popular search tools with clickable links.

3. Some search robots constantly scan the Web and add new sites to the database. Others work on the basis of having Web site information submitted to it by authorized persons. White and Yellow Page information is frequently purchased from telephone companies.

5. The Yahoo front page contains a large search box where you can enter your own keyword(s). The 14 main subject categories appear beneath the search box. There are links to sports pages that depend on the season—as of this writing in January, information appears about basketball, hockey, and professional golf. There are links to other Yahoo search categories including Yellow Pages, people search, maps, classified ads, personals, news, weather, jobs, homes, and more. At the bottom of the page are links to Yahooligans for kids, Yahoo store, stock viewer, MTV guide, and more. Finally, there are links to

World Yahoos in more than a dozen countries and specialized Yahoos for major metropolitan areas in the United States.

7. Add t: in front of the search keyword to restrict the search to document titles only.

9. First open the home page of the site. Type your name and e-mail address into the search boxes, then click on the Add E-mail Address link. Before your name is permanently added, you will get an e-mail message at that address asking you to confirm the placement in that directory. Thus, someone else cannot add your e-mail address without your knowledge. Many colleges and companies will automatically add your e-mail address to the organization's internal on-line directory.

11. An embedded search tool provides searching within a specific Web site. That is, if you want to find some information from that site only, use the embedded search tool. It doesn't give any information about other Web sites.

## Unit 6

1. A discussion group is an electronic forum where people with common interests share ideas and respond to postings. Responses can be made to an individual via e-mail or by posting an article to the entire group.

3. a. To subscribe to a news group, highlight the name of that group, then use the *Group→Subscribe* command. Or right-click the group and select Subscribe.

   b. To retrieve a list of articles within a news group, choose the desired news group by double-clicking with the mouse.

   c. To read an article, choose it from the list of articles by double-clicking its name.

   d. To post a new article, use the *Article→Post Article* command. Create the article by typing it in, then use the *File→Send* command to send it along.

   e. To unsubscribe from a news group, select its name in the list of subscribed news groups, then use the *Group→Unsubscribe* command. Or right-click the group and select Unsubscribe.

5. A thread is a set of postings that pertain to one another. For instance, someone might post an article. Someone replies to that article. Someone replies to the first reply. If your newsreader supports threads, you can read those postings one after another, without having to search for them yourself.

7. a. To subscribe to a mailing list, send an e-mail message to the Listserv address with a single line in the message body: "SUBSCRIBE groupname yourname." Not all list servers support use of "yourname" in the subscribe command.

   b. To read the postings of a Listserv group, do nothing other than check your e-mail. Postings are automatically sent to all members of that group as ordinary e-mail.

   c. To unsubscribe from a mailing list, send an e-mail message to the list server with "UNSUBSCRIBE groupname" as the message. Some listserv hosts require you to use the SIGNOFF command instead.

    d.  To start a new mailing list discussion group, prepare a proposal and develop a theme for the group. Unlike news groups that require that users vote on the group, you can begin a mailing list unilaterally. You will need to locate a mailing list host with appropriate software. Although that is beyond the scope of this book, you could check out the Lyris software Web site at *http://www.lyris.com*. Their commercial mailing list software has a free version for up to 200 members in a list.

## Unit 7

1.  FTP is used to transfer files without errors. Many of these files are shareware programs that are distributed freely. Some files contain frequently asked questions (FAQs) and answers. There are many learning materials available via FTP on the Internet.

3.  ASCII files contain text characters; binary files are usually programs, graphic images, or special data files. Binary files must be transferred in binary mode or else errors will occur. ASCII files are used for Readme files and other simple text files where the size is relatively short and no formatting is desired. HTML files used in Web documents are text files with HTML formatting codes placed as regular text characters within the document.

5.  A Web browser is simpler to use and is more available than a specialized FTP program that first must be downloaded. To navigate between levels of the FTP server, just click once in the browser on that line.

7.  a.  The **open** command will connect to a specific FTP host. You must specify the Internet address of the host after the open command.

    b.  **cd** is used to change to a new directory.

    c.  **cdup** is used on some systems to change to the parent directory. Some systems use **cd..** to change to the parent directory.

    d.  **pwd** will display the name of the current directory.

    e.  **status** will display the file transfer mode and other option choices.

    f.  **get** will transfer a file from the host to your computer. Specify the name of the file after get.

    g.  You can transfer multiple files with **mget**.

    h.  **put** is the command to transfer a file from your computer to the host computer.

9.  Telnet is used to connect your computer as a terminal to a remote host. You can issue commands to that computer as if you were present at that computer. Some university computers allow you to log in to a Telnet session with a special user name and check student personal information.

## Unit 8

1.  HTML stands for HyperText Markup Language, the standard language used for creating http documents, also known as Web pages. Web users do not need to know anything about HTML to surf the Internet. In fact, those who build

Web pages do not need to know much about HTML if they use a commercial HTML editor program or Netscape Composer to create Web pages; those are as easy to use as most word processors.

3. You can create a Web page as a file stored on your disk drive using Notepad or another text editor, and then display it on Netscape or your own Web browser. Place any graphic images in the same folder as the Web page document itself. You can test everything except anchor links to other Web resources found on the Internet.

5.  a. Inserts a horizontal rule (line) across the screen.

    b. Creates an ordered (numbered) list. Items starting with <LI> start a new line in the list.

    c. Creates an unordered (bulleted) list. Items starting with <LI> start a new line in the list.

    d. Ends the head section of the HTML document.

    e. Begins a paragraph that is centered horizontally on the screen.

7. If Netscape is your browser, use the *View→Page Source* command to examine the HTML codes within a home page. With Internet Explorer, use the *View→ Source* command. Or, save that page as a disk file and open the resulting text file with an editor like Notepad.

9.  a. HTML tables look like tables in a word processor, with borders between cells and around the outside of the table by default. They are an attractive way to present tabular data in rows and columns.

    b. Frames break up a Web document into panes, each independently scrollable. You can put a table of contents into one small frame, and use another frame to display text that is tied to each link in the first frame.

    c. An image map is a graphic image that is broken up into menu choices. An image map is usually more simple to use than a series of individual link lines. Images take much longer to download than text link lines.

    d. Java is the name of the programming language first developed by the Sun Microsystems. Java applets can be programmed to accomplish simple and complicated tasks.

## *Unit 9*

1. The "pre-sale" phase involves advertising products—goods and services—to potential customers. This can be targeted e-mail or Web sites. The "taking the order" phase is augmented by on-line business Web sites that display information in electronic catalogs and then permit buyers to add the items to their electronic shopping carts. Most on-line sites have secure payment systems. The phase involving "delivering the goods" *may* be executed over the Internet. Software and information represent the most common products that are delivered electronically. The final stage, "customer service," can involve e-mail for tech support, FAQs, driver library, and forums where customers can talk to other customers and leave messages for support personnel.

3. The mirror site in North Carolina represents a shorter path for packets to follow. Pages will download more quickly from North Carolina for North American viewers.

5. CU-SeeMe is a videoconferencing tool available on the Internet. With CU-SeeMe and appropriate hardware, you can transmit a slow-scan video image of yourself and your voice while you communicate with another user. The picture quality and speed (frames per second) depend on the bandwidth of the Internet connection.

7. Visit the Web site with your browser, and then follow instructions. Select a product category, and then choose a particular model. Go into the configure program and select the options for that model. When finished, the computer will update the price. Then you can buy the product electronically with a credit card or other payment method.

9. An intranet is a Web site that is limited to internal users only and protected from the rest of the Internet by a firewall. Intranets works just like the Internet and are used primarily to disseminate information. Someone who needs to access the intranet from outside the organization can do so by going through an authentication procedure, giving the user name and password. This is called an extranet.

# Glossary of Internet Terms

**ADDRESS**   An Internet address can appear in two formats. The domain name system (DNS) combines geographical and specific user information. For example, the author's e-mail address is mfbjm@befac.indstate.edu. Explanation: *mfbjm* is the user name, *befac* is the server name, *indstate* is the institution name, and *edu* refers to an educational institution. Most U.S. addresses omit the country segment that is placed on the end. The IP address is the other format. The author's IP address is the numeric location of a computer physically attached to the Internet, in this case 139.102.67.10. A static address is always the same and denotes a computer with a direct connection. A dynamic address is assigned each time the user connects to the network, usually through a dial-up connection.

**ADDRESS BOOK**   The local directory of nicknames and related e-mail addresses. The address book in Eudora can contain nicknames for individuals or groups.

**ALIAS**   A nickname for an individual's physical e-mail address. An alias is useful when your physical e-mail address changes, such as when assigned to a new server: users continue to use the alias to address e-mail.

**ALTAVISTA**   A search engine that catalogs the contents of all home pages it finds on the Internet.

**AMERICA ONLINE (AOL)**   A popular commercial information utility that offers some Internet access features. It is not necessary to have an Internet address when using AOL.

**ANCHOR**   A hyperlink found in an HTML document. The <A> command refers to another document or image found on your computer or on the Internet.

**ANONYMOUS FTP**   A method of transferring (downloading) files using FTP. When you do anonymous FTP, you log in with the "anonymous" user name and give your full Internet user name as the account's password. Anonymous FTP users have limited access to FTP host files.

**ARCHIVE**   A downloadable collection of older messages, articles, postings, or files associated with a discussion group or topic. *See FAQ.*

**ARTICLE**   Another term for a news group or Listserv group posting. You can browse through headers of the articles in a group and then download the desired one to your news reader.

ASCII FILE   A text file that can be viewed directly with Notepad and that can be read by most computer programs. ASCII files contain no formatting or special encoding. When doing FTP, you must specify whether a file is ASCII or binary.

ASYMMETRIC DIGITAL SUBSCRIBER LINE (ADSL)   Recently approved digital telephone service yielding data download speeds up to 1.5 Mbps. ADSL also allows normal use of the telephone at the same time as data transmissions. ADSL will cost significantly more than the usual $20/month ISP fees.

AUTHENTICATION   The process of verifying that the user logging in is authorized to use the resources requested. Authentication generally involves submitting a username and a password.

BANDWIDTH   Measurement of the capacity of the communications channel to carry information.

BIGFOOT   A search tool used with business and personal information such as address, phone number, e-mail address, and home page URL.

BINARY FILE   A coded file that requires a viewer to read. All executable programs and most word processing documents are binary files. When doing FTP, you must specify whether a file is ASCII or binary.

BITNET   A large academic network that has become an informal part of the Internet.

BLIND COPY   A copy of an e-mail message sent to another user without the original recipient's knowledge. In Eudora, Bcc: represents the blind copy recipient.

BOOKMARK   A list of frequently used Internet resources. You can retrieve information from a bookmark item without having to remember the exact address for that site.

BOOLEAN SEARCHING   Use of the keywords AND, OR, and NOT to make Web searches more explicit. A AND B means both A and B must be true; A OR B means either A or B may be true; NOT C means that C cannot be true. Boolean searching produces more true hits among the sites returned by a search engine.

BROWSER   A client program such as Netscape Navigator or Internet Explorer for viewing Web documents formatted in the HTML language.

BTW   A slang abbreviation for "By The Way."

CACHE   A temporary holding area in the computer that allows faster processing. In a Web browser, the disk cache holds graphic images and whole Web pages that have been previously viewed. The browser will load these items from the cache instead of going to the Web to fetch a new copy, speeding up loading of home pages. If the object on a page has changed from the version in the cache, the browser will load a fresh copy from the Internet.

CERN   The Institute for High Energy Physics located in Switzerland. CERN is largely responsible for the early development of the World Wide Web, which provided a way for scientists to communicate and share results around the world. CERN continues to act as an important research facility for WWW.

CERT   Computer Emergency Response Team. This group was established to help users repair damage done by viruses, computer hackers, and other threats.

CHAMELEON SAMPLER   An older TCP/IP software suite used in Windows 3.*x* systems. This suite included a Winsock, TCP/IP dialer, and individual programs for e-mail, telnet, FTP, Web browsing, and so forth.

CHANNELS   The organization for push technology information in modern Web browsers. You can subscribe to a channel from your browser; then, information pertaining to that topic will be automatically sent to your browser in the background. When you want to view that information, simply open the channel and view.

CHAT   A way for you to participate in Internet discussions via the keyboard. Enter a chat room, provide a handle to identify you, and participate. The submissions from others appear in one window on your screen, while your comments appear in another.

CLIENT   Another term for a software program that runs on the workstation or client computer. You might have an e-mail client program like Eudora or a WWW browser like Netscape Navigator or Internet Explorer. Server versions of programs will display information requested by client programs.

CLIPBOARD   The Windows feature that allows information to be transferred from one document or application to another. Users typically copy or cut text or images to the Clipboard, then paste from the Clipboard into another document.

COMMON GATEWAY INTERFACE (CGI)   The programming interface used with HTML documents that provides for some script to run on the Web server. CGI scripts are used to process user information submitted via a Web form.

COMMUNICATIONS CHANNEL   Medium used to carry information. Common channels include telephone line (dial-up modem), ISDN, and direct network connection. Wireless media include cellular telephone, microwave, and satellite.

COMPRESSED FILES   Compressed files have been processed to save space and thus take much less time to be transferred. Once received at their destination, compressed files are expanded to their original size. Popular compression methods include PKZIP and WinZip.

COOLTALK   A method of voice communication over the Internet. Similar to the telephone, CoolTalk lets you convert voice messages into digital pulses and replay them at the other end.

CSO   A style of phone book information named after the Computing Services Office at the University of Illinois. CSO describes a method for searching electronic phone books.

CU-SEEME   A method of video conferencing over the Internet. CU-SeeMe requires that you have a small video camera and video capture board to convert the video signal into a highly compressed digital pattern. CU-SeeMe provides for slow-scan TV signals with audio that can be transmitted in real time to another user.

CYBERSPACE    A term that describes the vast collection of information available to interconnected computers.

DEALERNET    A combination of automobile dealers that provide information about their businesses from one Web site. DealerNet contains information about automobile models as well as locations of individual dealers.

DIAL-UP CONNECTION    A network connection created by using a modem to dial in over telephone lines. A dial-up connection is much slower than a direct connection. Newer telephone technologies such as ISDN may make medium-speed connections possible over specialized phone lines.

DIGEST    A group of mailing list articles that are grouped into a single posting and periodically sent to your e-mail address. A digest results in many fewer e-mail messages from that group.

DIGITAL CASH    One method of prepaying money into an account and then spending that cash on the Internet without using a credit card number or providing other information that could be a security risk.

DIRECT CONNECTION    Refers to a direct network connection in which you have a high-speed dedicated connection. Most university computer labs have a direct connection to the Internet, whereas most home users and some offices must create a temporary connection by dialing in with a modem. A direct connection is preferred when transferring large files or downloading graphics, sound, and video images.

DISCUSSION GROUP    A group of Internet users with similar interests who post articles on the group's mailing list area. Group members react to the postings with discussion in the form of additional postings. News groups require that members download desired articles to their computer; mailing list groups automatically e-mail all articles to members of the group.

DOMAIN    The name associated with a particular computer site. The last letters in the domain usually give either the country of that site or the type of domain. We use .EDU to represent educational institutions, .COM for commercial companies, .GOV for government bodies, .MIL for military organizations, .NET for network providers, and .ORG for not-for-profit and other organizations.

DOMAIN NAME SYSTEM (DNS)    The DNS converts the location of a computer within a domain such as *www.indstate.edu* to an IP address. *See Address.*

DOOM    An adventure-type game played on the Internet among multiple players.

DOWNLOAD    The process of transferring a file from another computer *to* your computer.

DRIVER    A software program that enables a particular hardware device to function. Windows 95 comes with many drivers built-in, and most hardware devices come with drivers on a diskette. You can download updated drivers from the Web.

ELECTRONIC COMMERCE    Also known as e-commerce, includes the ways that the Internet is used to do business. This includes targeted advertising, mass e-mail campaigns, electronic catalogs, on-line order entry, electronic payments, and post-sale customer service.

ELECTRONIC SHOPPING CART   The figurative vehicle used to accumulate items selected for purchase at a business Web site. As you select an item, the computer adds it to the electronic shopping cart.

E-MAIL   An abbreviation for electronic mail. E-mail is a way to send and receive messages electronically using a network. E-mail is received almost instantaneously at little or no cost to the sender or receiver. Eudora Light is used to demonstrate e-mail in this book.

E-MAIL SIGNATURE   A block of text identifying the sender that is automatically appended to outgoing e-mail messages. The signature usually contains the sender's name, affiliation, telephone numbers, an Internet address, and sometimes a slogan or other humorous information.

EMOTICON   A text-based icon created from the keyboard, and meant to be read sideways, to give your e-mail message some emotional flavor. For instance, :-) can mean a grin, while :-( is a frown.

ENCRYPTION   Sending coded information over the Internet so that sensitive information such as credit card data cannot be intercepted and stolen. Netscape has an encryption mode for secured transactions.

EUDORA   A popular e-mail application that runs on the Internet. Eudora is based on the POPmail standard that allows someone to receive and answer e-mail messages off-line, away from the normal mail server. This book uses Eudora Light to illustrate electronic mail services.

EXTRANET   An intranet with restricted access that is available outside the borders of an organization. Thus, authorized users who travel or who are located outside the organization can access information from the intranet.

FAQ   Frequently Asked Questions. A FAQ is a compilation of frequently asked questions in a particular subject. Before posting a question or comment to a news group or mailing list, it is recommended that you read the FAQ in that group to see whether your point has already been addressed.

FAVORITES   Another term for bookmarks within Microsoft Internet Explorer.

FILTER   A rule for deciding which e-mail messages to read. Some filters reject mail from certain e-mail addresses, while others give rules for subject content that will be filtered.

FINGER   A UNIX command often found on the Internet that will provide certain identification information about an individual.

FIREWALL   A software or hardware device that keeps outside users from getting in to an organization's network. Firewalls are used for security purposes.

FLAME MAIL   Flamboyant e-mail messages that tend to arouse the emotions of the recipients. We recommend that you avoid flame mail.

FORM   A type of HTML document found on the Web that contains text boxes where you can fill in information. A form is used to gather information from a user that is subsequently sent to the provider of that document.

FRAME   An HTML object whereby the screen is divided into two or more windows called frames. The frames are independently scrollable, and Web designers typically put a menu in a smaller frame to the left or top and then use the larger frame to display information associated with a particular menu choice.

FTP   File Transfer Protocol. This method is used to transfer files between computers on a network.

FYI   Slang abbreviation representing "For Your Information."

GATEWAY   The name for a communications portal that allows messages to be sent to or received from other networks.

GOPHER   A user-friendly menu-driven method for distributing information to users, Gopher was originated at the University of Minnesota. Gopher can automatically fetch documents and files and perform remote log-ins.

GRAPHIC IMAGE FILE (GIF)   A graphic file format frequently used on the Internet. GIF files are moderately compressed but are a well-known standard. JPEG files are more compressed and are becoming the preferred way to store graphic images on the Internet.

GRAPHICAL USER INTERFACE (GUI)   The interface used in Windows and Macintosh computers. GUI screens use icons, windows, and buttons to represent user commands. Users select items by clicking them with the mouse.

HACKER   An individual who tries to damage or destroy information found in computer networks. Some hackers just "break in" and don't intend to do damage.

HANDLE   A temporary ID used to identify an individual in a chat room. CB radio enthusiasts often use a handle when talking to identify themselves without giving their proper names.

HIT   A Web document matching your search criteria that is returned by a search engine. A miss represents a matching Web document that does not prove to be helpful. To reduce the number of misses, be more specific with the search criteria key words.

HOME PAGE   A Web document that appears when you access a particular Internet location. The home page has links or jumps to other pertinent information stored on the Web.

HOST   Another term for server. A host computer maintains resources that client computers can request.

HOTBOT   A search tool that crawls around the Web finding and cataloging home pages according to their content.

HTML   Hypertext Markup Language. This is used to create documents with hypertext links to embedded resources such as other documents, graphics, animation, and sound.

HTML MAIL   The e-mail client included with modern Web browsers. HTML mail features rich formatting, graphics, and colors. However, not all e-mail clients can handle HTML mail.

HTTP   HyperText Transport Protocol. Used with World Wide Web (WWW), HTTP is the standard for transferring hyperlinked HTML documents from the Web server to your computer.

HYPERLINK   Also known as a link or pointer, a hyperlink represents the address of a resource that can be loaded by clicking the hyperlink. Hyperlinks can refer to other files on the user's computer, or to files found on the Internet. Once you load a new document by clicking its hyperlink, you can go back to a previous page by clicking the Back button.

HYPERTEXT   A way of displaying information in a hierarchical fashion with links to relevant information elsewhere in that document. WWW documents are examples of hypertext files. They often resemble an outline of the full document.

IMAGE   A graphic file found in an HTML document, usually denoted by its file extension. Common files types include *.gif* and *.jpg* file.

IMAGE MAP   A graphic image found in an HTML document that is subdivided into graphical menu choices. The image map contains hyperlinks to each menu item according to what region the user clicks in.

IN-LINE IMAGE   A graphic image that is displayed next to text in a WWW document.

INDEX.HTML   The default home page found on many UNIX-based Web servers. That is, if the URL address of a particular page contains the path but no file name, the Web server looks for a file called *index.html* at that address and loads it. Some other Web servers use *default.asp* or *default.htm* as the default home page.

INFORMATION SUPERHIGHWAY   Term that describes a large network connecting businesses, other institutions, and home users. Some people say that the Internet is the precursor to the information superhighway.

INFOSEEK   A search tool on the Internet.

INTERNET   A network of networks. The Internet contains more than 100,000 networks representing millions of individual computer users. The Internet is global with connections in over sixty countries worldwide. No single organization controls the growth, development, and operations of the Internet.

INTERNET EXPLORER   The Web browser developed by Microsoft for Windows 95, Windows 3.1, and the Macintosh. Internet Explorer contains modules for browsing, news groups, e-mail, and more.

INTRANET   An internal Internet protected by a firewall from the rest of the Internet. An intranet serves the internal information and communication needs of an organization.

IP ADDRESS   Internet Protocol Address is the numeric number assigned as the address of an Internet site. Any computer (server or client) attached to the Internet has a unique IP Address. For example, the Indiana State University *befac* server's IP address is 139.102.67.1. Specialized domain name servers are able to convert a name such as *befac.indstate.edu* into the proper IP address.

IRC   Internet Relay Chat. A method that allows groups of users to "chat" with each other over the Internet using their keyboards. Each participant in an IRC channel receives a copy of the messages sent to other members in that group. Some people believe it is similar to chatting on CB radio.

ISDN   Integrated Services Digital Network. ISDN is a medium-speed direct-dial digital telephone service becoming available at substantially extra cost. ISDN can transfer data in excess of 100 Kbps, whereas most high-speed modems are limited to 14,400 bps or 28,800 bps. ISDN will be popular for those who transfer large files or graphic images and who do not have a direct Internet connection.

JPEG   A highly compressed graphics file found on the Internet. JPEG files are more easily transferred over the Internet than GIF files.

LINK   The pointer that contains the URL address for the current item. In Web documents the links are usually underlined and appear in a different color. In Gopher documents each line represents a link or pointer.

LINK   *See hyperlink or pointer.*

LISTSERV GROUP   A mailing list type of discussion group. A Listserv group uses specialized software to administer the mailing list. You can use an e-mail message to subscribe or unsubscribe to that group. Some groups are moderated, meaning that someone reads and edits submitted articles before they are posted to the group s list. Accepted postings are electronically mailed to all members of the Listserv group.

LOCAL AREA NETWORK (LAN)   A communications network spanning a room or building. A LAN contains a server, individual workstations, communications cable, and network shared resources such as a high-speed printer, CD-ROM drive, communications gateway, and so forth.

LURKING   Where a member of a discussion group listens to the discussion but never submits any postings nor contributes to the discussion. New users frequently are lurkers until they become experienced with the way topics are discussed.

LYCOS   A popular index for Internet resources with search capabilities. Lycos can be found at *http://lycos.com.* Lycos is maintained at Carnegie Mellon University.

LYNX   A text-only viewer of Web documents. Lynx versions exist for DOS and UNIX computers.

MAILBOX OR FOLDER   A means of storing e-mail messages according to their content. Eudora automatically creates an In mailbox for incoming mail and an Out mailbox for copies of outgoing messages.

MAILING LIST   Another term for Listserv group. Postings to the mailing list are automatically sent as e-mail messages to all members of that group.

MICROSOFT FRONT PAGE   An easy-to-use Web page design and editing tool. Front Page allows the user to build complex Web sites without having to know HTML commands.

MID-LEVEL NETWORK   The high-speed communication channels that serve as the backbone of the Internet, carrying data between cities and continents. Commercial providers such as Sprint and MCI provide the mid-level network.

MISS   A site that is returned by the search engine but does not contain information about the topic you are researching.

MODERATED LIST   A mailing list or news group in which submissions are edited before being posted to the group. Messages may be examined to see if they are appropriate for that group or if they contain profanity or improper statements. Group members usually vote to determine whether the group will be moderated. It is a controversial issue to some people.

MOSAIC   The original graphical WWW hypertext viewer. Mosaic was developed at the University of Illinois and is available for Windows and the Macintosh. Other companies have licensed Mosaic for their own browsers.

MPEG   Although not formally covered in this book, MPEG files represent a highly compressed form used for full resolution video clips with sound.

NCSA   National Center for Supercomputer Applications. Located at the University of Illinois, this center has been a leader in the development of Internet applications, particularly the Mosaic Web browser.

NETIQUETTE   A set of suggestions or guidelines for proper etiquette on the Internet when submitting e-mail or discussion group messages. Look in Units 3 and 6 for netiquette rules.

NETSCAPE   The company that developed Netscape Navigator, the most popular Web browser, created by some of the original Mosaic programming team. Netscape Communicator is the most current version. Netscape Communicator is available for Windows, Macintosh, and UNIX computers. A copy can be obtained via anonymous FTP at *ftp.netscape.com*. This book uses Netscape Communicator to demonstrate Web services. Netscape produces Web server software as well.

NETSCAPE COMPOSER   The intermediate WYSIWYG HTML editor for creating home pages. Netscape Composer is used to demonstrate some HTML skills in this book.

NETWORK   A system of data communication channels, software, and hardware resources that work together to facilitate exchange of information.

NETWORK NEWS   Another name for news groups that belong to the seven categories: *alt, comp, misc, news, rec, sci,* and *soc.*

NEWBIE   A slang term meaning a new Internet user.

NEWS GROUP   A discussion group in which postings are made to the news group. You can view the subjects of the postings in a group and then decide whether to download the entire article to your computer.

NEWS XPRESS   The name of the Windows newsreader client used in this book. News Xpress lets you subscribe to desired news groups and then will display those messages you wish to view. You can create regular postings to the group with News Xpress, or create an e-mail message to the sender of the original posting.

NEWSRC   The file stored on your own computer that contains the names of news groups you have subcribed to and the last message you have read. Although you can edit this file to change news group subscription information, it is easy to make mistakes.

NEWSREADER   The client software used to fetch and display postings for your subscribed news groups. This book uses the News Xpress newsreader software.

NICKNAME   Another name used for an e-mail address in Eudora. Nicknames can represent a single user or a group of users and are stored in Eudora's address book.

NNTP   Network News Transport Protocol. The news group protocol used to handle submissions to the group and dissemination of news group articles to news servers. Your campus probably has an NNTP-compliant news server.

NOTEPAD   The Windows text editor used to view text files and to create HTML documents in this book. Notepad is found in the Accessories program group.

ONLINE CAREER CENTER   A Web site containing information about jobs and careers.

ORDERED LIST   A numbered list in an HTML document, denoted by <OL>. Each item in the list is numbered incrementally, starting with 1.

PACKET   A portion of a computer message that is transferred across a network such as the Internet. TCP/IP is responsible for splitting the message into packets and transporting them without error from the sender to the receiver.

PAGE   Another term for a Web document. A page represents a single HTML document.

PING   An Internet utility program used to test your Internet connection. It works by sending a packet to another computer on the Internet and measuring how long it takes for the message to return. You can send a message to a domain name and Ping will return the IP address for that domain name. Windows 95 includes a Ping program.

PKZIP   The file compression program frequently encountered when using FTP. Files encoded with PKZIP usually have the .ZIP extension. You decompress ZIP files with the PKUNZIP program. PKZIP files can contain multiple files and are easier and quicker to transfer with FTP. Some self-extracting files have the .EXE extension, signifying they have the PKUNZIP program built into them. See WinZip.

PLUG-IN   Another name for a viewer for a particular kind of Web file. Plug-ins are associated with the file type of the file, and can be downloaded and installed in your Web browser.

POINTER   Another term for link. It gives the actual Internet address associated with the item attached to the pointer.

POPMAIL   Post Office Protocol. An e-mail protocol whereby you can dial in to your e-mail server and download your messages. You can disconnect from the mail server and then read your messages off-line, reducing connection costs. When replies are ready, you can reconnect to the mail server and upload the replies.

POSTING   An article or message submitted to a news group or Listserv mailing list.

POSTMASTER   A special e-mail address used when you don't know the specific e-mail address of your recipient. Send mail to *postmaster@domain-name* with a subject line containing the real name of the recipient at that institution. The e-mail postmaster will look up the name locally and forward your mail to that individual.

PPP   Point to Point Protocol. PPP is a dial-up protocol that enables your computer to be connected to the Internet through a modem attached to a serial port. PPP contains error-checking capability and is generally considered superior to the SLIP protocol when the quality of telephone connections is less than perfect. Windows 95 comes with a built-in PPP connection.

PRETTY GOOD PRIVACY (PGP)   A method of encrypting information before it is sent over the Internet. PGP can be used to make e-mail messages and other files nearly impossible to read without the key.

PRODIGY   A well-known dial-up commercial information utility. Prodigy now offers many Internet features as part of members' monthly service contract.

PUSH TECHNOLOGY   Where personalized information is automatically and continuously sent to your browser by the Web server, rather than after you click a link. Push technology is implemented as channels in the Netscape Communicator and Internet Explorer browsers. Channels contain HTML documents.

QUICK MENU   In Windows 95, the menu that results from clicking the right mouse button in a browser, e-mail client, or newsreader. The quick menu is also known as the context menu. It contains relevant commands that can be used in that situation. For instance, in a browser the quick menu contains choices for saving an image, copying something to the clipboard, and so forth.

REALAUDIO   The company that developed a method of transmitting compressed audio content over the Internet. Radio and other audio-only programs can be heard in real time using the RealAudio player, available for free from the RealAudio Web site.

ROUTING   Involves switching data packets in networks so that they arrive at their proper destination. Routers perform this function.

SCRIPT   A program, written in Visual Basic or PERL, that processes information on a Web server.

SEARCH ENGINE   A program used to find Web documents containing the searcher's key words on the Internet or within an intranet. Yahoo, Lycos, AltaVista, and WebCrawler are examples of search engines.

SEARCH TOOL   A Web site that contains catalogs of information about home pages in the Internet. You can use the search tool to locate Web sites that meet your criteria. Yahoo and Lycos are the two best-known search tools.

SELF-EXTRACTING FILE   A compressed file that has the decompression or decoding code built into it. To extract the compressed files in the self-extracting file, run the .EXE file.

SERVER   A host computer that provides information to other computers that are called clients. A local area network has a file server on which users store data. A Web server stores home pages and transmits them to clients on demand.

SHARED RESOURCE   Typically a network resource such as a file server, tape drive, printer, or communications gateway that is used by many users.

SHELL ACCOUNT   A text-based Internet account typically found on a UNIX computer network. Internet users with a shell account do not have a true TCP/IP address; the host computer has a TCP/IP address and handles distribution of data packets through the network operating system.

SIMPLE SEARCH   A net search in which a single keyword is used as the search criteria.

SLIP   Serial Line Internet Protocol. SLIP is the original dial-up protocol that enables your computer to be connected to the Internet through a modem attached to a serial port. You must have a SLIP or PPP account in order to use the dial-up connection for full Internet services. Most users select PPP today.

SMTP   Simple Mail Transport Protocol. SMTP is the mail protocol used by many e-mail systems to exchange messages with other mail servers.

SPAM   Junk e-mail usually sent to many users at the same time.

SPORTSZONE   The ESPN Web site containing nearly all the sports information you might want to have, including news, scores, statistics, feature stories, and links to other sports Web sites. Other companies have similar sports Web sites.

STAND-ALONE COMPUTER   A client computer that is not attached to a network.

STORE AND FORWARD   The technique in which a packet is received at an intermediate node, stored for a short time, and then forwarded toward its destination. Consecutive packets may not follow the same physical path.

SUB-CENT CHARGES   Represent a way to charge visitors for use of the Internet or particular Web sites. These charges would be subtracted from some electronic money account. Few providers have instituted sub-cent charges.

SUBDIRECTORY   A group of files stored together on the disk drive. The drive is organized in a hierarchical fashion, starting with the root directory. It is subdivided into subdirectories, and so forth. Windows 95 and Macintosh refer to subdirectories as folders.

SUBSCRIBE   The command to join a news group or mailing list (Listerv) group. Send an e-mail message to the administrator of the group with a single line in the body of the message: SUBSCRIBE *<group-name><your first name><last name>*

SURFING THE NET   A slang term representing the way many people use the Internet. A user will visit a particular page, see useful links to other pages, and then follow a particular link. When reaching that page, the user might find more useful or interesting information and follow more links. In this way you may end up far from where you started. This is the way in which much useful information is discovered.

TABLE   An HTML formatting code that represents a tabular view of information in rows and columns.

TAG   An HTML formatting code. Most HTML tags come in pairs, one to activate the feature and another to disable that feature. For instance, <H1> is the tag for Heading 1 and </H1> is the tag to turn off the Heading 1.

TALK    A method of chatting between two users over the Internet. The screen is divided into two sections, one for your comments and the other for your partner's messages.

TCP/IP    Transmission Control Protocol/Internet Protocol. This is the standard communications protocol used by computers connected to the Internet. TCP makes sure that all data arrives at a node in the correct order. IP refers to the format for data packets as they are transferred across the Internet. TCP/IP stacks refer to the specific communications software used by a computer connected to the Internet.

TCP/IP STACK    The set of protocols on a computer that permit it to communicate with other computers on the Internet. For Windows machines, this means the Winsock and related utility programs including PPP dial-up networking.

TELNET    This is a way to perform a remote login to another computer on the Internet. Windows 95 comes with a Telnet client.

10BASE-T    The most common direct network medium. 10Base-T stands for 10 megabits per second transfer rate using baseband transmissions over telephone wiring.

TEXT FILE    An unformatted file containing text characters. HTML documents are text files and usually end with the *.htm* or *.html* file extension.

THREAD    A set of discussion group postings that begins with the initial article followed by the set of replies to that article. There may be *replies* to the replies. Most newsreader clients can display threads so that you can follow the discussion about a particular topic.

TIMED OUT    When your Internet connection is dropped by your Internet Service Provider because you have not entered a command or downloaded any information for a preset time.

TRASH    In graphical user interface computers, trash represents an intermediate folder or area where items to be discarded are placed. In Eudora, the Trash folder holds messages that will be deleted in the future; you can remove them from the Trash folder before they are permanently removed.

TRUMPET    The well-known TCP/IP stack software with Winsock capability for Windows 3.1 users. Trumpet allows you to dial in to the Internet with a modem and create a SLIP or PPP session. Windows 95 comes with its own TCP/IP software.

UNORDERED LIST    A bullet list in an HTML document, denoted by <UL>. Each item in the list begins with a bullet.

UNSUBSCRIBE    The command to leave a Listserv discussion group. Some groups require that you use the SIGNOFF command. Send an e-mail message with the UNSUBSCRIBE *<group-name>* command in the body of the message.

UPLOAD    The processing of transferring a file *from* your computer to another computer.

URL    Uniform Resource Locator. It provides for the Internet address of a site, including the protocol used to access that site and the name of the file to be retrieved. Protocols include *http* for Web documents, *Gopher* for Gopher pages, *ftp* for FTP documents, and *Telnet* for Telnet sites.

USENET NEWS    A set of news groups corresponding to the User's Network. Not all news groups belong to UseNet.

V.32BIS    The 14,400 bits per second (bps) modem standard. V.32 represents the 9600 bps modem standard.

V.34    The 28,800 bps modem standard. Most Internet providers installed V.34 modems by mid-1996. V.34+ refers to speeds up to 33,600 bps. To connect at the fastest speed, you must have a good telephone connection.

V.90    The 56k modem standard approved in February 1998. V.90 modems connect for downloading at speeds up to 56 Kbps when used over compatible phone lines. Uploads are done normally at speeds up to 33.6 Kbps. The V.90 standard is a compromise between the competing x2 and K56Flex modem technologies.

VIDEOCONFERENCING    Using the Internet to transmit one-way and two-way video and sounds between users at two or more sites. True videoconferencing is difficult to accomplish due to the limited bandwidth of most Internet users.

VIEWER    A software program used to display the contents of a certain kind of application file. Examples include viewers for sounds, video, word processing files, HTML files, and so forth.

WEB    Abbreviation for the World Wide Web. *See WWW.*

WEB SERVER    The combination of hardware and software that provides HTML documents on request from users. You must place your HTML-formatted home page on a Web server in order for others to access it.

WEBMASTER    The person responsible for development and administration of a Web site. You may notice references to the Webmaster at the end of large Web pages.

WHOIS    A method of searching for information about a user on the Internet. WHOIS will return name, user name, and related information for a specific user or for a domain name such as a university.

WIDE AREA NETWORK (WAN)    A network that covers an area larger than a building or campus. WANs include networks covering cities, states, and even continents.

WINSOCK    Windows sockets. Winsock is a programming standard that makes TCP/IP (Internet) services available to Windows applications programs. Most of the Internet tools described in this book are Winsock compliant. Windows 95 comes with built-in Winsock software.

WINZIP    Similar to PKZIP, WinZIP is a user-friendly file compression program designed specifically for Windows. The Windows 95 version is able to compress long file names. Download a trial copy from *http://www.winzip.com/.* See PKZIP.

WORKSTATION    Another term for client computer. A workstation represents a user's computer that is usually attached to a network.

WS_FTP    The most popular FTP client for Windows 3.1 and Windows 95. The limited edition version is free, and the Pro version is for sale over the Internet. For more information, see *http://www.ipswitch.com.*

WWW   World Wide Web (The Web). This portion of the Internet is used for hypertext documents that include multimedia contents. View Web documents with a browser such as Netscape or Mosaic. Most Web documents are prefixed with *http:*.

YAHOO   Yahoo is an extremely popular catalog or index of Internet resources. Yahoo is accessed at *http://www.yahoo.com*.

ZINE   A Web magazine available on the Internet. Zines frequently present avant garde or unconventional views of life.

ZIP   The file compression protocol frequently used when transferring files on the Internet. *See PKZIP and WinZip.*

# INDEX